797,885 Books
are available to read at

Forgotten Books

www.ForgottenBooks.com

Forgotten Books' App
Available for mobile, tablet & eReader

ISBN 978-1-332-05663-7
PIBN 10277463

This book is a reproduction of an important historical work. Forgotten Books uses state-of-the-art technology to digitally reconstruct the work, preserving the original format whilst repairing imperfections present in the aged copy. In rare cases, an imperfection in the original, such as a blemish or missing page, may be replicated in our edition. We do, however, repair the vast majority of imperfections successfully; any imperfections that remain are intentionally left to preserve the state of such historical works.

Forgotten Books is a registered trademark of FB &c Ltd.
Copyright © 2015 FB &c Ltd.
FB &c Ltd, Dalton House, 60 Windsor Avenue, London, SW19 2RR.
Company number 08720141. Registered in England and Wales.

For support please visit www.forgottenbooks.com

1 MONTH OF FREE READING

at

www.ForgottenBooks.com

By purchasing this book you are eligible for one month membership to ForgottenBooks.com, giving you unlimited access to our entire collection of over 700,000 titles via our web site and mobile apps.

To claim your free month visit:
www.forgottenbooks.com/free277463

* Offer is valid for 45 days from date of purchase. Terms and conditions apply.

English
Français
Deutsche
Italiano
Español
Português

www.forgottenbooks.com

Mythology Photography **Fiction** Fishing Christianity **Art** Cooking Essays **Buddhism** Freemasonry Medicine **Biology** Music **Ancient Egypt** Evolution Carpentry Physics Dance Geology **Mathematics** Fitness Shakespeare **Folklore** Yoga Marketing **Confidence** Immortality Biographies Poetry **Psychology** Witchcraft Electronics Chemistry History **Law** Accounting **Philosophy** Anthropology Alchemy Drama Quantum Mechanics Atheism Sexual Health **Ancient History Entrepreneurship** Languages Sport Paleontology Needlework Islam **Metaphysics** Investment Archaeology Parenting Statistics Criminology **Motivational**

THE HISTORY

OF THE

United Parishes

OF

GILES IN THE FIELDS

AND

St. George Bloomsbury,

COMBINING

STRICTURES ON THEIR PAROCHIAL GOVERNMENT, AND A VARIETY OF INFORMATION OF LOCAL AND GENERAL INTEREST.

By ROWLAND DOBIE.

London:

Printed for the Author, 13, Kenton Street, Brunswick Square.
And may be had of all Booksellers.

1829.

Br f: 889.27
~~94/3/14~~

Phillipo gift.

PREFACE.

In the early part of 1828, an Association was formed in the United Parishes of St. Giles in the Fields and St. George Bloomsbury, for the laudable purpose of investigating and correcting the abuses which had too long prevailed under the government of a Select Vestry, possessing no claims to power but what were founded on assumption and usurpation.

"Friends of Elective Vestries, and Publicity of Accounts," the object of this Association was to carry these principles into practical effect; and it has been already seen, that its views have been eminently successful, with the best prospect eventually of their complete consummation.

As a member of the Committee, I sought for information connected with the cause we espoused, when it soon appeared evident how much the absence of local knowledge contributed to perpetuate the evils we were opposed to, and I gradually contemplated the writing the Work now offered to the Public.

Mr. Parton, the late clerk of the Vestry of these parishes, collected materials for a work of this description, which was published in an imperfect state after his decease, under the title of " Some Account of the Hospital and Parish of St. Giles in the Fields, Middlesex."

The general utility of this quarto volume is, however, more than questionable : a great portion of it involves uninteresting details of the Hospital grants and charters ; and the price prefixed being five guineas, placed it beyond the reach of most readers ; indeed, it is a fact, that very few among the parishioners are aware that such a publication is before them.

Mr. Parton had exclusive advantages to aid him in such a work, having the custody of the parish records, to which he alone had free access—a privilege of the highest importance, and without which any history applicable to the district we are treating of must necessarily prove essentially defective.

Occupying a station both lucrative and influential, Mr. Parton too frequently forgot the impartial province of the historian in his zeal for advocating the cause of the assumed Vestry under whom he held his appointment. It has been my care to evince a contrary conduct, by combining principle with the candour of truth, without which history has no claims to philosophy, teaching by example. Whilst, therefore, it was necessary to avail myself of his researches, it has not been with a slavish adherence to his sentiments and opinions, by which " the worse is often made to appear the better reason ;" but I have combated them wherever they have appeared to be founded in sophistry and error.

Since the completion of my manuscript copy, the decision of a British Jury has established the long-lost rights of the parishioners of St. Giles, by the overthrow of a pretended Select Vestry, whose authority had been exercised uncontrouled, with some deductions, during more than two hundred years.

This glorious triumph was achieved on the 23rd of July, 1829, a day ever to be recorded in the annals of these parishes: and, I had thought it essential to give a full report of the Trial from the best sources in my power, to perpetuate so memorable an event. It is, however, in the nature of power to be tenacious, and an effort is now in progress to reverse the verdict by a new trial, it would therefore be premature until a future period to enter on that subject, when the whole proceedings may be completely embodied.

With regard to the subjects introduced in

this volume, they are too numerous to particularize here. Among them will be found, details on the antiquity of the Village and Hospital of St. Giles—the first institution of its Parish—progress in building—political occurrences—extension of its population—division into two parishes in consequence—history of Bloomsbury—its amazing increase accurately delineated—public institutions—places of worship of the joint parishes—the vestries—parochial acts—biographical sketches, &c. &c.

Finally, no exertion has been spared to render the Work both instructive and entertaining; and, above all, to make it a faithful record of a parochial government, where abuses and malversations are notorious, and thereby guarding the parishioners in future from similar evils. If I have succeeded in these objects, even in a remote degree, my end is answered—they are more invaluable in my estimation than the hope of profit, or the gratification of vanity.

R. D.

December 15th, 1829.

ERRATA.

10th page 25th line *for* " seven years" *read* " two years."
11th .. 2nd .. *for* " twenty-seven" *read* " twenty-five."
12th .. 15th .. *for* " was" *read* " is."
87th .. 29th .. *for* " cutilage" *read* " curtilage."
101st .. 24th .. *for* " a consecration" *read* " as consecration."
114th .. 25th .. *for* " ear" *read* " year."
163rd .. 29th .. *for* " Oxford" *read* " Orford."
179th .. 14th .. *for* " 38" *read* " 28."
188th .. 20th .. *for* " George III's. reign" *read* " George IV., &c."
190th .. 4th .. *for* " is only, &c." *read* " are only."
230th .. 22rd .. *for* " D. W. Robinson" *read* " T. D., &c."
272nd .. 17th .. *for* " 1625" *read* " 1635."
327th .. 20th .. *for* " £2,776 " *read* " £264,770"
416th .. 22nd .. *for* " 8th February, 1823" *read* " 8th February, 1616."

Note in last line to Lady-day, 1826, the sums denote the gross rental, the two last columns the assessed ditto.

HISTORY

OF

ST. GILES IN THE FIELDS,

AND

ST. GEORGE BLOOMSBURY.

CHAPTER I.

The Manor of St. Giles and Boundaries described—Its Hospital for Lepers and their Disease defined—Name derived from a Grecian Saint—Charters and Grants of Hospital, dissensions of its Inmates, final Dissolution—Cruel Execution of Lord Cobham at St. Giles's Gallows, &c. &c.

THE Manors of St. Giles and Bloomsbury were anciently divided by a great fosse or ditch, called Blemund's Ditch, and were bounded on the south-east, by the Manor of Holborn, or Oburn; on the north-east, by the Manor of Portpole; and on the south, by the Liberty of the Dutchy of Lancaster; on the south-west, by the Manor of St. James, Westminster; on the north-west, by the Manor of Mary-le-bone;

and on the north, by the Manor or Prebend of Tottenhall.

In the celebrated register of estates contained in Doomsday Book, made by order of William the Conqueror, anno 1070, no mention is made of this district, except indeed a reference to a vineyard in Holborn, as belonging to the Crown. This was probably the site where stood, a few years since, the Vine Tavern, a little to the east of Kingsgate Street.*

These Manors of St. Giles and Bloomsbury, under a different designation, were vested in the Crown, probably previously, but certainly immediately subsequent to, the conquest; as

---

* Doomsday Book. it should be observed, minutely details the particulars of our towns and cities, whilst it is wholly silent in regard to London, it only mentioning the above vineyard and ten acres of land, nigh Bishopsgate, belonging to the Dean and Chapter of St. Paul's. Mr. Ellis, in his Modern London, p. 15, says, " no mutilation of the manuscript has taken place, since the account of Middlesex is entire, and exactly coincident with the abridged copy of the survey, taken at the time, and now lodged in the office of the King's Remembrancer in the Exchequer." Mr. Brayley argues, that a " distinct and independent survey of the City itself might have been made at the time of the general survey, although now lost or destroyed, if not yet remaining among the yet unexplored archives of the Crown."

There can be no question that many important documents remain concealed among the ancient records : some have been occasionally discovered by accident, and otherwise. A short time since, the Charter of the Artillery Company was found by accident in the Rolls Chapel, after being lost 200 years.

may be deduced from the grant of eight acres* of land by Queen Matilda to found the hospital, which was expressly stated to have been a portion of the royal domains.

According to Pennant, the neighbourhood of London, and especially towards the north, consisted in the time of the Romans of immense forests, and even as late as Henry II. these extended down to the Thames, and were filled with various species of beasts of chace. The City was defended by fosses on every side except to the south, which was guarded by the Thames, and it is most probable that the great fosse, or ditch, which separated the Manors under our notice, was part of the continuation of such a line of defence, running nearly parallel with the north side of Holborn, and in an easterly direction connecting itself with the creek which ran along Fleet Ditch. "The Britons," he says, "sought for security in places surrounded with woods or morasses; and added to their natural strength by forming ramparts and sinking fosses: but they preferred spots fortified by nature; and made artificial works only where nature shewed herself de-

---

* First styled "Sancti Egidij in Campis" in Henry VIII.'s grant to Lord Lisle. In the exchange previously made with Radcliffe, it was called "Villa Sei Egidij."

ficient. Within such precincts they formed their towns."—*Pennant's London*, 4th edit. p. 3.

A great proportion of the soil to the north-west of London is described to have been very marshy, wet, and unhealthy, of which character these Manors partook at an early period, till draining and cultivation had rendered them otherwise; much of this was effected by the formation of ditches in different directions at an early period.

About the time of the Norman conquest, the loathsome disease of leprosy was very prevalent, which has been oddly ascribed to the eating of sea-fish. Orivalle, Bishop of London, among many of the higher classes, was greatly afflicted with it anno 1075, and never could be cured, although it is said he underwent a peculiar operation.

In the present day this disease is but little understood, and medical men seem scarcely able to comprehend its symptons with accuracy. We may notice some of the opinions on this subject.

" Leprosy, or Lepra," says Dr. Willich, "is a cutaneous disorder, in which the skin is rough, with white eschars resembling bran, though they are sometimes beneath the surface, and accompanied with an intense itching."

Among the Jews it existed to a formidable degree, and the Levitical laws were very strict in separating the diseased from the tabernacle, and from the eating of the holy things. *See* xxii *and* xxiii *of Leviticus.* Some have imagined it to have been the itch, contracted by this people, partly from their filthiness, and partly from drinking water of a bad and bituminous quality, which greatly augmented the disease.

Calmet and other commentators have differed greatly on this subject, but the exact nature of the malady has been much questioned; there is, however, little doubt but its inveteracy was engendered by uncleanliness—dirty linen—and want of baths during their wanderings in the desarts.

Voltaire assures us, that there are about thirty diseases of the skin from the *simple itch* to the *direful cancer,* and many of them are of a formidable nature.

"That species of the leprosy, which is called elephantiasis, came not into Italy before the time of Pompey the Great: it commonly began in the face, or at the nostril, no bigger at first than a small pea; it spreads itself all over the body, which it deforms with divers spots, unequal skin, and a rough scab: at last it turns black, and wastes the flesh unto the very bones, making the fingers and toes in the meantime swell. The disease is peculiar to Egypt, and if it falls upon the king, is fatal to the people, for baths of human blood are the usual and frequent remedies that are prepared for it."— *See a curious passage in Wanley's History of Man.*

This disorder, modern medical men say, was an inveterate stage of the scurvy. Its effects render the limbs swollen and tuberous, the skin bloated, rough and wrinkled, the callous parts of the feet and other members ulcerated and varicated. A cleanlier system, and different modes of living, have almost extinguished this malady.

Hospitals were founded and endowed in many parts of the kingdom for persons thus afflicted, and among these institutions St. James's was founded, before the conquest, as a hospital for fourteen maidens that were leprous. Henry VIII. first procured it for a palace, and it was greatly added to by Charles I.

Among the earliest of these was the celebrated Hospital of St. Giles, which was founded in 1117 by Matilda, (or, as she is called by some historians, Maud), daughter of Malcolm, King of Scotland, Queen of Henry I. It was built for the reception of forty lepers, one clerk, and one messenger, besides matrons, the master, and others on the establishment, and she gave sixty shillings a year to each leper.*

The site of the hospital was the site of the original parochial church, as is evident from the words of King Henry II.'s charter, which expressly states it to have been founded " ubi Johannes bonac memoriæ fuit capellanus," which is " upon the spot where John of good memory was chaplain." The ground given by the crown (together with the Manor of St. Giles), was eight acres, upon which, says Leland, Queen Matilda caused to be built " a house or principal mansion with an oratory (chapel) and offices." That these buildings, at first few and small, were afterwards increased and enlarged as well as the hospital boundaries, when charity added to its revenues, there seems no doubt, but at this distance of time we can only conjecture. In the licence to Wymond Carew, which we shall advert to hereafter, there is mention made of a close, or enclosure,

---

* Maitland and other antiquarians have been much puzzled to account how they were maintained with so scanty a sum, after allowing for the difference of the value of money at that and the present period. It is well known, however, that lazar houses when first built were allowed to augment their means by sending every market-day to the markets a *clapdish*, to beg corn. Other means were also resorted to to increase their income. Matilda founded another hospital for poor maimed persons at Cripplegate; the Priory of the Holy Trinity within Aldgate; and the Church and Hospital of St. Catherine, below the Tower, (now removed to Regent's Park.)

lying within the precincts of the hospital, and one before the *great gate*, is stated at sixteen acres, late in the occupation of Thomas Magnus, clerk, and another, same tenant, called Newland, twenty acres.

Another called Le Lane, late in the occupation of George Sutton, gentleman. It has been inferred from hence, that the hospital buildings were much of the same character at the foundation and dissolution.

But among all the establishments of this kind, the most celebrated in magnitude and consequence was that of Burton St. Lazar in Leicestershire, which was built in 1135 (eighteen years after that of St. Giles) during the reign of King Stephen. This hospital was erected by general contribution, and Roger de Mowbray was a munificent benefactor to it; and we have records to show how intimately it was connected with that of St. Giles.

The latter hospital comprised, with its garden, a considerable extent, and was situate near to the present church, a little to the west, and, according to Maitland, where Lloyd's Court now stands, and its gardens between High Street and Hog Lane (now Crown Street) and the Pound which stood nearly opposite to and west of where Meux's Brewhouse now stands. It was surrounded by a wall nearly of a triangular form, being a boundary to the hospital and its precincts, running in a line with Crown Street, to somewhere near the Cock and Pye Fields (now Seven Dials) thence in a line with Monmouth Street, and thence east and west up High Street, joining at the north end of Crown Street where St. Giles' Pond stood subsequently.

The hospital was dedicated to a Grecian Saint, bearing the name of "St. Giles of the Lepers": it had a chapel attached to it, a house for its master and other officers, and continued under flourishing circumstances, with some variations, owing partly to the quarrels of its loathsome inmates, till its dissolution under the rapacious reign of Henry VIII.

In the Hospital Chapel (or Church as it was afterwards called) a great taper was superstitiously burnt before its patron Saint Giles, which stood on a high altar at its east end.

It would seem that this disease increased in virulence: the council of Lateran having decreed in 1179, that persons so afflicted should have churches, church-yards, and ministers of their own, and kept distinct from society.

On the removal of the gallows from the elms in Smithfield in the first year of Henry V. 1413, it was set up at the north corner of St. Giles's Hospital Wall, between the termination of High Street and Crown Street, opposite where the Pound stood, at which place it continued till it was transferred to Tyburn.

A remarkable custom is on record connected with the execution of criminals at St. Giles. A bowl of ale was provided by the hospital, which was given to the culprit at its great gate, as his last refreshment in this life, he being allowed to stay there for that purpose. This ale was given probably where the Resurrection Gate now stands, that being supposed to be the point of entrance to the hospital The name of " St. Giles's bowl" is derived from this custom, and Pennant says, that a similar one prevailed at York, which gave rise to the saying, " that the sadler of Bawtry was hanged for leaving his liquor." Had he stopped as criminals usually did, his reprieve, which was actually on the road, would have saved him.

It may not prove uninteresting to remark here, that Pennant and others have been incorrect in their account of St. Giles's gallows. Their authority seems to be founded on the fact of Lord Cobham having been hanged and barbarously treated here during the reign of Henry V. anno 1418, seven years after the removal of the gallows from the elms, Smithfield. Now it is upon record, that Judge Tressilian* and Sir Nicholas Brember were

---

* The following account of that transaction is taken from the State Trials, which I copy, to show the uncivilized taste of

executed at Tyburn as early as 1388, being twenty-seven years prior to the transfer from the elms to St. Giles!

In regard to Tyburn, I have taken some trouble to ascertain when it first became a place of execution, but have not been able to trace it earlier than the period when these eminent individuals suffered there, and I doubt whether any authentic record of a prior date can be adduced on this point.

Fuller, in his Church History, speaking of Lord Cobham's execution, says " at last he was drawn on a hurdle to the gallows, his death, as his crime, being double, he was

---

that period. " Immediately Tresillian is taken from the Tower, and placed on a hurdle and drawn through the streets of the city, with a wonderful concourse of people following him. At every furlong's end he was suffered to stop that he might rest himself, and to see if he would confess or acknowledge any thing, but what he said to the friar his confessor is not known. When he came to the place of execution, he would not climb the ladder until such time as being soundly beaten with bats and staves, he was forced to go up; and when he was up he said ' so long as I do wear any thing upon me I shall not die'; whereupon the executioner stripped him, and found certain images painted like to the *signs of the heavens and the head of a devil* painted, and the names of many of the *devils* written on parchment; these being taken away, he was hanged up naked, and after he had hanged some time, that the spectators should be sure he was dead, they cut his throat, and because the night approached they let him hang till the next morning, and then his wife, having a licence of the king, took down his body and carried it to the Grey Friars, where it was buried."

hanged and burned for a traitor and heretick." "Hence" he adds " some have deduced the etymology of Tyburn, from ty and burn, the necks of offending persons being tyed thereunto, whose legs and lower parts were consumed in the flame." If this definition has any foundation, the question is set at rest at once. Be this as it may, it is pleasing to reflect on the total abolition of the disgraceful spectacle of criminals being dragged publicly through the streets of the metropolis to receive the punishment of death. Even the site where Tyburn tree (as it was called) stood for ages, would be found at the present period with much difficulty, although it was only forty-six years since the last criminal, Ryland, was executed here for forgery (1783.) As a matter of historical curiosity, I learn, that it is identified with a house occupied by a Mr. Fenning, being No. 49, Connaught Square, which is built on the spot where the gallows stood, and in the lease granted by the late Bishop of London, this is particularly mentioned. In the year 1784, the mode now adopted was first introduced, called the New Drop, by which much of the horror of these executions has been obviated.

The first notice of this is however a most melancholy specimen of the prevalence of crime, no less than fifteen being executed on that occasion, June 23rd, 1784, and on the following year, from February to December 1st, no fewer than the unprecedented number of ninety-six individuals suffered at Newgate by this novel process!

In reference to the hospital, King Henry II. for the health of the souls of his grandfather, Henry I. and his grandmother, Queen Matilda, and for his own health, and the health of his ancestors and successors, confirmed to the said lepers the place where the said hospital was built, with the donation of sixty shillings yearly receivable, which Queen Matilda had given them, and granted them sixty shillings more, to be paid also yearly at the feast of St. Michael the Archangel, out of the Exchequer, to buy them clothes, and thirty shillings more out of his rents in Surry, in perpetual alms, to buy them lights, and then confirmed all the other gifts and benefactions which had been by others granted and bestowed upon them, among which he confirmed to them the church at Feltham.*

Nothing important enough to narrate occurred during the reigns of Richard I. and King John, embracing a period of twenty-seven years, namely, from 1180 to 1216, being 109 years

---

* This village is situate near Hounslow, twelve miles south-west from London; the church thus confirmed *inter alia* to the hospital was a gift of Hawysia, Countess of Rumaze. We shall have to advert to it again.

subsequent to the founding this hospital, but in regard to Henry II. his charters are still extant.

Henry III.'s reign commenced in 1216, and continued till 1272, being of the extroardinary length of fifty-six years; but, in regard to this hospital, was a barren period of events, except that a bull issued by Pope Alexander IV. confirmed its privileges, and he also took it under his holy protection, whence its donations increased.

Edward I. granted it two charters in 1300 and 1303, and, from the tenor of the latter, it appears to have been in the wane, which is attributed to the dissensions of the inmates.

In Edward the II.'s reign another charter was granted in 1315, and there were more grants of estates to it in this than in any other reign. It then possessed most of the district of the parish as now formed, exclusive of a great portion of many other parishes in London, which thus became endowments to it. It appears, however, that in proportion as it grew rich, it increased in irregularities, and quarrels prevailed amongst its inmates.

By this King's charter, bearing date the second year of his reign, anno 1309, he granted to the hospital permission to stop up a certain way in the village of Feltham, which extended from the said village by the *middle court* of the said master and brethren unto the spring in the same village for ever, with a certain other way leading thereto also. Parton supposes, that the middle court mentioned, formed part of some building of magnitude on the hospital estates here, which was kept as a lazar-house, or place of retirement, for the master or such of the members who were convalescent: the manor or advowson of the church being vested in the hospital.

Edward III.'s reign produced a new era in its history, he making it a cell to Burton St. Lazar by a charter, dated at Westminster, 4th April, 1354, in the twenty-seventh year of his reign. By this instrument he invested the master and brethren of that hospital with the custody of that of St. Giles, in consideration of the remission of four marks and the arrearages thereof, which was to be paid them yearly out of his Exchequer.

Of the dissensions of this period we may gather something from the five charters issued by this monarch, and especially from the last, which was directed to his beloved and faithful Walter de Gloucester, Roger de Mathcote, and John de Foxelyere. It recites, that a complaint had been made to the King " by brother John Cryspin, Keeper of the *Hospital of St. Giles without London*, that of late certain evil doers and disturbers of our peace, opposing themselves against our subjects, and the exemptions of the said hospital, forcibly seized possession of the same hospital and the gates thereof, and the same held by force and arms, against Robert, Archbishop of Canterbury, who, coming there to perform his official duty of visiting the said hospital, was thereby prevented and shut out, to the prejudice of us and the said hospital, and certain papal letters, writings, charters, and other monuments, as well of privileges as other rights and possessions of the said hospital, or touching or concerning the same, were taken and carried away, and other outrages repeatedly committed, as well in contempt of us, as to the damage of the said keeper, and against our peace, &c.; and because we may not permit contempts and offences of this kind to be acted with impunity, we have assigned you our justices to inquire thereof, on the oath of true and lawful men of the county of Middlesex, by whom the matter may be better made known, together with the names of such offenders, and the nature of their crimes, and such contempt and offences heard and determined according to the laws and customs of our kingdom, &c."

Such are the proofs of outrage of these leprous brethren, founded no doubt on the barter this hospital had undergone to Burton St. Lazar, and from which we come at the fact of their being subject to the visitation of the Archbishop of Canterbury.*

King Edward III. also commanded the wards of the city to make proclamation for the removal of all lepers, and not to shelter those so diseased. This seems to have arisen from the plague raging in this kingdom to an alarming extent, after destructively depopulating half the inhabitants of Asia, Africa, and Europe, of which Hume gives us the following account. " In the midst of the festivities of the court of Edward III. on the institution of the Order of the Garter, a sudden damp arose in consequence of a destructive pestilence invading France, as also the rest of Europe. It is computed to have swept away near a third of the inhabitants in every country which it attacked. It was probably more fatal in great cities than in the country, and according to Stowe, 50,000 souls are said to have perished in London alone.

" This malady first discovered itself in the north of Asia, was spread over all that country, made its progress from one end of Europe to the other, and sensibly depopulated every state

---

* Stowe notices the refractory spirit of these periods, and narrates the opposition to the Archbishop of Canterbury, Boniface, on his visitation of St. Bartholomew's Priory, Smithfield, when he was compelled to enforce his authority against the canons by *blows*. These Lepers probably acted in a similar manner, by which the hospital books and records were destroyed.

through which it passed. So grievous a calamity, more than the pacific disposition of the princes, served to maintain and prolong the truce between France and England."—*Hume's England, Cadell's edition, vol.* 2, *p.* 448.

Stowe's Survey, p. 478, states, that "There were buried 50,000 bodies in one churchyard, which Sir Walter Manning had bought for the use of the poor." The same author says, "There died above 50,000 persons of the plague in Norwich, which is quite incredible."—*Ibid.*

After the sale of the hospital to that of Burton St. Lazar,* it gradually sunk in importance so

---

* This hospital must have been a most splendid establishment, judging by a paragraph which appeared in " The Dispatch" of 29th June, 1828, as follows:—

"Thursday, 26th June, 1828, the Manor and Estate of Burton St. Lazar, and formerly a hospital which was anciently called Burton St. Lazar, and situate in Leicestershire, was sold at the Mart. It was founded in the reign of King Stephen for poor leprous brethren. The estate is principally meadow and pasture, and is celebrated for the cheeses made there, and which are carried to Stilton for sale. The property contains 1100 acres—a manor, with the freehold tithes of the whole estate. The manor abounds with game, and the principal fox cover for the Leicestershire hunt, which is part of the property, is held by Col. Lowther. 362 acres of the estate is freehold, and the remainder is held under the Bishop of Ely during three lives, aged 27, 54, and 63, renewable according to the custom of church of England leases."

The estate was sold in one lot at £30,000, timber to be taken at a valuation. This magnificent endowment for loathsome lepers flourished 412 years, when, like other monastic institutions, it was suppressed by the rapacious avarice of Henry the Eighth.

that it was entirely under the controul of that foundation previous to its dissolution, and its final fall was completed by the exchange of its best estates by Henry VIII. in 1537, 191 years after the above sale.

In the exchange made by that monarch, the interests of the hospital were completely sacrificed. By deed dated anno 1537, Thomas Ratcliffe, then master of Burton and warden of St. Giles, with the consent of the brethren, granted at the instance of the king, the greater part of the hospital, land, &c. in St. Giles's, with the manors of Feltham and Heston, and other premises, to the crown, in consideration of receiving the manor of Burton St. Lazar, &c. in Leicestershire, late the property of the monastry of St. Mary de Valdy, in the county of Lincoln, and which only two years after came into his hands in consequence of the dissolution. The estates of St. Giles's hospital, so exchanged, may be here noticed to shew the extent of its endowments at this period.

1. The manors of Feltham and Heston, in Middlesex.

2. Two acres of land in the fields of St. Martin, Westminster.

3. Twenty-five ditto, lying in the *village of St. Giles*.

4. Five acres ditto, lying in Colman's-hedge field, and five ditto in a close near it.

5. One close called Conduit Close, containing about five acres.

6. One ditto, called Meersheland, one messuage called the Whyte Hart, and eighteen acres of pasture to the same messuage belonging.

7. One messuage, called the Rose, and one pasture belonging thereto; and

8. One ditto, called the Vyne, situate and being in the said village of Saynt Gyles.

In *St. Gyles's village* forty-eight acres were thus transferred, exclusive of the marsh lands, and Rose closes, and the several messuages mentioned above. There are omitted,—the Hospital and its site; the manor of St. Giles; the Pittaunce Croft; Le Lane; New Land; and some lesser places.

The ten acres in and about Coleman's Hedge, were in the parish of St. Martin in the Fields. The church of Feltham and its glebes, lands, tythes, and oblations, were reserved to the said master, and probably the hospital estates at Edmonton, in the city of London, and the various parishes in its suburbs, no mention being here made of them.*

---

* According to Parton, the transfer of St. Giles's hospital to Burton St. Lazer, in 1354, operated much to the detriment of the village, by its extinguishing the small landholders, as may be verified by reference to the old deeds relative thereto still extant. The dissolution and the grant to Lord Lisle effected a further change both in population and extent.

The history of the hospital of St. Giles, from the dissolution of Burton St. Lazar, with its dependant cell of St. Giles's hospital, anno 1539 to 1547, when the site of the hospital and its appendages were thus parcelled out to various possessors, is short.

As it required no separate deed of surrender in resigning the hospital into the king's hands, it being included in that of Burton St. Lazar, some information is lost which it might have been gratifying to know, namely, as to the number of officers, &c. then on the foundation, who, (if not lepers) would have been required to sign such deed. That the establishment was much reduced there is little doubt, from several circumstances before stated.

Henry kept the hospital and its precincts six years in his own possession, as he retained for a length of time those of St. John of Jerusalem, St. Bartholemew, and others, apparently from their nearness to town, and in 1545, bestowed it on Lord Lisle, together with Burton St. Lazar, by the following grant. Rent to the crown £4 : 6s. : 3d.

"The king, to all whom it may concern, sends greeting. Be it known, that we, in consideration of the good, true, faithful, and acceptable counsel and services to us, by our beloved counsellor John Dudley, knight of the most noble order of the garter, Viscount Lisle, and our great Admiral of England, before time done and performed, of our special grace, and of our certain knowledge and mere motion, have given and granted, and by these presents do give and grant, to the said John Dudley, Viscount Lisle, all the late dissolved hospital of Burton St. Lazar, otherwise called the hospital of Saint Lazarus of Burton, with all its rights, members, and appurtenances, in our county of Leicester, lately dissolved, and in our hands now being, and all that the late hospital of St. Giles in the Fields, without the bars of London, with all its rights, members, and appurtenances, in our said county of Middlesex, in like manner dissolved of late, and in our hands now being. And also all that our rectory and church of Feltham, with all its rights, members, and appurtenances, in our said county of Middlesex, to the late hospital of Burton aforesaid, belonging and appertaining, or being part or possession thereof, and the advowson, donation, free-disposition, and right of patronage of the vicarage of the parish of Feltham, in our said county of Middlesex, of the possessions of the late hospital of Burton aforesaid, being, belonging, and appertaining.

"And also all and singular their *manors, messuages*, rectories, churches, &c. (amongst others) in the parish of St. Giles in the Fields, without the bars of London, and in Holbourne, Feltham, and Edmonton, (Edlemeton,) in our said county of Middlesex, and in the city of London, and elsewhere, and wheresoever, within our kingdom of England, to the said late hospital of Burton St. Lazarus, otherwise the hospital of Burton St. Lazar, and of the said late hospital of St. Giles in the Fields, without the bars of London, or either of the same late hospitals of Burton aforesaid, in anywise belonging, or appertaining, or as parcel, or possession of the said late hospital of Burton aforesaid, and the said late hospital of St. Giles in the Fields, or either of the said late hospitals heretofore possessed, known, accepted, used, are reputed to belong."

By this grant, all the possessions of the hospital of St. Giles, (not expressly mentioned in the exchange with the king) were vested in Lord Lisle. They consisted of the hospital, its site, and gardens, the church and manor of St. Giles, the Pittaunce Croft, Newland, Le Lane, and other lands in the parish of St. Giles. Also of the church of Feltham, and lands at Edmonton, and of the several rent charges, and hereditaments in the city of London, and in the suburbs thereof, and in the fields of Westminster, and at Charing, as described in the hospital possession.

After this grant Lord Lisle fitted up the principal part of the hospital for his own residence, leasing out other subordinate parts of the structure, and portions of the adjoining grounds, gardens, &c. and at the end of two years he conveyed the whole of the premises to John Wymonde Carewe, Esq. by licence from the king, in the last year of his reign.

"The king, to all whom it may concern, sends greeting. Know ye, that we, of our special grace, and in consideration of the sum of seven pounds and sixteen shillings, paid to us in our hanaper, do grant and give licence, and by these presents, have granted and given licence, for us and our heirs, as much as in us lies, unto our beloved John Dudley, Knight of our Order of the Garter, Viscount Lisle; and our great Admiral of England, to grant and sell, dispose of, alienate or acknowledge by fine in our court, before our justices of our common bench, or in any manner whatsoever at his pleasure, unto John Wymonde Carewe, Esq. all that his mansion, place, or capital house, late the house of the dissolved hospital of St. Giles in the Fields, in the county of Middlesex," &c. &c.

This charity, founded by royal munificence, had subsisted under varied circumstances from 1117 to 1547, forming a period of 430 years, when it finally fell a prey to the rapacity of a monarch, whose "catalogue of vices," as Hume remarks, "would comprehend many of the worst qualities incident to human nature."

The capital mansion or residence which Lord Lisle fitted up for his own accommodation, was situate where the soap manufactory of Messrs. Dix and Co. now is, in a parallel direction with the church, but more westward. It was afterwards occupied by the much celebrated Alice, Duchess of Dudley, who was buried therefrom in the reign of Charles II. anno 1669, aged 90. This house was afterwards the town residence of Lord Wharton; and Strype notices it thus, " Lloyd's Court is divided from Denmark Street by Lord Wharton's house and gardens, which fronts St. Giles's Church." The house appropriated to the master of the hospital, was situate where Dudley Court has been since built, and is mentioned as occupied by Dr. Borde, in the transfer from Lord Lisle to Sir Wymonde Carewe, which is said to have been afterwards the rectory house, being given by the Duchess for that purpose. It was known by the name of the White House, and since the Court has been substituted, the rents have been to this day collected by the rectors, it being their property for ever.

There were various buildings connected with the hospital precincts,[*] and the wall which surrounded them, and its gardens and orchard, was not entirely demolished until the year 1639.

---

[*] See Aggas's Plan of London.

The first historical fact of importance, in which the name of St. Giles's village is mentioned, is the pretended conspiracy of the Lollards, and the cruel death of their supposed leader, Lord Cobham, in 1418, as before alluded to, and which, for its local interest, may well claim our attention at some length, before we proceed to other parts of our history. Lord Cobham was charged with the heresy of Wickliffe,* whose followers were stigmatized with the name of Lollards, and he was much persecuted by the Primate Arundel, who, according to Bale, gave him, for his instruction, the following tests, and allowed him two days to consider of them.

"The fayth and the determinacion of holy church, touchyng the blissfull sacramente of the aulter is this: That after the sacramentall wordes ben sayde by a prest in hys masse. The materiell bred that was before, is turned into Christes verray body, and the materiell wyne that was before, is turned into Christes verray blode, and there leweth in the aulter, no materiell bred, ne materiell wyne, the wych wer there before the seying the sacramentall wordes. How lyve ye this articul? Holy Churche hath determyned that every christen man lyving here bodilie, in erthe oughte to schryve to a prest ordeyned by the churche, if he may come to hym: How fele ye this articul?

---

* This celebrated reformer, among other tenets, held, "That all the sins committed in the world are inevitable and necessary, that God could not prevent the sin of the first man, nor pardon it without the satisfaction of Christ, all being matters of necessity; that God approves of our becoming sinners; that he obliges us to commit sin; and that man cannot act better, or otherwise, than he does act," &c. &c. *See Vaughan's Life of Wickliffe.*

Christe ordeyned St. Petir the Apostell to bene hys vicarie in erthe, whos see ys the Church of Rome, ordeyning and graunting the same power that he gaf to Petir shuld succede to all Petir's successours, the wych we callyn now Popes of Rome; by whose power in churches, particular special ben ordeyned Prelates, Archbyshoppa, Byshopps, Curates and other degrees, to whom christen men oughte to obey after the lawes of the churche: How fele ye this articul? Holy churche hath determyned that it is needfull for a christen man to goo a pylgrymach to holy places, and ther specially to worshyp holy reliques and ymages of seyntes, apostells, martirs, confessours, and all seyntes approoved be Churche of Rome. This is determinacion of holy church: How fele ye this articul?"

Such are some of the dogmas our ancestors were called upon to believe, under pain of being burnt to ashes!

"Lord Cobham was brought before the Primate, Bishops, and Doctors, September 25, 1414, and repeatedly refused to profess his belief of the several articles contained in the above paper. The Archbishop then "*modestly, mildly, and sweetly,*" as he says himself, pronounced a sentence of condemnation against him as an obstinate heretic, and delivered him over to the secular arm, the meaning of which was well known. He found means to escape from the Tower the night previous to his intended execution, and escaped into Wales, were he remained concealed four years. Soon after his escape, a report was industriously circulated by the clergy, that he was at the head of 20,000 Lollards in St. Gyles Fields," which appears to have had no foundation whatever, although Hume seems to give credit to it.

Fuller, in his Church History, says, "It is laid to the charge of Lord Cobham, that though not present in person, with his counsel he encouraged an army of rebels, no fewer than 20,000, which in the dark thickets, expounded in our age into plain pasture, *St. Giles's Fields, nigh London,* intended to seize the king's person, and his two brothers, the Dukes of Bedford and Gloucester. Of this numerous army thirty-six are said to have been hanged and burnt, though the names of three only are known, and Sir Roger Acton, knight, the only person of quality named in the design. For mine own part, I must confess myself lost in the intricacies of these relations: I know not what to assent to. On the one hand, I am loath to load Lord Cobham's memory with causeless crimes, knowing the perfect hatred the clergymen of that age beared unto him, and all that looked towards the reformation in religion. Besides, that 20,000 men should be brought into the field, and no place assigned whence they were to be raised, or where mustered, is clogged with much improbability. The rather, because only the three persons as is aforesaid are mentioned by name of so vast a number.

"This is most true, that Lord Cobham made his escape from the Tower, wherein he was imprisoned, and fled into Wales, where he lived four years, being at last discovered and taken by the Lord Powis; yet, so, that it cost some blows and blood to apprehend him, till a woman at last, with a stool, broke Lord Cobham's leggs, whereby being lame, he was brought up to London in a horse litter. At last he was drawn on a hurdle to the gallows: his death, as his crime being double, he was hanged and burned for a traitor and heretick, &c. Stage poets have themselves been very bould with, and others very merry at, the memory of Sir John Oldcastle, (Lord Cobham) whom they have fancied a boon companion, or jovial royster, and yet a coward to boot, contrary to the credit of all chronicles, owning him a martial man of merit. Sir John Falstaff hath derived the memory of Sir John Oldcastle,[*] and of late is substituted buffoone in his place, but it matters as little what petulent priests, as what malicious poets, have written against him."

As whatever regards this celebrated martyr is interesting, I subjoin a further account of him. "A reward was offered the 11th of January, 1415, soon after his escape from the Tower, of 1000 marks to any who should apprehend him, and other tempting offers were held out through the influence of Chichely, who suc-

---

[*] He obtained his Peerage by marrying the daughter of Lord Cobham, who so firmly opposed Richard II.

ceeded Arundel as primate. None of these had any effect for several years; but at length he was apprehended, after some resistance, by Lord Powis, in December, 1418, and brought to Westminster, where a Parliament was sitting, by which he was condemned on his former sentence, to be strangled and burnt." " Upon the day appointed he was brought out from the Tower, the 25th of December, with his arms bound behind him, having a very chearful countenance. Then was he laid on a hurdle, as though he had been a most haynous traitoure to the crowne, and so drawne forth into Sainct Gyles Felde, whereat they had set up a new paire of gallowes. As he was comen to the place of execution, and was taken from the hurdle, he fell downe devoutly upon his knees, desyring Almighty God to forgive his ennemies. The cruel preparations of his torments, could make no impression of terror upon him, nor shock his illustrious constancy, but in him were seen united the fearless spirit of a soldier, and the resignation of a christian Then he was hanged up ther by the middle in chayns of yron, and so consumed alive in the fyre, praysing the name of God so long as his life lasted."—*See Hume and Henry's History of England, Fox's Acts and Monuments, State Trials, &c.*

The first toll ever imposed in England had its origin in St. Giles's, of which the following account is given :—In 1346, King Edward III. granted a commission to the master of the hospital of St. Giles, and to John de Holborne, empowering them to levy *tolls*, ("perhaps," says Anderson, "the earliest known by any remaining records,") "upon all cattle, merchandize, and other goods for two years, passing along the public highways leading from the bar of the old Temple," (i. e. Holborn Bar, between which and Chancery Lane, then called New Street, the ancient house of the Knight Templars stood) to the said hospital, and also along the Charing Road, (probably St. Martin's Lane,) and another Highway called Portpoole, (now Gray's Inn Lane,) for the purpose of repairing the said highways, which, by the frequent passing of carts, wains, horses, and cattle, hath become so miry and deep as to be nearly impassable." The rates upon the several articles amounted to about one penny in the pound on their value, and were to be paid by all, except lords, ladies, and persons belonging to religious establishments, or the church.—*See Rymer's Foedera.*

Chapter II.

St. Giles viewed as a Suburb Village—Its rural Character—Gradual Extension of Buildings—and a variety of other Information, Illustrations, &c.

HITHERTO our attention has been chiefly drawn towards the history of the Hospital, an object of veneration to the antiquarian, and of some interest to the local residents; we will now devote ourselves to St. Giles, in its progress from a village to its present consequence. In doing which, it may not be unuseful to premise some notices of the metropolis and its vicinity at an early period.

The suburbs of London and Westminster, and the parishes thereunto belonging, may be considered anciently as forming so many distinct villages. For instance, the village of Tyburn, or Tyborn, formed part of the district we are treating of, and it is said to have stood where the north-west part of Oxford Street now is; Mary-la-bonne Court House, near Stratford Place, being supposed, from the number of human bones dug up there in 1729, to stand upon the site of the old church and cemetery.

Mary-la-bonne owes its rise to the decay of

Tyborne, it having with its village church fallen into decay and desertion, and been robbed of its vestments, bells, images, and other decorations. There was a brook or rivulet near this decayed church, which was of such antiquity as to be made mention of in Doomsday Book; and in the decretal sentence of Stephen, Archbishop of Canterbury in 1222, it is expressly called Tyburn, from which it doubtlessly derived its ancient names.

Near the east end of this village, in what is now Oxford Street, there was a bridge over the rivulet alluded to, and near it stood the Lord Mayor's Banqueting House, in the vicinity of which the citizens had nine conduits erected about the year 1238, for supplying the city with water; but having been better supplied from the New River, the citizens in the year 1703, let the water of these conduits on lease for £700 per annum.

Malcolm, and other writers on the metropolis, have remarked on the rural state of its vicinity, even at an early period of Queen Elizabeth's reign, and aided by the much celebrated Plan of Aggas, published in the year 1578, it is competent for any one to observe how much has been effected in buildings and extension up to the present time. In her reign the chief part of London lay between Cornhill and the Thames. Cornhill was then a corn market, and had been so time out of mind, from which it derived its name. Goodman's fields was a tenter ground, and Smithfield used for bleaching cloth; Goswell Street was the high road to St. Albans; Covent Garden was the rich garden of the Convent of Westminster; whilst magnificent rows of trees lined Long Acre and St. Martin's Lane, leading from the mansion of the Lords Cobham at the village of Charing, near which stood the Spring Gardens. At Queenhithe was the large structure for bull and bear baiting, the favourite amusement of the Queen and the court; Gray's Inn Lane only extended, at this period, to a short distance beyond the Inn; whilst the ground from the back of Cowcross towards the Fleet river, and towards Ely House, was either entirely vacant or occupied in gardens. From Holborn Bridge to the vicinity of the present Red Lion Street the houses were continued on both sides, but farther up to about Hart Street, Bloomsbury, the road was entirely open; a garden wall there commenced, and continued to near Broad St. Giles and the end of Drury Lane, where a cluster of houses, chiefly on the right, formed the principal part of the village of St. Giles, only a few other buildings appearing in the neighbourhood of the church and hospital, the precincts of which were spacious and surrounded with trees. Beyond this all was country, both north and south, and the Oxford and other main roads were distinguished only by avenues of trees. From the Oxford road, southward to Piccadilly, called the way from Reading, and thence along the highways named the Haymarket and Hedge Lane, to the vicinity of the Mews, not a house was standing; and St. James's Hospital and three or four small buildings near the spot lately occupied by Carlton Palace, were all that stood near the line of the present Pall Mall. St. Martin's Lane had only a few houses beyond the church, abutting on the Convent Garden, (now Covent Garden), which extended quite into Drury Lane, and had but three buildings in its ample bounds. Not a house was standing either in Long Acre, or in the now populous vicinage of the Seven Dials, nor yet in Drury Lane, from near Broad Street, Giles, (as it was then called) to Drury House, at the top of Wych Street. Nearly the whole of the Strand was a continued street, formed however of spacious mansions and their appropriate offices, the residences of noblemen and prelates. Those on the south side had all large gardens attached to them extending down to the Thames, and have mostly given names to the streets, &c. that have been built on their respective sites.

Among the suburb villages stood anciently that of St. Giles in the Fields, or, as it has been called in old records ' *the verie pleasant* *village of St Giles.*' The name it bears was evidently derived from its hospital being called at an early period of its history, " St. Giles of the Lepers",* and " the Parish of the Hospital of St. Giles of the Lepers." On the suppression of the hospital it assumed the name of " St. Giles in the Fields," or " *in campis,*" to distinguish it from St. Giles Cripplegate, and other churches so dedicated, and as descriptive of its rural situation in regard to the city. In ancient records, according to Newcourt, it is written " St. Giles, extra London;" and Parton

---

* St. Giles, the patron of this hospital and parish, and also of many others both in England and other countries, is said by Butler, in his Lives of the Saints, and by others, to have been an Athenian by birth, and of noble extraction. He flourished, say they, in the seventh and eighth centuries, and was possessed of piety and an extreme love of solitude. Quitting his own country he retired to France, and formed an hermitage near the mouth of the Rhone. He afterwards retreated finally to a deep forest, and immured himself in the neighbourhood of Nismes, where, secluded, he passed many years. It is said the hunters pursued a tame hind who flew to this Saint for protection, when an arrow intended to kill it, wounded him, but he continued his prayers, and refused a recompence offered him for the injury. This hind had long nourished him with her milk, and had accidentally strayed into danger. This adventure made him a great favourite with the French king, but nothing could induce him to quit his retirement. Towards the end of his life he admitted several disciples and founded a monastery, where excellent discipline prevailed. It became afterwards a Benedictine Abbey, and since a Collegiate Church of Canons. A considerable town was built about it, called St. Giles. This Saint is commemorated in the Martyrologies of Bede and others. St. Giles and his hind has often been a favourite subject for artists.

supposes, with reason, that its boundaries were in remote times much more extensive than now,* but in point of population truly insignificant, containing, in the early part of the fourteenth century, including the hospital inmates, only 100 inhabitants.†

In its ancient state, like its surrounding vicinity, St. Giles's district presented a marshy wet aspect, as is apparent from its ditches and neighbouring brookes or bournes, as they were then denominated, instance Old-bourne, West-bourne,

---

* Tottenhall or Totnam Hall, from whence Tottenham Court Road takes its name, was formerly included in the bounds of St. Giles's parish. It stood where the Adam and Eve now stands, and was a mansion of eminence in Henry III.'s time. Its owner was William de Tottenhall. It was a house of entertainment in 1645.

† In the first plan of London extant drawn by Aggas, before spoken of, and re-published by Vertue in 1748, is the following description. "The part of the north-west suburbs of the City of London, since called St. Giles in the Fields, was, about the time of the Norman conquest, an unbuilt tract of country, or but thinly scattered with habitations. The parish derived its name from the hospital dedicated to that saint, built on the site of the present church by Matilda, Queen of Henry I., before which time there had only been a small church, or oratory, on the spot. It is described in old records as abounding in gardens and dwellings, in the flourishing times of the hospital, but declined in population after the suppression of that establishment, and remained but an inconsiderable village till the end of the reign of Elizabeth, after which it was rapidly built on, and became distinguished for the number and rank of its inhabitants." The latter part of this statement, at least, was evidently added by Vertue, and there are also prefixed further remarks on the increase of this parish, and the taking from it the new division of St. George Bloomsbury.

Tybourne, &c. It became, however, healthy in proportion as it became drained, and as it increased in sewers, and as early as the reign of King John, 1213, it was laid out in garden plots, cottages, and other buildings to a certain limited extent.*

As early as Henry III.'s reign, it assumed the appearance of a scattered country village, having shops and a stone antique Cross, where High Street now stands, and its probable dependance was chiefly on the hospital, which had been rendered the more important by the endowments of the preceding monarch. In 1225, or thereabout, stood a country blacksmith's shop at the north-west end of Drury Lane, which continued till 1595, when the progressive buildings rendered its demolition necessary.

The lower part of Holborn was paved in the reign of Henry VI. (1417), and in 1542, in the twenty-third of Henry VIII. Stowe says, that " High Oldburn Street leading from the bars towards St. Giles was very full of pits and sloughs, and perilous and noisome to all that

---

. * " It is worthy of remark," says Anderson, " that in the year 1372 (Edward III.) at least twenty houses in Borcher (Birchin) Lane, in the very heart of the city, came under the denomination of cottages, and were so conveyed to St. Thomas's Hospital in Southwark. The shops also at this time appear to have been detached and separate tenements, or at least separate properties unconnected with houses, as they are at this day in several cities and towns."

repaired and passed that way, as well on foot as on horseback, or with carriage, and so were other lanes and places that led out of or into High Oldbourne, as Shoe Lane, Fetter Lane, New Street, or Chancery Lane. Upon complaint whereof an act was made in the thirty-second of Henry to pave all those parts with paving from the farther part of Oldbourne unto St. Giles in the Fields, as also on the east-side of the city, the way from Aldgate to Whitechapel Church which had the same ill passage, all to be paved and made by the feast of St. John the Baptist, 1542, in manner and form as the cawsey or highway leading from Strand Bridge to Charing Crosse had been made and paved."

During several successive reigns the village of St. Giles probably bore the same character, no material alteration taking place in it till the reign of Henry VIII. and especially during that of Queen Elizabeth, after the land was no longer vested in the hospital. In her reign we have mention of the immense line of thick forests extending from the Village of St. Giles westward towards Tybourne and Wickham, and reaching almost interminably to the north. This was the great black forest of Mary-la-bonne into which she used to send the Muscovite ambassador to hunt the wild boar, when she found him such a *bore* that she wanted to get rid of him.

Stowe gives a curious account of a visitation to the conduits at Tyborn in 1562, of the Lord Mayor, Harper, and Aldermen, and many other citizens, masters, and wardens of the twelve companies, accompanied by their ladies in waggons, it being usual after examining the state of them, to give a grand entertainment at the banqueting house. On this occasion, says Stowe, " afore dinner they hunted the hare and killed her, and thence they went to dine at the head of the conduit. There was a good number, entertained with good chear by the chamberlain, and after dinner they went to hunting the fox. There was a great cry for a mile, and at length the hounds killed him at the end of St. Giles's; great hallowing at his death and blowing of horns, &c." This account is sufficient to show the rural character of this neighbourhood at that period, and must excite our admiration on contrasting it with its present crowded and populous state.

Judging by the plan of Aggas, the metropolis was neither extensive in buildings, which were mostly of wood and plaister, nor seemly in appearance; and, according to Hume, London was even ugly in every respect at a much later period than the plan in question was published.*

---

* " Not any plan or view of the metropolis is known with certainty to be extant of an earlier date than Queen Elizabeth, although Bagford, in his letter to Hearne prefixed to " Leland's

The first increase of buildings in this district seems to have been on the north-side of St.

Collectanea," has mentioned a view or ground-plot of London, as being noticed in a manuscript inventory of Henry VIII.'s furniture. Vertue, speaking of a plan and view of London with the River Thames, &c. which he describes as " the most ancient prospect in point," says " this was reported to have been done in Henry VIII.'s or Edward VI.'s time; but from several circumstances it appears to have been done early in Queen Elizabeth's reign, about 1560, being cut on several blocks of wood; the plates thereof are now of the greatest scarcity, no copies, perhaps, preserved, being put up against walls in houses, therefore, in length of time all were decayed or lost." Whether that " prospect" was the identical " Civitas Londinum, Anno Domino 1560," which Vertue " re-engraved to *oblidge* the curious," and " shew posterity how much was built of this populous city" in Elizabeth's reign, is somewhat questionable, and the engraver's notes are not sufficiently explicit to enable us to determine the question. Of the " Civitas Londinum" his words are " probably this was published by Ralph Aggas, as he himself mentioned in that plan of Oxford done after this was begun." But it must be observed, that this very impression is a second publication, with the date 1628, and that there are several alterations from the first in this, and particularly, instead of the arms of Queen Elizabeth those of James I. (of England, France, and Scotland) are put in the place of them. (See Walpole's Catalogue of Engravers under Aggas.) Vertue's plan was executed in 1737, and eventually purchased of his widow by the Society of Antiquarians. He describes the original printed plan of Aggas as " 6-feet 3-inches long by 2-feet 4-inches wide, contained in six sheets and two half sheets ;" but with " notes of explanation printed," he imagines, " on slips of paper to be added at bottom." His own plan was engraven on eight pieces of pewter, and printed on eight sheets corresponding together with the size of the original. From this very curious representation, many interesting particulars may be deduced of the state of the metropolis in the early part of Elizabeth's reign. (*See much more on this subject in Brayley's Londiniana.*)

Giles's Street, now Broad Street, with Blemund's ditches, about 100-feet in the rear, and that the metropolis was gradually extending during the reign of Elizabeth, is inferrable from the proclamations issued by her at three different periods, namely in 1582*, 1593, and 1602, to prohibit building under severe penalties, on the plea of its being wickedly presumptuous as restraining agriculture, and above all engendering pestilence. In despite of the authority of the crown, and the mistaken ground of these restrictions, aided by the *orders* of the city authorities, the suburbs were greatly extended before the end of Elizabeth's reign, and many of the large mansions of the nobility and others within the city itself, which now began to be deserted for the more courtly air of Westminster, were separated into divers tenements, or pulled down to make way for streets. Population under this extension of buildings could not fail to increase, aided as it was by the great influx

---

* The first proclamation was issued from Nonsuch Palace, and dated 7th July. Three especial reasons were assigned for it: 1st.—The difficulty of governing a more extended multitude without device of new jurisdiction, and officers for that purpose: 2nd.—The improbability of supplying them with food, fuel, and other necessaries of life at a reasonable rate: and 3rd:—The danger of spreading plague and infection throughout the realm. Various regulations were ordered to prevent any further resort of people from distant parts of the kingdom; and when the Lord Mayor went to the Exchequer to take the usual oaths, he was strictly enjoined by the Lord Treasurer to enforce the proclamation.

of foreigners at this period, the consequence of a wiser policy which this princess evinced by her encouragement of commerce and manufactures.

In 1580 the resident foreigners in the capital were numbered by an order of council, by which the amount was found to be 6462; of these 2302 were Dutch; 1838 French; 116 Italians; 1542 English born of foreign parents, and about 664 of countries not specified. This return was an increase of 3762 persons (foreigners) within the space of thirteen years. Many of these had fled from different parts of France after the fatal Vespers of St. Bartholomew. *(See more on this subject in Brayley's London.)*

St. Giles's Parish, among others of the out-villages, augmented in houses towards the termination of this Queen's reign, especially towards the precincts of the former hospital. It had been suppressed in 1547, but a considerable portion of the wall which surrounded it remained in 1595, according to Stowe, after which it was mostly demolished, and residences were built on the east and west ends towards the year 1600. Holborn, even as early as 1595, had extended west so as to nearly join St. Giles's Street, and the latter street was still increasing. " On the High Street (Holborn) have ye many faire houses builded, and lodgings for gentlemen, inns for travellers, and such like, up almost (for it lacketh but little) to St. Giles-in-the-Fields."—*Stowe's Survey*, 1595. In Aggas's plan a considerable space is exhibited of fields and gardens extending from St. Giles's hospital wall to Chancery Lane easterly, with scarcely a house intervening, if we except a few houses opposite where Red Lion Street now stands, in Holborn, and the same at the north end of Drury Lane, now Broad Street. From thence southward we see not the vestige of a house till we arrive at the north-side of the Strand, with the exception of two or three in Convent Garden, Drury House at the bottom of Drury Lane, and an inconsiderable cluster a little to the south-east of it. Cattle are seen grazing amidst intersecting footpaths, where Great Queen Street now is, and in the intermediate fields reaching to the boundaries described. A different scene now began to develope itself, and at the commencement of the reign of James I. these pastures began to be covered with buildings. In 1606 Great Queen Street was begun, and Drury Lane,* which had hitherto

---

* Drury Lane derived its name from the knightly family of the Druries, who, before the reign of Henry VIII. were settled at Drury Place, near the bottom of the Lane, in the grounds now occupied by Craven Buildings and the Olympic Theatre. In a statute of 34th and 35th of that king, for mending the roads " without Temple Bar," the way leading to Clement's Inn and New Inn Gates and to Drury Place, and also one little lane (probably the present Holiwell Street), " stretching from the said way to the sign of the Bell at Drury

been a country lane or road to the Strand, became built on the east-side, so that by an assessment made in 1623, the whole number of houses rated amounted to 897, and upwards of twenty courts, yards, and alleys are mentioned by name ; a considerable accession since Edward the VI.'s reign, when the housling* people amounted to 305 only. On the north-side of

---

Lane end," is described " as very foul and full of pits and sloughs." Pennant believed Drury House to have been built in Elizabeth's reign by Sir William Drury, Knight, an able commander in the Irish wars, who " fell in a duel with Sir John Burroughs, in a foolish quarrel about precedency; and whose son, Sir Robert, being a great patron of Dr. Donne, assigned to him appartments in this mansion."

This house was the rendezvous of the associates of the Earl of Essex in 1600, whose residence at the north-west side of Essex Street, the site of the present Unitarian chapel, extending to Devereux Court, and southwards its gardens and offices reached the Thames, rendered it a convenient place of resort for them, and which ended in the public execution of the Earl, Sir Christopher Blunt, Sir Charles Davers, Sir Gelly Merrick, and Henry Cuffe. *(See Brayley and State Trials.)*

* " Housling people" is a phrase of doubtful import in the present day, the first word being obsolete. Shakspeare, it is well known, causes the Ghost in Hamlet to say,

" Thus was I, sleeping, by a brother's hand,
Of life, of crown, of queen, at once dispatched :
Cut off even in the blossoms of my sin,
Unhousell'd"—

Which has been rendered, the not taking the sacrament. If this be a correct definition, the number here mentioned formed but a small proportion of the population, inasmuch as many, from a variety of circumstances, were not qualified or allowed to partake of that sacred rite.

St. Giles's Street 100 houses were soon after added, and on the south-side of Holborn 71. Also in Drury Lane and the adjacent neighbourhood, on the west-side 56 residences are named, supposed to be first-rate chiefly, to which may be added 15 in the whole in Great Queen Street, and at Holborn end 10 were assessed. In Bloomsbury 136 were now built, making a total of 1285.

These are the amount stated as erected in the principal thoroughfares, and will afford an idea of the increase in other parts of the parish not assessed.

"The accession of James I. was quickly followed by a destructive plague, the spreading of which, there can be no doubt, was highly accelerated by the narrowness of the streets, and the crowded state of the houses; yet every extension of the suburbs seems about this period to have been resisted by successive administrations, with a pertinacious obstinacy, for which at the present time we know not how to account."* Proclamation followed proclamation, restricting the proprietors of decayed dwelling houses and other premises, in re-building to the identical limits formerly occupied; and all edifices reared in the city or suburbs, contrary to the tenor of the proclamation, were ordered to be demolished. In defiance, how-

---

* Survey of London, p. 329.

ever, of these prohibiting restraints, the metropolis increased, although the delinquents were prosecuted and fined, the building speculation continued, till it became necessary, in consequence of the rapid decay of wooden structures, and the vast consumption of timber, to order, that in future the outer walls, fore-fronts, and windows of all edifices should be either of brick or stone.*

"The principal ground on which recourse this restraining policy was the danger of pestilence, and notwithstanding the continued injunctions for the "voiding of inmates" from the capital, it is most certain that if London was at any time " overthronged with inhabitants it appears rather to have had its population decreased by pestilential diseases, than spread over a wider district by royal and civic precaution."

"During the whole of Queen Elizabeth's reign industry had progressed to a considerable degree, and the working classes had greatly augmented by the multitudes redeemed by the Reformation, from the idleness of the cloister." When her successor James came to the throne, many of his countrymen flocked with him to

---

* Lilly's Sculptura informs us that the Earl of Arundel was the first who brought over from Italy the new way of building with bricks, which tended to the safety of the city and the preservation of the wood of the nation. This was in Charles the I.'s reign.

the metropolis, so that these concurrent causes tended to add greatly to its population and consequent extension. During the first ten years of Charles I. building went on with spirit; but the disastrous wars which followed produced a total suspension until the Commonwealth was established, when it was again checked by a parliamentary ordinance.

During the Interregnum the buildings in our district did not much increase, except that the chief streets were gradually completed, the same state policy of Elizabeth and James being again enforced. An act passed in 1657, had for its object the restraining such speculations, enacting "that every house-building, out-house, or other building erected within the suburbs after 1620, not having four acres of land at least therewith used, there should be paid to the Commonwealth one full year's rent; and all who built after this a house or cottage upon a new foundation within the said suburbs, or within ten miles thereof, should forfeit £100, and every person that should uphold the same was to be subjected to the fine of £20 for every month that such building should remain standing."

The augmentation of the capital on the settlement of the Commonwealth appears to have advanced with accelerated rapidity, which fact we gather from the preamble of the act referred to, which runs thus:— " Whereas the *great* and *excessive number* of houses, edifices, out-houses, and cottages, *erected and new-built* in and about the suburbs of the City of London, and the parts thereunto adjoyning, is *found* to be *very mischievous* and *inconvenient*, and a great *annoyance* and *nuisance* to the *Commonwealth;* and whereas, notwithstanding divers prohibitions heretofore had and made to the contrary, yet the said *growing evil is of late so much multiplied and encreased*, that there is a *necessity* of taking some *further* and *speedy course* for the *redress thereof*. The act then proceeds to state, that by the law the said houses and nuisances ought to be abated, that is, removed or pulled down; and the builders, occupiers, and tenants thereof, ought to make fines for the same; so that if the severity of the law should be inflicted, it would tend to the undoing of divers persons who have laid all, or a great part of their estates in such new buildings." From this consideration, therefore, it was enacted, that one year's rent, or year's value, at the full and improved yearly value of such dwelling-house, out-house, and other building built and continued upon any new foundation within the city of London, or in any other place or places within ten miles of the walls of the said city, since the 25th March, 1620, and not having four acres of land, at least, according to the statute or ordinance,

De Terris mensurandis, should be paid for the use of the Commonwealth, in full satisfaction and discharge of all fines, forfeitures, and penalties incurred by the said builders, &c."

" Among the exemptions from these forfeitures which concern the metropolis were William, Earl of Bedford and his brothers, John and Edward Russell, the sons of Francis the late Earl, who were allowed £7,000 out of the fines payable by them in respect of the buildings in Covent Garden parish. This considerable remission evinced that this neighbourhood was now greatly advanced. About this time also Long Acre was built on an extensive field, which had previously borne the name of the Seven Acres."

It is also on record, that James Cooper, Robert Henley, and Francis Finch, Esquires, and other owners of certain parcels of ground in the fields, commonly called Lincoln's Inn Fields, were exempted from forfeits or penalties, in regard to any new building they might erect on three sides of the said fields, previous to the 1st of October, 1659, provided that the said named persons paid for the public service one full year's value for every such house within one month of its erection; and provided that they conveyed the residue of the said fields to the society of Lincoln's Inn, for laying the same into walks for common use and business, whereby the great annoyances which formerly have been in the said fields* will be taken away, and passengers there, for the future, better secured.

Thus we see, with surprise, the frequent restrictions upon the enterprise of builders enforced, by pains and penalties, upon the most mistaken principles of legislation and philosophy, during a period of nearly eighty years; and yet, with all these impolitic restraints, the British Capital grew expansively to an amazing degree. But this spirit of our ancestors, thus excited, sinks into insignificance when compared with what has been effected since that eventful period, and they would contemplate their former opinions with compunctious astonishment, could they behold the stupendous work of extension in buildings at the present

---

* Faithorne's plan, published 1658, exhibits no traces of houses on the north, except a single one called the gaming house, in Piccadilly. Windmill Street, standing in a field on the north side, points out the etymology of its present name. The Haymarket and Hedge Lane are to be seen literally as lanes bounded by hedges, and all beyond was one entire country; and even in Charles II.'s reign, we find the Judges, on the first day of term, stopping to breakfast at the village of Charing. A great fete being given at the summer house, called *Spring Gardens*, the flirting of the Duchess of Shrewsbury occasioned a duel, in which two of the combatants were killed.

day, unaccompanied by the baneful consequences which they anticipated.*

At the restoration, a new and grand era commenced in building, and Lincoln's Inn Fields assumed an appearance of magnificence, having arisen under the auspices of the masterly hand of Inigo Jones. These fields had long been the resort of the disorderly, and were known by the appellation of Ficket's Fields; and it appears there had been houses erected there,

---

* Captain John Graunt, who was the first English writer who turned his attention to political arithmetic, published a book at this period called "Observations made upon the Bills of Mortality," in which he says, "London is, perhaps, a head too big for the body, and possibly too strong; that this head grows three times as big as the body to which it belongs; that our parishes are grown madly disproportionate; that our temples are not suitable to our religion; that the trade and very city of London removes *westward;* that the walled city is but a fifth of the whole pyle; that the old streets are unfit for the present frequency of coaches; and that the passage of Ludgate is a throat too straight for the body."

In illustrating these ideas, he states, that "the encrease of the ninety-seven parishes within the walls, was scarcely discernable, but of the out parishes, then called ten, formerly nine, and before that eight, St. Giles's and St. Martin's in the Fields, were most encreased, notwithstanding St. Paul's Covent Garden had been taken out of them both." He adds, "when Ludgate was the only western gate of the city, little building was westward thereof; but when Holbourn began to encrease, New-gate was made, but now both these gates are not sufficient for the communication between the walled city and its enlarged western suburbs, as daily appears by the intolerable stops and embaresses of coaches near both these gates, especially Ludgate."

about 1609. The privy council at that time, at the desire of the benchers and students of Lincoln's Inn, directed a mandate to certain magistrates of the County of Middlesex, stating that it was the king's express pleasure and commandment, that the erection of new buildings "should be restrained," and ordering the said justices to apprehend and commit to goal any who should be found so offending, and to take sureties of him or them, to appear before the privy council, to answer the charges. This curious mandate was not in force many years. The cause of its having been issued, may be partly seen from the special commission, bearing date 1618, and in which, after the most grossly false assumption, that *more public works* near and about London had been undertaken in the sixteen years of that reign than in ages heretofore, it was alleged, that the grounds called Lincoln's Inn Fields, were much planted round with dwellings and lodgings of noblemen and gentlemen of quality, but at the same time were deformed by cottages and mean buildings, encroachments on the fields, and nuisances to the neighbourhood. Certain commissioners, therefore, who were the Lord Chancellor Bacon, the Earls of Worcester, Pembroke, and Arundel, and other noblemen and gentlemen, were directed to reform these grievances, and according to their discretion to frame and reduce those fields, both for sweetness, uniformity, and comeliness, into such walks, partitions, and other plottes, and in such sort, manner, and form, both for public health and pleasure, as should be drawn up, by way of map, by Inigo Jones, who was then Surveyor General of his Majesty's works. Under the superintendance of this able architect, the present square of Lincoln's Inn Fields was laid out, and the buildings were began, but many deviations were subsequently made in the original plan.*

This square contains three sides of handsome houses, being bounded on the east, by the wall of the Inn gardens. The whole of it is in St. Giles's parish, and is confessedly the largest square in the metropolis, being by a whimsical conceit of the celebrated architect, in extent equal to the base of the largest pyramid founded by Cheops, in Egypt,† which was built accord-

---

* In Rymer's Foedra, vol. 18, p. 67, is another commission, directed to the Earl of Arundel, Inigo Jones, and others, for the prevention of any building on new foundations, within two miles of the city of London and palace at Westminster, and in the Strafford papers, are some letters of Mr. Gerrard published, which contain an account of proceedings under that commission, under whose orders and authority twenty newly-erected houses in St. Martin's Lane were entirely pulled down.

† Walpole says "Lincoln's Inn Square is laid out with regard to so trifling a circumstance, as to be of the exact dimensions of one of the pyramids. This would have been admired in those ages, when the keep of Kenilworth Castle

ing to Diodorus, 1050 years before Christ, and is 700 feet in length on each of its four sides, and 500 feet high. Had it been finished according to the plan laid down, it would have surpassed every modern square in London, as it is the most extensive in Europe, comprising, in its area, ten acres of land.*

We may remark, that as St. Giles's parish contains the largest square, so it also *may boast* of the smallest, which is situate near it, namely, Prince's Square, containing only one house! It is situate in a little avenue, called also Prince's Street, leading to Little Queen Street and Gate Street.

The slip of ground between the north side of Lincoln's Inn Fields and Holbourn, now occupied by the avenue called Whetstone's Park, in the parish of St. Giles, is in old deeds named " Le Spencer's Lond," and a deep ditch, which anciently divided it from those fields, and ex-

---

was erected in the form of a horse fetter, and the Escurial in the shape of St. Laurence's gridiron."

* " Babington's plot was concocted at Southampton house, Holborn, as it is called in the indictment, in the parish of St. Giles in the Fields, and at other places in the said parish. He and his accomplices, seven in all, were hanged, bowelled, and quartered in Lincoln's Inn Fields, on a stage, or scaffold of timber, strongly made for that purpose, even in the place where they used to meet, and to conferre of their traitorous purposes." *See State Trials and Stowe.*

tended nearly to Drury Lane, had the appropriate designation of "Spencer's Dig." On this ground, which, from lying waste, was frequently the scene of low dissipation, houses were first erected on the eastern part, by Mr. Whetstone, a vestry-man of St. Giles's, and from him it obtained the name of Whetstone's Park. On the other half, the houses were continued by Mr. Phillips, and called Phillips's Rents. Several of the courts communicating with Holborn were built about the same time, particularly Pargiter's Court, by a person of that name, which is now called Feathers Court, from a neighbouring sign in Holborn.

Gate Street, and Great and Little Turnstile, were, as their names imply, avenues leading into Lincoln's Inn Fields.* Strype, in 1723, de-

---

* Great and Little Turnstiles, both in this parish, are much frequented thoroughfares, the former a straight passage, the other a crooked alley, derived their names from the *turning stiles*, which 200 years ago, stood at their respective ends next Lincoln's Inn Fields, and which were so placed, both for the conveniency of foot passengers, and to prevent the straying of cattle, the fields being at that time used for pasturage. In Charles I.'s reign " Europea Speculatum, or a View or Survey of the state of religion in the western part of the world," a curious work by Sir Edwin Sandys, printed in quarto, 1637, was "sold by John Hatton, at the *Turning stile* in Holborn." Also, the English Translations of Bishop Peter Camus's "Admirable Events," printed in quarto 1639, was "sold in Holborn in Turnstyle Lane."

Strype says, (anno 1638) " Great Turnstile Alley is famous for shoe-makers, sempstresses, and milliners, for which it is of

scribes Whetstone Park, at the back of Holborn, as being noted for its once infamous and vicious inhabitants, which some years since were forced away; and Butler, our inimitable satirist, has thus alluded to its profligacy:—

> "And make a brothel of a palace,
> Where harlots ply, as many tell us,
> Like brimstones in a *Whetstone ale-house.*"

The early attention of the legislature, on the restoration of Charles II. was directed to the lighting and cleansing the streets, repairing the highways and sewers of the capital, the salutary effects of which were gradually communicated to our parish, and the novel exhibition of candles, or lights in lanthorns, was directed by the act to be hung out by every householder, from the time of its becoming dark, till nine every evening, from Michaelmas to Lady-day.

The south side of Great Queen Street was now completed, which contained, with many other parts of the parish, various mansions of the nobility. Lord Herbert, of Cherbury, had been one of the first inhabitants of this street,

---

considerable trade, and well noted." Its present occupants can hardly be classed, their trades being mostly different, as dealers in cutlery and hardware, and butchers, dress, bonnet, and glove-makers, a tobacconist, pastry-cook, fruiterer, &c. Little Turnstile is chiefly inhabited by brokers and petty chandlers. Near it is New Turnstile, built 1685, which has been lately thoroughly repaired, and is occupied by small shop-keepers.

residing at the south side, near the east corner of Wild Street, where he died in 1648. The house is still standing, and is one of the fifteen built in the third year of James I. (1603.) This spirit of building continued till the reign of Queen Anne; the marsh, and other portions of land belonging to the crown, being leased out for that purpose, and the injudicious restraints of former periods no longer continuing.

In the sixth year of the reign of this princess, the whole parish, except the neighbourhood of Bedford Square, and part of Bloomsbury, became generally covered with houses, including St. Giles's Street and Broad Street, from the Pound to Drury Lane,* on both sides, the south-

---

* Drury Lane is now, when contrasted with its former state, an extraordinary instance of the change effected. In Aggas's and Hogenburgh's plans of about 1570 and 1584, it is represented at the north end, as containing a cluster of farm and other houses, a cottage, and a blacksmith's shop, and the lane, in continuity to Drury Place, forms a separation from the fields by embankments of earth, something like those of Maiden Lane, Battle Bridge. It was in fact a country road to Drury Place, and the Strand, and its vicinage. It was anciently called via de Aldewych. "Nearly opposite to Crown Buildings, is a low public house, bearing the sign of the Cock and Pye' (being a contraction for the Cock and Magpie) which two centuries ago, was almost the only house in the eastern part of Drury Lane, except the mansion of the Druries. Hither the youths and maidens of the metropolis, who, in social revelry on May-day, threaded the jocund dance round the may-pole in the Strand, were accustomed to resort for cakes and ale, and other refreshments." Pope, in his Dunciad, has immortalized

east side of Tottenham Court Road, Hog Lane, (now Crown Street) from the north end to the then Greyhound Tavern, seven streets diverging from the Seven Dials, and Castle Street, the east side of Drury Lane, south, to the Maid in the Moon Tavern, two doors south of the Horseshoe Tavern, all inclusive, and all its west side to Princes Street, both sides of which were complete, thence to Wild Street end, north side of Duke Street, and on the south side to the Portuguese Ambassadors, to Lincoln's Inn Fields, the three sides of which were completed, thence to Louches Buildings, now Portsmouth Street, to the Black Jack. The south side of Holbourn was finished, extending from St. Giles's Broad Street to the Boot and Gridiron, a little east of Great Turnstile, and on the north side, two doors east of the Vine Tavern; Kingsgate Street, both sides to Eagle Street, and to

---

this neighbourhood, by naming it as the scene of the "high heroic games, devised by dullness to gladden her sons."

"Amid the area wide they took their stand,
Where the tall may-pole o'erlooked the Strand,
But now piety and Anne ordain,
A church collects the saints of Drury Lane."

Londiniana.

Nell Gwynne is said to have been born in the Coal Yard, part of a passage leading out of Drury Lane to Holborn. She is well known to have been a favourite mistress of Charles II. and from her sprang the Dukes of St Albans. Whatever were her vices, she has the merit of first suggesting the founding Chelsea Hospital for superannuated soldiers.

the corner on the west side, and all King Street and Great Russell Street, to Tottenham Court Road. Such is the outline of the vast increase, including the intermediate spaces, not mentioned here, mostly effected during little more than a century! I purposely omit Bloomsbury, till I expressly treat on that portion of this parish, but I may here state, that towards the termination of Queen Anne's reign, the whole district was calculated to comprise about 3000 houses, being an addition of 2203 since the death of James I. 1624.

In the early part of this vast increase of St. Giles's parish, the south and east sides of the hospital site proceeded slowly. Mr. Abraham Speckart, and Mr. Breade, two eminent parishioners in the time of James and Charles I. had residences and grounds here, and afterwards Sir William Stiddolph; these seem to have been almost the only inhabitants on the spot. About the year 1697, the suburbs of the metropolis were much increased, through the settlement of about 14,000 French protestants, who had fled from the bigoted intolerance of Lewis XIV. on his revocation of the edict of Nantz. Many hundreds of these refugees fixed their abode in the neighbourhood of Long Acre, the Seven Dials, Soho, &c.*

---

* The district thus named, was formerly known by the name of the Cock and Pie Fields, and noted for assemblages of

New Compton Street, when first formed, was denominated Stiddolph Street, after Sir Richard Stiddolph: it afterwards changed its name from a demise of the whole adjoining marshland, made by Charles II. to Sir Francis Compton, who built a continuation of Old Compton Street. All this, and the intermediate streets, formed part of the site of the hospital and grounds,* as did the west side of Monmouth Street, so named after the Duke of Monmouth, who was very popular at that period.

The reigns of William III. and Queen Anne, were important periods for building, when the

---

dissolute and idle persons. Here was also a large laystall for soil from the streets for many years. At length, in the reign of William III. a Mr. Neale took the ground to build upon, and completely metamorphosed this sink of filth and iniquity. Under the date of the 5th of October, 1694, Mr. Evelyn, in his Diary says, "I went to see the building near St. Gyles's, where Seven Dials make a star from a doric pillar, placed in the middle of a circular area," said to be by Mr. Neale introducer of the late lotteries, in imitation of Venice, now set up here, for himself twice and now once for the state." The Doric pillar was afterwards surmounted by a clock, having seven dials, and hence the name by which this neighbourhood is known. This same Mr. Thomas Neale, took a large piece of ground on the north side of Piccadilly, of Sir Thomas Clarges, agreeing to lay out £10,000 in building, but he did not do so, and Sir Walter, son of Sir Thomas, after great trouble, got the lease out of his hands. Clarges Street was subsequently built on the same plot of ground. *Brayley's Londiniana and Malcolm's Lond.*

* In a scarce ground plan, published after the fire in 1666, the north side of the hospital site seems only to have been built on, the back or south side being all laid out as gardens.

metropolis greatly expanded, and especially towards the west. " *The distant* villages," Mr. Brayley observes, " as they had been of St. Martin's and St. Giles in the Fields, were now incorporated with the capital, which began to stretch away towards the yet remote village of Mary-la-bonne. The increase was so abundant, that in the ninth year of Queen Anne, the legislature deemed it expedient to pass an act for the erection of *fifty new churches* within the cities of London and Westminster, and their respective suburbs. By a statement laid before parliament during the progress of the bill, it appeared that the metropolis and its suburbs contained, at that time, about 200,000 persons more than could be accommodated in churches and chapels belonging to the establishment."

As the buildings progressed, Bedford Square arose, from a cow yard, to its present magnificent form, and has been the residence of several of our lord chancellors and judges during many years. This square, with its avenues and neighbouring streets, mostly in St. Giles's, have been chiefly erected since 1778, comprising Caroline Street, Bedford Street, Tavistock Street, the east side of Tottenham Court Road, Store Street, Alfred place, North and South Crescents, Chenies Street, Thornhaugh and Gower Streets, &c. These erections, amounting to about 420 houses, have made a considerable addition, and are mostly of a genteel description.

The village of St. Giles has been celebrated for its early inns and houses of entertainment;* and as some account of them cannot fail to interest the lovers of antiquities, I shall notice a few of them here chiefly on the authority of Parton, and especially as illustrative of several particulars in this history.

CROCHE HOUSE is said to have been one of the earliest inns in the parish, and is mentioned in the hospital grants, by the name of "Le Croche Hose," or the Crossed Stockings, the sign of which it bore. (This sign is still retained by the hosiers, and exhibits a *red and white* stocking crossed, after the manner of St. Andrew's Cross.)

It belonged to the hospital cook, anno 1300, who afterwards presented it to this establishment, and was situate opposite the present entrance to Monmouth Street, north end. It not being mentioned in the deed of exchange in Henry VIII.ths reign, leads to the supposition of its being destroyed, or that it had ceased to be known at that period.

THE SWAN ON THE HOP was another house of entertainment, mentioned in a demise of the master and brothers to John de Potton and

---

* See quotation from Stowe, p. 43.

wife, (34 Edward III.) in which it is called, "Le Swan on le Hop," and from the description therein, it must have stood eastward from Drury Lane end, and on the south side of Holborn. Little else is known of it, it being also omitted in the deed of exchange.

THE WHITE HART. In the exchange, this inn is described as "one messuage called the Whyte Hart, with eighteen acres of pasture to the same messuage belonging." It stood on the north-east corner of Aldewych, or Holborn end of Drury Lane, and was an Inn as lately as 1720. *See View of London*, 1708, *and Strype's Stowe*, in whose plan it is shewn under the name of the White Hart, 1720. In Aggas's Plan, 1560, the site of this inn is marked by a cluster of buildings, standing at the corner of Holborn and Drury Lane, surrounded on three sides by a wall. Attached to them is pasture land, which might be the eighteen acres described, being bounded on the west by Drury Lane, on the east, by the way now called Little Queen Street, and on the north by Holborn, from which last it appears fenced by an embankment.

The court called White Hart Yard, where the inn stood, has been recently demolished, having been taken by Messrs. William and Edward Cleaver, who built thereon, and conditioned to widen the west end of Holborn fifteen feet, and the north end of Drury Lane seven.

Parton designates this as one of the greatest improvements, in public accommodations, that has taken place in these parishes for a century.

THE ROSE. This and the Vine were enumerated amongst the hospital possessions, in the exchange with Henry VIII. and are described to have then stood in the "village of St. Giles." The Rose is mentioned in a deed in the time of Edward III. but not its situation; but by a deed of bargain and sale, dated 1567 (Charles II.'s reign) Edward Tooke conveyed to Luke Miller, "all the tenements, with the yards, gardens, or backsides thereto belonging, situate in Lewkner's Lane, in the parish of St. Giles, which said two tenements do abut on the tenement formerly known by the sign of the *Rose*, late in the tenure of Walter Gibbons." Hence we may conjecture that it stood on the south side of Holborn, not far eastward from the White Hart.

THE VINE. The Vine was, till September, 1816, a house of public accommodation, on the north side of Holborn, a little below the end of Kingsgate Street, and a few doors to the east. It was originally a complete roadside house, having nothing at its back but fields and country.* In some parish entries it is called "The

---

* This house, mentioned in Doomsday Book, (see p. 2,) became a nuisance of the lewdest description, during many years previous to its demolition. The new erection comprised

Kingsgate Tavern," probably from its standing near the king's-gate, or turnpike, at the entrance of the adjoining road. It was taken down 1817, and two houses were erected on its site.

TOTEN, OR TOTTEN HALL, or as it is sometimes in ancient records termed "Totham Hall," and from which Tottenham Court Road took its name, was formerly within the boundaries of St. Giles's parish, as was also a considerable portion of the prebend of Totten Hall. It was in Henry III.'s reign the residence of William de Tottenhall, and was a mansion of eminence, as the court house, probably, of that manor. It is noticed as a house of entertainment in 1645, when the following entry occurs :—

1645. "Received of Mr. Bringhurst, constable, which he had of Mrs. Stacye's maid and others, for drinking at Tottenhall Court on the sabbath-day, xijd. a piece" £0 3 0

At this period, and from thence to the restoration, if a judgment may be formed from entries of similar fines, it was a place of much resort on Sundays for drinking, but little else is known of it. The Adam and Eve, Tottenham

---

one house only, which was occupied, first, by a respectable timber merchant, (a Mr. Semple) and afterwards by Probert, the accomplice of the murderer Thurtell. Subsequently it has been divided into two dwellings, one of which is occupied by Mr. Easterby, and the other by Mr. Kleft.

Court Road, (or rather New Road,) is built on the spot, and part of the old building and a fine spring still remains there.

THE MAIDENHEAD INN was situate in *Dyot Street* at least as early as the reign of Queen Elizabeth, and formed then part of the estate of Lord Mountjoy. In the deeds of that period it is described as "one large tenement, called the Maidenhead, so thence divided into two tenements," and during many years, the house at which the parish meetings were chiefly held.

In Charles II.'s reign it mostly flourished, when the parish books frequently notice these meetings; and at a later period, about 1700, it became a house much resorted to by mealmen and farmers. When it lost its respectable character is doubtful, but it is known to have been, during more than half a century, a liquor-shop and public-house of the vilest description, and the haunt of beggars and desperate characters. It bore marks of having been a handsome house to the last, it having been demolished, together with a great part of the east side of Dyot Street, and the ground on which they stood has been converted into a stone-yard, under the direction of the paving-board, of which more notice will be taken hereafter.

TURNSTILE TAVERN. This was situate on the south side of Holborn, on the west side corner of the footpath leading into Lincoln's

Inn Fields, since called Great Turnstile, and is now a butcher's shop. As a tavern, it was of great celebrity, and, by will, four pounds annuity was left issuing therefrom, and from an adjoining house, as an endowment to the alms-houses. This bequest was made by Anthony Bayley, a parishoner, in 1640; and there is a parish entry in 1693, which proves that it had then ceased from being a tavern. It is as follows:—

"Received at the house, *formerly* the Turnstile Tavern, in clear rent, taxes allowed"............... £3 6 6

THE COCK AND PYE. This public-house stood, according to tradition, at the west corner of the marsh land, now the junction of Little St. Andrew Street, West Street, and Castle Street, and afterwards originated the name of Cock and Pye Fields, to the spot called the Seven Dials. The sign was the Cock only, to which, probably, the Magpie was afterwards added.

According to ancient records, the district under our consideration comprised six divisions, which have been considered naturally formed, and it is essential to our history to notice them in detail, as illustrative of the progressive changes it has undergone at different periods. In pursuing this course, it is impossible to avoid some anticipations in regard to the Parish of

St. Giles, which we shall hereafter treat of more particularly.

The FIRST DIVISION comprised the southern side of the hospital from *Town's-end* to *Aldewych west* with a lane which ran under the hospital walls denominated in old records *Oldestrate* and *Eldestrate*, now Crown Street, being the great road from *Tottenhall* to *Westminster:* it contained the *Marsh-land*, or *Merslade; New-londe*, and *Aldewych;. west Marshland*, or *Le Merslade*. The hospital occupied much of this tract, and the estates lay behind it, and comprehended the whole of the ground by the Seven Dials and its neighburhood, it was a *mere* or. *lake* probably at an early period, but certainly wet and marshy.

Le Newelond, or *Newland*, probably separated the eastern end of *Marsh-land* from the west side of *Aldewych*, (Drury Lane) and derived its name from being newly drained (as conjectured) from the Marshlands, a continuation of which it anciently formed.

Aldewych west comprised the land to a considerable extent on both sides of the *via Aldewych*, or Drury Lane, and in this division it comprehended that on the west side, bounded by the *via regia de Aldewych;* on the east, *Newland;* on the west, the land of the *Abbots of Westminster;* (Long Acre) on the south; and the *Street of St. Giles* on the north.

All this district remained mere pasture land till subsequent to the Dissolution, except a few scattered houses near the north end of Drury Lane, or *Aldewych* About anno 1600, the whole north side of the hospital had given way to a row of houses, and in 1623, other houses were continued from Drury Lane to the east end of this row, amounting to forty-seven, exclusive of six courts or alleys branching from them into Aldewych west, all of which ground was, until now, unbuilt on. At *Town's-end*, which lay to the west of the church, there were now, including eleven in *Rose and Crown Yard*, on the same site forty-nine houses more. *Middle-row*, which is supposed to have stood near the Church, was well inhabited, *Rose and Crown Yard*, corner of Crown Street, was occupied by Mr. Alderman Bigge when the Church was built. It has been rebuilt, and is called *Farmer's Rents*, inhabited by very low people.

Dudley Court, so named from the Duchess Dudley, is now become an obscure thoroughfare, inhabited also by low people *Lloyd's Court*, the site of the hospital mansion, according to Maitland, and where Lord Lisle, Duchess Dudley, and Lord Wharton resided, was so named from the builder.' *Denmark Street* runs into *Hog Lane*, or Crown Street: this was not entirely built on till after 1687. *Stedwell Street* is spoken of by Strype as very ordinary for buildings and inhabitants, as is *Stacie Street,. Kendrick Yard, Vinegar Yard, Phœnix Street,* &c. In his time they were mostly French, and of the poorer sort. *Hog Lane, the Eldestrate* of ancient deeds, is of the same date as Denmark Street. Hogarth has given a degree of celebrity to this Street, and the adjoining Hog Lane, the scene of one of his sets of prints, called "The Four Times of the Day."

Belton Street was erected in 1683, and from the age of the houses and other concurrent circumstances is but poorly inhabited, and has several courts branching therefrom, some of which are of antiquity.

Bowl Yard and Canter's Alley, about where the brewery stands, at the north end of Belton Street, were first built on about 1623, the rest of the land about here being mostly cultivated ground, known by the name of the great garden, which name the ground now occupied as the Workhouse formerly bore, in a lease granted to Anthony Baskerfield, when it was described as enclosed with a brick wall.

Short's Gardens and Brownlow Street, with their neighbourhood, was garden ground in 1623, having only three houses, occupied by gardeners, as mentioned in the assessments of that period. The northern side assumed the name of Short's Gardens, from a mansion built there by Dudley Short, Esq. an eminent parishioner in the reign of Charles II. with garden attached. The above street received its name from Sir John Brownlow, Bart. a parishioner in the same reign, whose house and garden also then stood there; and from the minutes of vestry it appears that a serious dispute occurred with St. Martin's parish in 1682, about the rates due on these premises, which was decided in favour of St. Giles's parish.

Monmouth Street, anciently called *Le Lane*, with Hog Lane or Crown Street, surrounded the south and west sides of the hospital. It was so named in compliment to the unfortunate James, Duke of Monmouth, who had a house in the adjacent Soho Square, (called also Monmouth Square.) The custom of living in cellars is peculiar to this and some other parts of the parish; and here the superstitious practice of nailing *horse-shoes* on the door thresholds, to exclude the entrance of witches, is still retained. Every body knows it is noted for second-hand apparel.

THE SECOND DIVISION is situate on the south side of the parish, and on the east side of *Aldewych* (Drury Lane.) It includes the ground now covered by *Lewkner's Lane, Parker Street*, &c. as far as the back of *Great Queen Street south*, being bounded by *Drury Lane west, Holborn north*, and *Little Queen Street east*. In early times this division was separated into nearly two equal parts by *Spencer's Dig*, or Ditch, which commenced at the entrance of *Lewkner's Lane*, and ran eastward as far as *Holborn Bars*. The part of land between the ditch and Holborn was then most inhabited.

1623. The assessment for re-building the Church, mentions ten housekeepers in *Aldewych east;* and Philip Parker and family had a seat in Parker's Lane; and Sir Lewis Lewkner had another, with garden, in the lane which bears his name; and these are the only parishioners who can be named with certainty as then resident here. The *Rose Inn* has been already spoken of.

"*Lutner's Lane*, at the lower end of *Newton Street*, falls into *Drury Lane*, and is a very ordinary place: It is a corruption of the name of *Lewkner*." Sir Roger L'Estrange called it a rendezvous and nursery for lewd women, but first resorted to by the roundheads. It is now called *Charles Street*.

Parker's Lane runs from Drury Lane west, to Little Queen Street east. The Dutch Ambassador had formerly stables and premises here. *Newton Street* and *St. Thomas's Lane* have nothing extraordinary appertaining to them. *Little Queen Street* is described by Strype as coming out of *Great Queen Street*, and from thence falling into *Holborn*, and being much pestered by coaches. *Great Queen Street*, which bounds the division on the south, is a handsome and spacious street, built on the site of the common path which anciently separated *Aldewych Close* from the northern division of *Aldewych*, which extends to *Holborn*. Its south side was probably built in a straggling manner near the close of Elizabeth's reign, from whence, no doubt, it was designated *Queen Street*, but its best houses were built for people of quality in James I.'s reign, under Inigo Jones, about the time he laid out Lincoln's Inn Square. Powlet, Cherbury, and Conway houses were among them, and are still remaining.

Freemason's Tavern is an elegant modern building, and one of the best conducted houses in town; and has unquestionably, under the superintendance and guidance of Mr. Cuff, far more public dinners than any other tavern in town. The other courts about this spot and division, *New Turnstile Alley, Monmouth Court,* &c. are of little note.

THE THIRD DIVISION. "*Campum de Aldewych*," or *Oldwick Close*. This comprised the site of the present *West Street, Princes Street,* and their neighbourhoods, being bounded north by *Great Queen Street;* south, by the back of *Princes Street,* part of *Duke Street,* &c.; west, by *Drury Lane;* and east, by *Lincoln's Inn Fields.* On the sale and dispersion of the hospital, this track of land came into the possession of the

Holford family, a descendant of which held it in the reigns of Elizabeth and James I. at the same period when Sir John Drury, Knight, held the north end, or St. Clement's half. He left a sum of money to be paid to the poor of the parish annually, founded on some conscientious scruples on account of its having belonged to the hospital, a charitable foundation. Part of this land came into the possession of Sir Edward Stradling and other persons about the beginning of the reign of Charles I. Houses had however been previously raised on the side next the highway, together with the play-house called the "*Cockpit Theatre.*" Both sides of *Princes Street* also (which had been a path dividing *Aldewych Field,* between the parishes of St. Giles and St. Clement's Danes) had been built on as early as the latter end of the reign of Queen Elizabeth, or thereabout. The spot had then acquired the name of *Oldwick Close,* and had fourteen houses standing on its west side, or the east side of Drury Lane, as well as a second theatre called the *Phœnix,* which succeeded the *Cockpit,* after it was destroyed in 1617.* *Oldwick Close,* by a deed of 1629, containing two acres, enclosed on the north, towards Queen Street, with a ditch; on the east, towards Lincoln's Inn, with a common sewer;

---

* This theatre stood in a court denominated Pitt Place, an avenue running out of Drury Lane to Wild Street.

on the south, with a ditch or fence dividing it from other parts of the same close; and on the west, towards the back of Drury Lane, with a ditch or mud wall. It was in the possession of Sir Edward Stradling in 1632, and the celebrated Sir Kenelm Digby; and the former built on his part a large mansion and offices. There was a ditch and mud wall, or embankment, with a few scattered buildings on the Drury Lane side, among which were the *Cockpit*, and afterwards the *Phœnix Theatres*.

Queen Street and Princes Street, with *Weld Street*, (now Wild Street,) are the principal streets erected on *Oldwick Close*. In the latter site, the respectable family of the *Welds* of Lutworth Castle, and a magistrate, resided in a large mansion. *Holford Court*, now *Stewart's Rents*, is a thoroughfare from Drury Lane to Wild Street.

THE FOURTH DIVISION. South side, *Fikattesfield and Holborn Bars*. This division included the whole of Lincoln's Inn Fields, and the streets, &c. in its vicinity, (forming part of St. Giles's parish,) to the east and north, with the land next Holborn Bars, now *Whetstone's Park*, &c. as far east and west as from ten houses beyond Turnstile to Little Queen Street, with the half of Holborn on that side.

Fikattesfeld, or Ficket's Field. This enclosure stood near the *old Temple*, of which it formed

part of the grounds previous to the removal of
that foundation. It derived its names probably
from some early proprietor, and was called also
the Templars' Field, from its having been in the
possession of the *Knights Templars*, before the
dissolution of that order. It was certainly laid
out early as a walking place, and planted as far
back as Edward III. (about 1376) when it was
a common walking and sporting place for the
clerks of the chancery, apprentices and students of the law, and citizens of London. During the Interregnum, a petition was sent to
parliament respecting these fields, in which it
was shewn, that at that early period, one Roger
Legit had privily laid and hid many iron engines
called *caltrappes* in the trenches of *Ficket's
Fields*, with a malicious intention to maim the
said clerks and others, for which he was punish-
ed by fine and imprisonment. This was recited
to shew the right the students and others had to
recreate themselves in these fields.

Holborn, in the reign of Queen Elizabeth,
began to be built on; and Turnstile, in the assessment of 1623, is said to contain, on both
sides, thirty one houses; and a "*Thornton's
Alley,*" somewhere near the spot, has therein
forty houses mentioned. "*Partridge Alley,*"
coming from Holborn to the back of the houses
in Lincoln's Inn Fields, now called *Newman's*

Row, is mentioned to have forty-nine houses; but no notice is taken of *Little Queen Street, Princes Street, Turnstile Alley, &c.* to the westward of *Gate Street*: they were probably not built. *Whetstone Park* was built in Charles II.'s time, and the whole site was covered with dwellings.

Holborn was a highway of great publicity in the reigns of Henry II. and John. The *village of Holbourn*, being erected on the bank of the *bourne or brook*, extended itself gradually westward, and communicated its name to the long and spacious street which attaches it to *St. Giles's Street*, that part of it being distinguished by the denomination of *High Holborn*.

THE FIFTH DIVISION comprised the north side of the parish, or *Bloomsbury west*, and reached from *Tottenham Court Road* west, to *Charlotte Street* and *Gower Street* east, bounded north by *St. Pancras* parish, and south by *St. Giles's Street*.

This northern district, in the early times of the hospital, formed two parts—the land belonging to the foundation, and the land called *Blemund's Land*, and afterwards *Blemundsbury*: the first comprised the *Pittaunce Croft*, or *Hospital Close*, and its adjoining land, and the latter of the present *Bloomsbury*. Their extent, lengthways, was from *Tottenham Court Road* west, to *St. Andrew's, Holborn*, parish east; and breadthways, *from St. Giles's Street* and *Holborn* south, to the parish of *St. Pancras* north.

The division we are treating of commenced westerly with the *via de Tottenhall*, and ran eastward to *Russell's and Blemund's Land*, its south and north sides being formed by *St. Giles's High Street*, and the prebend of *Tottenhall*. The following were its ancient estates:—

Pittaunce Croft contained about sixteen acres, and was situate before the *Hospital Gate*, and formed principally the gardens of the master and brethren. The north side of *St. Giles's Street*, part of which is in that parish, was about 100 feet deep from the road side, to the *Pittaunce Croft Ditch*. This slip of land and its continuation eastward, was the most inhabited part of the village, as remotely as during the reigns of John and Henry III. when its houses had gardens extending to the ditch.

East of *Pittaunce Croft* was mostly the property of *Seman Russell*, whose residence was there in an inclosure, some distance from the north side of *St. Giles's Street*, nearly in a direct line from *Monmonth Street*.

In 1623 forty houses were assessed at the north-west end of *St. Giles's Street*. "In *Dixon's Alley*" twenty-one, and "*Eagle and Child Alley*" thirty-seven. *Bainbridge* and *Buckridge Streets* were built on the above sites prior to 1672, and derive their names from their owners, eminent parishioners in the reign of Charles II. (*See Strype.*)

The former gentleman left a sum of money to build a gallery to the Church, the rents of which were to be applied towards the relief of the poor, which we shall notice hereafter. *Church Street* and *Church Lane* runs out of *Bainbridge Street* into *Dyot Street*, (now George Street): these take their names from nearly facing the church, having an avenue to them from thence formerly through *Bannister's Alley*, which now forms Mr. Remnant's timber yard.

Near to the timber yard is the *Hampshire Hog Yard.*

Dyot Street, now *George Street*, running from *Great Russell Street* to *Broad Street*, is the west boundary of *Bloomsbury parish*. It received its name from Richard Dyot, esquire, who resided upon the spot, and was a vestryman in the reign of Charles II.; and it was inhabited, till within these few years, by his descendant, Philip Dyot, esquire. This street, and its contiguous neighhood on the west side, has been remarkable for poverty and depravity, being the general resort of Irish, and where they first colonized at an early period.

Plumtree Street takes its name from Henry Plumtree, esquire, its builder, in 1686, or thereabout. This spot, so designated in the demise to him from John Buggin, esquire, in that year.

" *The old town of St. Giles.*" This street and its continuation, *Charlotte Street*, is of a respectable description, especially the latter.

THE SIXTH DIVISION. *North side of the parish. Bloomsbury east.* This extends from *Charlotte Street* west, to the extremities of the parish east, and bounded north and south as above, including the remainder of the present parish of *Bloomsbury.*

This division, with part of the fifth ditto, comprises the manor of Bloomsbury east and west. In the early part of the reign of Elizabeth, Southampton House was the only building in this part of the manor. In James I.'s time, it is denominated *a certain parcel of land called Bloomsbury*, nor was it till 1623 that a neighbourhood began to accumulate both in the east and west parts. *(For more on these divisions, see Parton's History, &c.)*

Chapter III.

St. Giles in the Fields noticed as a Parish—Antiquity of, examined—Its three successive Churches—High Church Politics—Puritanical Spoliations—Curious Parish Memorandums, &c.

Hitherto we have avoided treating on St. Giles as a Parish, a subject which comes next under our consideration, and a matter of no trifling importance to this History, involving, as it does, a question of much controversy.

Newcourt, in his Repertorium, which is considered a work of much research and corresponding authority, seems to be of opinion that it never was a parish till after the dissolution of the hospital. "I find," he says, "no institution to any Church in this parish (St. Giles), till after the hospital was suppressed, which makes me conclude, that the church belonging to the hospital was the place to which the inhabitants of this parish did, in those days, resort to perform their religious worship."—"The first institution I find to this church as *parochial* and a *rectory*, was in the first year of Edward VI.'s reign, the 20th of April, 1547, at the presentation of Sir Wimund Carew, as true and undoubted patron thereof; upon the death of whose clerk, William Rowlandson, (Bonner being Bishop of London) his successor was instituted November 8th, 1571, at the presentation of Queen Elizabeth, as true and undoubted patroness, from which time the advowson of this rectory hath continued all along in the Crown to this present."

On the founding of the hospital, it was very natural that a place of worship should be added to it; and Leland has established the fact by stating, that Matilda provided it with an oratory, but he says nothing of its church, nor of St. Giles as a parish, although he lived and wrote about the time of the suppression; and it is recorded of him, that he proposed the securing all the monastic manuscripts by placing them in the king's library, which, unfortunately, was not acceded to. In the charters extant, and especially in the deed for exchanging the hospital estates before quoted, St. Giles is called a village, and not a parish, the usual designation in all ancient and modern deeds, had it been so.

If we revert to early authorities, the existence of a parish will appear very doubtful prior to 1647, as the following inquiries will clearly shew:—

1st. *Doomsday Book*, a record of the highest importance, is silent on the subject, nor does it, under the head *Ossulveston*, (Ossulston) even mention the name of St. Giles, or indicate a parish in that suburb situation—a proof of its non-existence in 1066.

2nd. *The valor of Pope Nicholas* is a celebrated valuation of all the ecclesiastical benefices in England and Wales, taken in 1291, and recorded the taxation of the tenths of all those preferments, and also regulated the exaction of the kings and popes, until the twenty-sixth year of Henry VIII.'s reign, when it was superseded by the *Valor Ecclesiasticus*. No mention whatever is made in the above record of the parish of St. Giles, although ample notice is taken therein of the whole archdeaconry of Middlesex, which is the ecclesiastical division to which it is appended.

3rd. *The Nona Rolls*, records certain grants made in the fourteenth of Edward III. (dated twenty-sixth of January 1341) by the parliament of that monarch, of the ninth lamb, the ninth fleece, and the ninth sheaf, and was taken by assessors and others, throughout twenty-seven counties. St. Giles and Bloomsbury are here mentioned; the latter as Bilumond, or Blemund, but under the designation of a soke or liberty only, and not as a parish; neither in the ancient grants of kings, popes, bishops, &c. is it so named.

4th. *The Charter of Henry* II. confirming the institution of the hospital, states that it was built "*Ubi Johannes bonae memoria fuit Cappellanus.*" (When John of good memory was Chaplain."*) This, instead of establishing the idea of a parish, tends to prove that St. Giles was a royal manor about the time of the conquest, as has been before remarked, for not only did Matilda give to the hospital inmates a perpetual grant of it when she founded that charity, but she made them lords of the manor, and proprietors, under the crown, of the whole, or nearly so, of the soil. As a corroboration of these facts, it is well known that they held courts in their own jurisdiction, and exercised all the usual manorial rights. All payments of rent, and the various acknowledgments they were entitled to by their several grants, were made at the hospital court; and tenants holding, by service of bodily labour, and other servile tenures peculiar to that time, rendered them to the master, brethren, and sisters, as lords of the fee. In the ancient deeds now extant, we learn that nearly all the householders of the hospital domains lived under the master and paternity of that foundation, and were subject to them.

All the charters down to Edward III. speak of St. Giles's hospital without any allusion to a parish.†

---

* See page 7.

† The definition of the word parish, &c. has been generally admitted to bear the following construction. Parochial bounds

5th. *The confirmatory bull of Pope Alexander,* in the reign of Henry III. only mentions this district as "*locum ipsum in quo fundamentum est ipsius hospitalis, cu gardinis et octis que adjacent eid hospitalis exparte australe et exparte aquilonari.*" ("The place where the said hospital is founded, with the gardens attached to the same, and eight acres of land which adjoin the said hospital on the south and on the north.")

Newcourt says, "In the hospital of St. Giles was a chapel, wherein King Edward I. in the first year of his reign, 1272, founded a chauntry, (tis like for his father and ancestors) for which this hospital took yearly of the exchequer, for the maintenance of it, sixty shillings, and twenty shillings more at the hands of the sheriff of Surry;" and "I no where find this chapel

---

having been long fixed by custom and settled usage, were sometimes found so extensive, as to render it inconvenient for remote hamlets to attend the church. It was therefore a practice to relieve and ease such inhabitants by building oratories, or chapels, in many such remote hamlets, in which a *cappelane* (chaplain) was sometimes endowed by the lord of the manor, who was generally maintained by a stipend from the parish priest, to whom all right and dues were reserved. These chapels, though endowed, were not *parochial*, but dependant on their mother churches, to whom all dues were paid of an ecclesiastical kind, except the portions of such endowments. The privilege of administering the sacrament, (especially that of baptism) and the office of burial, were the proper rights and jurisdiction that made it no longer a dependant chapel of ease, but a separate parochial chapel. (*See Jacob and others.*)

charged with first fruits and tenths, but with procurations and synodals."

If, according to this writer, there was no institution to St. Giles's Church till 1547, (and it would certainly appear from the register if it were so) it is a strong presumption that there could not have been an independant parish priest before that period; the institution of the parish priest being positively necessary by the canon law, and was only to be dispensed with under particular circumstances; one of which was, when licences were granted to monks, or the ecclesiastical religious fraternities, to serve a parochial cure by themselves, by reason of the contiguity of the churches, or poverty of the houses; and this seems to have been the case in St. Giles. It had no church or place of worship for the inhabitants of the manor but what was poor, and the advowson which was appendant to the manor and hospital, appears to have been purely donative, and conferred successively on one of their own fraternity.

In this view we may account for a few solitary instances wherein St. Giles, at early periods, has been denominated a parish, rather by reputation than otherwise, in the hospital deeds and other documents.

In the reign of Henry III. it is recorded that "a house and cutilage was granted by William

Thrillam, situate in St. Giles's parish." (No date.)

Premises were granted to the hospital by William Christemasse, a messuage and land, in the parish of St. Giles. (Date unknown,)

A plot of land of hospital fee, in the parish of St. Giles. (Grantor and date unknown.)

A curtilage, situate in the parish of St. Giles, a grant of William de Tottenhall. (Date unknown.

Half an acre of land, &c. in the parish of St. Giles, without the bars of *Holeburn*, a grant of Thomas Osgood. (Date unknown.)

It is worthy of notice, that out of the number of ninety-two grants on record,[*] applicable to the hospital, known to be situate in St. Giles's parish, none of them except the five enumerated are so described! This would not have been so had St. Giles been a regular parish, instead of one by reputation,—a distinction in law, which is evidently in point here.

Out of ten anniversary obits, for which bequests were given, only two individual donors (William Christmasse and John de Garderoba, anno 1200) mention the parish of St. Giles.

But independant of other considerations, it should be observed, that the deeds referred to

---

[*] The hospital estates lay in no less than sixty-three parishes and places, and yet the greater number were in its own parish, and in fact it owned the most part of it.

on this question are no longer in existence, none but copies remain, and we have noticed that those quoted are without dates, and even the kings' reigns when the grants were made, are only known by probability.

The result of our inquiries leads us therefore to the conclusion of Newcourt, as to the first institution of a parish, and that the hospital church was the place of religious worship for the inhabitants at an early period.

It is conjectured that this church included that of the parish, and was divided by a screen, one portion of it being the resort of the inhabitants, and the other that of the hospital inmates; but when it was erected is uncertain, but probably in the prosperous days of that institution; or it was an addition to the chapel, or oratory, which originally belonged to it. Although it was of no great magnitude, superstition had furnished it with several divisions for altars and chapels, wherein different priests are said to have officiated, exclusive of others employed in the chantries and singing masses for the repose of the dead. From the Minutes of Vestry, we gather that it had a body and choir, or nave and chancel, a middle and side aisles: That the middle was divided by pillars and arches, above which arose walls, probably lighted by clerestory windows, called in the Minutes "the mayne wall over the arches, which wall ran the whole length of the church, or ranged through the church and chancel, into the crown of the arch, and the arches sprung from pillars extending also to an equal length."

From these several particulars Parton remarks, "we may conclude that this first structure was of some magnitude and beauty, though not of the largest class. Whether it was built with the *round* or *pointed* arch, is no where hinted at in the minutes from which we have quoted, otherwise we might have guessed at its general style of architecture; but if it was actually the church erected by Matilda, of which there seems no doubt, it must have been of that kind usually termed Norman. After the dissolution of the hospital, the ancient partition walls, or screen, being removed, the whole church was formed into a parish church, and a new steeple was built with a ring of bells, to accommodate the parishioners."

The principal object on entering that division called the hospital church, must have been its high altar of St. Giles, which stood at its east end, and was probably adorned with the image of the patron saint: before this burnt a great taper called "St. Giles's light," towards which, about the year 1200, William Christemas bequeathed the annual sum of twelve-pence.

The chapel of St. Michael and its altar, formed another prominent feature in the same building, and had its own proper priest, or chaplain. These both belonged to that portion of the structure appropriated to the use of the infirm of the hospital, and which, as most convenient for that purpose, it is reasonable to conjecture, occupied the southern division or half of the church.

The account of this church when it became entirely parochial is very meagre. The hospital church, or southern division of this fabric, became decayed with age and lay in rubbish, there being a void space at the upper end of the chancel, which was stored with lumber, as the boards of coffins, &c. when Lady, afterwards Duchess Dudley, added the becoming ornament of a screen, which divided the nave from the choir, or chancel, at her own expense.

From the Minutes of Vestry, 1617, four persons were appointed by vestry to inspect the account of Mr. Bigg concerning the charges of building the steeple and casting the new bells, when £125 : 19 : 5, due to him for money expended thereon, was ordered to be paid;* and at the next vestry, " the upper churchwarden was ordered to be assistant to the late churchwarden in the hanging of the said bells in the new steeple."

The church originally, before the erection of

---

* This refers to the first minute extant.

this steeple, is conjectured to have had merely a small round bell tower, with a conical top at its western entrance ; and there was only one bell, the customary appendage of hospitals and religious houses. The parish becoming, however, now more populous, a larger and more ornamental steeple was judged necessary, and was accordingly erected and furnished with additional bells, a full peal. Six years afterwards (viz. anno 1623), an order of vestry was made for pulling down " divers parts of the said church, the same being ruinous and decayed ; as also for the building and re-edifying of the same." The preamble to this order states that " whereas upon diligent view taken by men of skill, the walls of the north and south aisles, together with the main roof of the middle aisle, and walls thereof, as well as all the pillars in the church and chancel, were found so rotten and decayed, as to be in manifest danger of falling down ; it was by general consent agreed upon, that the said north and south aisles, together with the main roof of the middle aisle, should be wholly pulled down and re-edifyed with all convenient speed." Another vestry was called after a second inspection, and the following minute was entered.

" That the parts of the church before determined to be pulled down and rebuilt, viz. both the side aisles, and the *mayn wall over the arches* ranging through the church and chancel, unto the crown of the church, and no further," would be insufficient " the general pillars, as well within the chancel as within the church, being found to be so decayed and ruined in their very foundations, as by the opinion of surveyors and workmen, no further building might be raised upon them without imminent danger to the whole frame of the church. It was ordered that all the pillars, both in the church and chancel, should be wholly taken down and raised up again of free stone from the foundation to the crown of the arches."

Collectors were appointed to collect the money which should be assessed, and regulations agreed on for conducting the repairs, when they were found impracticable to execute, and finally the church and fabric was demolished.

A petition was presented, stating the necessity of wholly re-building St. Giles's church; the expense would, according to estimate, amount to £1500 more than the parish could raise, and humbly praying his majesty to recommend to the right reverend the Bishop of London, to write to the clergy of his diocese to raise contributions in their respective parishes for the finishing thereof; which the king, by an order dated at the court of Greenwich, 9th of June, 1624, was pleased to do. In consequence of this sanction, the Bishop (George Abbot*) by letter dated from his palace, London, on the 16th of the following July, directed his clergy to " move their several congregations liberally to contribute all in their power towards so good a work, and the rather to do it with all expedition, for that the winter coming on, the parishioners (to the number of *two thousand souls*) would be utterly destitute and deprived of spiritual comfort." The preamble of this letter states, " that through the injury of time and weather, as also for want of due reparation in ages past, there had a general wrack befallen the ancient parish church of St. Giles in the Fields, where not only the roofe and walls of the said church, but also the arches and pillars throughout the church and chancell, were, upon view taken by men of skill, found to be so ruinous and decayed, that of necessity the whole structure of the same was to be, and had been pulled down and demolished to the very foundation ; for the re-edifying whereof, in part, the parishioners and inhabitants having strained their abilities beyond example, did nevertheless find that the work would much exceed their

---

* I have here quoted Parton, but I find he was in an error as to the Bishop. Abbot had long ceased to be Bishop of London, having been promoted to Canterbury in 1611. King succeeded him in the metropolitan see, and on his dying in 1621, he was succeeded by George Mountain, who was in fact, Bishop of London at the time above alluded to.

power to finish, the charge of the whole being in estimate for the sum of £2,500," and he concludes (after some further directions) with ordering that " all monies collected should be entered in a vellum book to be provided by the parish of St. Giles for that purpose, as a perpetual memorial of the benevolence of each individual contributor." This was accordingly done in a register still remaining, intitled, " Liber Domus Dei Anglice,* or Doomes-day Booke." This book, through the politeness of the vestry clerk, I have seen and perused, and I consider it a curious parish record. The title continues—" *Thesaurus caelij* Reposit, Sive liber Dom Dei res memorata dignas parochiam hanc Sci Egidij in campis, Et imprimis: Nupera templi hujus instaura eo' em tangentes (breviter complectus.)" " Treasure deposited in heaven, or the book of God's house, of things worthy to be remembered in this parish of St. Giles-in-the Fields; and in the first place of the church now lately restored, some account touching the same."

It then gives an inscription commemorating

---

* Doomsday Book, or Dom Bec (the judicial book) a name applied to the inquisitions made by Alfred and William the Conqueror. It has been said to derive its name from Domus Dei, from the church or cathedral of Winchester, in which Alfred's survey was first deposited. It simply means, the Doom-book or Register, from whence judgment might be given in the tenure of estates.—*Kennet.*

the great liberality of Lady Dudley towards the expense of the new church, which afterwards was engraved on a marble tablet, and fixed against the *north gate* of the churchyard.

<table>
<tr><td>Surge re Caepit an 1623.
Adumbelicos Deductu, 1625.
Muro undiquaq valutie 1631.</td><td>Quod Foelix Bonusque Sit:
Posteris
Hoc Templum Loto Veteris ex Annosa Vetustate
Collapsi, Mola et Splendore Auctum
Multo Parocoerum
Charitas Instauravit
Inquibus Pientissima Heroinac
D. Alicia Duddeley
Munificentia Gratum Marmoris Hujus
Meretur Eloquium
Huic etiam accessit beneficia aliorum Quorundam
Pietas
Quibus Provisae in Coelo Sunt Grates.</td><td>Heus! Viator an effectum est bonis operibus Hoc Seculum?</td></tr>
</table>

TRANSLATION.

<table>
<tr><td>The Building commenced Anno Domine 1623.
Finished in 1625.
And encompassed with a wall in 1631.</td><td>This Temple (may it be a blessing to posterity), was built in the place of a former one, which had fallen from the effects of time. But augmented in size and with greater splendour by the christian beneficence of the parishioners, among whom the munificence of the pious Lady Alice Dudley deserves the grateful tribute of this marble.
The pious contributions of some others whose reward is in heaven, aided the work.</td><td>Say! Traveller! is this age barren in works of munificence?</td></tr>
</table>

Various particulars are next given in regard to the collecting money for the church, the names of the contributors, the sums subscribed, with the treasurer and wardens appointed to overlook the progress of building the church, as follows:—

" Money to re-build the present church, how collected and applied, namely, from the parishioners and others, with the particulars of the collection made in the churches of this diocese towards this work."

" Names* of those who, during the time of re-building the present church and the vestry house, constitued the vestry. First, Roger Manwayring, D.D. chaplain to the most serene prince Charles, King of Great Britain, a man of probity of manners and singular condition, and treasurer for the money collected."

---

* " A second book is among the parish records," (Parton informs us), " containing a further list of the names and residences of every inhabitant, with the sums they were assessed at; to which is prefixed this notice, viz. ' The inhabitants of the parrish of St. Gyles in the Fields in the countie of Middlesex, being at sundrie times warned and summoned both publiquelie at divine service by the parson, and particularlie at their howses by the churchwardens and others of the parish, to assemble themselves for the ratinge and assessinge of themselves, and the rest of the said inhabitants, towardes the re-edifieinge and buildinge of ther church, being then fallen in parte, and judged necessarie to be wholly pulled downe, the charge whereof was estimated by the view and survey of skilful workemen, to be likelie to amount to the sum of £2,000 and upwards. Uppon the 23rd day (xxiij) of September, 1623, and upon severall daies after, the said parishioners did accordinglie meete and assemble, and did rate and assesse themselves and the rest of the said inhabitants of the said parrish towardes raisinge of the same, as followeth."

Mr. Parton adds, " N.B. *This assessment was unauthorized by law.* It was made and signed by many of the then principal inhabitants, and contains the name of every individual inhabitant, as well householders and inmates, as servants, with such sums affixed against their names, as in the opinion of those signing the assessment, they respectively ought to pay towards the new church. But the payment or subscriptious were voluntary, at least optional. Some in their subscriptions exceeded the amount expected; others gave not half the sum expected for them to pay, and many gave nothing." *(Parton's St. Giles's Parish, p. 196.)*

The following names appear next in succession, forming the vestry of that period:—

Sir William Seager, Knight, Garter, King at Arms.
Lawrence Whitaker   Zacherie Bethel
Thomas Shepherd   Hanns Claxton
  and Abraham Speckart, Esquires.
Martin Basil   John Shelberry
Richard Bigge   James Pert
Humphrey Gardiner   William Mew
Nicholas Bragge   Andrew Robinson
Andrew Browne   John Brewer
Robert Johnson   Matthew Quier
Robert Hope   Richard Syer
Edward Rice   Jeremie Cocke
Thomas Harvye   William Chapman
Jeremy Turpin   George Hope
—— Howland   —— Jepp
       and William Edmondes.
Edward Alleyn, alter Guardia optim merita-oies et Singuli.
Charles Robinson, Clericus Parochialis.*

---

* In the progress of the suit pending between Mr. G. Rogers and the vestry, it became necessary, under a judge's order, to examine the minutes of the vestry and other parish records, when it appearing that the above book was missing, the following advertisement for its discovery was inserted in the Examiner, 21st December, 1828. "St. Giles in the Fields Parish Records.—Information is wanted as to the existence of a Book of Record of this parish called Domesday Book. This book is of vellum or parchment, and was made in 1624, by direction of the then Lord Bishop of London, as a perpetual parish record. It is repeatedly referred to in the parish books since that time, and can be proved to have been in the possession of Mr. Parton, the vestry clerk, in the year 1821. Any person giving the requisite information for its production will be amply rewarded for his trouble, by applying to Mr. George Rogers, 58, High Street, St. Giles's." The book was afterwards found: Earle had taken it away by mistake.

A second treasurer was afterwards appointed to assist Dr. Manwayring; and, in addition to the vestry, there was a committee formed, consisting of the two late churchwardens, two overseers, and various gentlemen of respectability in the parish. An index of names of benefactors, who were parishioners of St. Giles's at this time, follows, some of whom were persons of note, and in some instances some comment is added; a few of them are here subjoined:—

"*Parishioners, Contributors towards re-building the Church in 1623.*

	£.	s.	d.
The Right Hon. the Duchess of Lenox, her Grace	40	0	0
Lawrence Whytaker, Esq. one of the surveighers of the said church, besides his great care and pains, and solicitac'on of his friends and acquaintance............	25	10	0
Abraham Speckart, Esq. (besides his extraordinay care and paines in soliciting and procuring from his friends and acquaintance above the sum of £200)	23	6	8
Mr. Jeremy Cocke, of the Prince's councell	10	0	0
Dr. Roger Manwayring, Rector of the said parish, besides his exceeding labour and paines, both in the pulpitt and with his friends abroad	7	4	0
Sir Anthony Ashelye, Knight	10	0	0
Sir John Cotton, Knight	10	0	0
The Lady Ann Duddelye............	6	0	0
The Lady Frances Duddelye	4	0	0
The Hon. the Lady Alice Duddelye, besides the paving of the church and chauncell with freestone, the charge whereof appeareth in the end of the booke	250	0	0
The plaiers of the Cockpitt Plaiehouse	20	0	0

The whole collection thus made was £1065: 9s., which sum, Parton says, was subscribed by 415 householders, exclusively of inmates; and among whom are persons of almost every rank in life. The first donation entered in the book is £250 by Duchess Duddelye,* the last is two pence given by " mother Parker!"

" The total number of souls," he adds, " in the parish did not exceed, perhaps not reach. 2,000. The subscriptions, therefore, upon an average, exceeded 10s. 6d. for each parishioner, old and young, at a time when that sum was

---

* Dr. Boreman, in her funeral sermon, says, " Besides all this she was at the charge of paving the upper end of the church with *marble stones*, and gave the *great bell* in the steeple, which as oft at it rings sounds her praise; and was at the charge of casting and hanging the other five bells." In addition to these acts of munificence, she caused great part of the *ancient wall* surrounding the church, which had become ruinous (and had belonged to the hospital), to be re-edified. Her gifts of plate and church ornaments were, the communion plate in silver and gilt, as large and rich as any in the city or suburbs; for the back of the altar, a rich green velvet cloth with three letters of gold, I.H.S. embroidered on it. Item, two service books in folio, embossed with gold; a green velvet cloth with a rich deep gold fringe, to cover the alter over with on Sundays. Item, a cambrick altar cloth, with a deep bone lace round about; another fine damask altar cloth; two *cushings* (cushions) for the altar, richly embroidered with gold; a large Turkey carpet, to be spread in the week over it; and likewise, very costly handsome rails to guard the altar or Lord's table from profane uses."—*Dr. Boreman's Sermon.* We may remark here, that however laudable the beneficence of this estimable lady, it appears extremely trifling in the divine to enumerate these church trappings so much in detail in his sermon.

equal to forty shillings of our present money:—
an example of liberality and munificence rarely
equalled!!"

	£.	s.	d.
The second class of benefactors consisted of persons not resident in St. Giles's parish; from 106 of whom was collected the sum of	455	10	2
The third class of donations consisted of gifts from various parishes in the diocese of London, there particularized, amounting collectively to	236	19	1
Add contributions of the parishioners............	1065	9	0
Ditto ditto strangers..................	455	10	2
Ditto ditto collected at the church	44	10	2
Received oute of the box there	4	11	9
Ditto for ould materials, and £200 borrowed on interest	209	11	6
The vestry advanced a farther advance of	51	14	8
The whole expense of building was............£2,068		7	2

The church was not consecrated until 26th
of January, 1630, although it was finished, according to Maitland, after the demolition of the
little old church (as he calls it) in 1623, in
two years, namely in 1625, and this is confirmed by the inscription referred to in page
96. A consecration generally precedes divine
service, or opening a church, as it is called:
one is a little surprised by so long a lapse before that ceremony was administered, nearly
five years. That the church was used by the
parishioners is evident, inasmuch as Dr. Manwayring is known to have preached three ob-

noxious sermons in it, two of them entitled "Religion and Allegiance," and the third, May 4th, 1628, in which he defended them in his parish church of St. Giles in the Fields. These sermons were deemed highly offensive, and he was in consequence fined and suspended from his clerical functions.*

---

* Fuller, in his Church History, says, " This charge against Manwayring was made by Pym, 9th of June, 1628, purporting that he had persuaded the subjects of the realm to obey illegal commands on pain of damnation. That like Guy Faux and his fellows, he sought to blow-up parliament, and its power, making up a mischievous plot to alter and subvert the government, &c."

" June 20th, 1628, he came to the house, and on his knees submitted himself with sorrow of heart and true repentance for the errors and indiscretions he had been guilty of, in preaching two sermons, which he calls ' Religion and Allegiance,' and his fault in rashly, scandalously, and unadvisedly handling the same in his parish church of St. Giles in the Fields, on the 4th day of May. He farther acknowledged these three sermons to be full of dangerous passages and aspersions; after which he craved pardon of God and the King." Fuller adds, " that he was afterwards promoted to the Deanery of Winchester, and finally to the Bishoprick of St. Davids."

Hume, who has been censured for his adherence to the Stuarts, has given us the following candid sentiments on this affair :—" There is nothing which tends more to excuse, if not to justify, the extreme rigour of the Commons towards Charles I. than his open encouragement and avowal of such general principles as were altogether incompatible with a limited government. Manwayring had preached a sermon, which the Commons found, upon enquiry, to be printed by special command of the King, and when this sermon was looked into, it contained doctrines subversive of all civil liberty. It taught, that though property was commonly lodged in the subject, yet whenever any exigency required supply, all property was

"The new church being finished," says Parton, "26th of January, 1630, was appointed for its consecretion." Bishop Laud (of London) performed the ceremony, and was enter-

transferred to the sovereign; that the consent of parliament was not necessary for the imposition of taxes; and that the divine laws required compliance with every demand, how singular soever, which the prince should make upon his subjects."

For these doctrines the Commons impeached Manwayring, and the sentence pronounced upon him by the Peers was, " that he should be imprisoned during the pleasure of the house, be fined £1000 to the King, make submission and acknowledgment of his offence, be suspended during three years, be incapable of holding any ecclesiastical dignity or secular office, and that his book be called in and burnt." He adds, " It may be worthy of notice, that no sooner was the session ended, than this man received a pardon, although he was so justly obnoxious to both houses, and was promoted to a living of considerable value. Some years after he was raised to the see of St. Asaph." At what period he became Rector of St. Giles is unknown. *(See Newcourt's Repertorium, and other writers.)*

The gross adulation of the clergy, and their subserviency to kingly power, was very conspicuous at this period of our history. Abbot, Archbishop of Canterbury, was a striking instance of this, and a fit precursor of Laud. His biographer gives us some sickening instances of his obsequiousness. He told James I. that he was zealous as David and wise as Solomon; religious as Josias; careful of spreading Christ's gospel as Constantine the Great; just and meek as Moses; undefiled in all his ways as Jehosaphat and Hezekiah; full of clemency as Theodosius," &c. &c. He it was, who, on being asked whether a protestant king might assist the subject of a neighbour, labouring under tyranny and oppression, replied, " No, for even tyranny is God's authority." Lord Clarendon, who was contemporary with him, tells us " he was a man of very morose manners and a very sour aspect, which in that time was called gravity, and under the opinion of that virtue, and by the recommendation of the Earl of Dunbar, James the I.'s favourite, he was promoted to the Bishoprick of Litchfield, and

tained, at the parish expense, at Mr. Speckart's house, adjoining the church. Two tables were provided to dine thirty-two persons in the whole, under the direction of a committee, and a subscription was entered into for the purpose of conducting this affair with splendour. The breach in the church-yard wall was fenced up with boards, the church made clean, the communion table adorned with the best damask table cloth, the green velvet cushion, and all the plate, the gift of Duchess Dudley, a rail was made to keep off the press of people from the west door, and a train of constables attended with bills and halberts (the appendages of that day), to maintain order; in short, the ceremony so long retarded, appears to have been very imposing.*

In the course of the following year, we learn from Strype, the wall of enclosure was completed; and by the vestry minutes, so early as

---

Coventry, and presented afterwards to that of London, before he had been parson, vicar, or curate of any church in England, and was, in truth, totally ignorant of the true constitution of the Church of England, the state and interest of the clergy, as sufficiently appeared throughout the whole course of his life afterwards." *See History of the Rebellion, vol. 1. page 38.*

* Laud, afterwards created Archbishop of Canterbury by Charles I. was the promoter of the following superstitions, and was supported in enforcing them by the authority of the king, viz. kneeling at the Sacrament—wearing the surplice—confirmation—keeping of saint's days—and bowing at the altar. He also formed and compiled the Book of Sports; and Charles and the bishops abolished preaching on Sundays, that the people might have more time to enjoy their diversions.

anno 1637, some decays in the new church were ordered to be repaired.

The high church politics of this period had been exemplified in the doctrines inculcated by Dr. Manwayring; whilst, on the other hand, there is little doubt of the reaction of the principles of puritanism. Dr. Heywood, the now rector of St. Giles, had been chaplain to Laud, Bishop of London, and being a favourite of his, it is probable he imbibed some of his notions, which are known to have approached to the grossest superstition. In 1630 he was presented to this rectory, having been previously, like Dr. Manwayring, chaplain to Charles I.; and in 1640 "a petition and articles" from the parishioners, was exhibited to parliament against him, which stated that "he had set up crucifixes and divers images of saints in his church, and likewise organs, with other confused music, &c. hindering devotion, which were maintained to the great and needless charge of the parish." In one of these articles, these "popish reliques," as they are termed, are enumerated, and appear to have consisted of the gifts of Lady Dudley principally. The beautiful screen given by her, (which is described as a *beautiful skreene* of carved wood, which was placed where the former one in the old church stood) was described as particularly obnoxious. The description contained in the articles exhibited is worth transcribing, as illustrative of the church and its ornaments at this junction. It stated that "the said church is divided into three parts, the *sanctum sanctorum* being one of them, is separated from the chancel by a large skreene, in the figure of a beautiful gate, in which is carved two large pillars, and three large statues; on the one side is Paul with his sword, on the other, Barnabas with his book, and over them Peter with his keys. They are all set above with winged cherubims, and beneath supported with lions." " Seven or eight feet within this holy place is a raising by three steps, and from thence a long rail from one wall to the other, into which none must enter but the priests and sub-deacons. This place is covered before the altar with a fine wrought carpet; the altar doth stand close up to the wall on the east side, and a deske raised upon that with degrees of advancement. This deske is overlaid with a covering of purple velvet, which hath a great gold and silk fringe round about, and on this deske is placed two great books, wrought with needle work, in which are made the pictures of Christ, and the Virgin Mary with Christ in her armes, and these are placed on each side of the deske; and on this altar is a double covering, one of tapestry, and upon that a fine long lawne cloth, with a very rich bone lace. The walls are hanged round within the raile with silk taffia curtaines." All the above ornaments being deemed popish and superstitious, were demolished and sold by an ordinance of parliament, with the reserve of the plate and great bell. An inventory being first taken of them, in which it was specified that the *surplesses* had been previously given away. As a specimen of the temper of the times, it is on record what was the charge for defacing the organ loft, and displacing the fine painted glass window :—

"1643. To the painter for washing the twelve Apostles off the organ loft,"................... £0 4 6

"To the glazier for taking down the painted glasse in the chancel and church, and fitting-up new glasse,".................................. £1 9 6

The following memorandum is appended to the accounts :—" Also we, the auditors of this account, doe find that the accomptant, Edward Gerrard, was commanded by ordinance of parliament, to take downe the *screene* in the chancell, it being found superstitious; which was accordingly done, and it sold for fortye shillings, and that fortye shillings, and with twenty that Mr. Cornish gave, and three pounds tenn shillings given by the accomptant, of their own proper monies, was given to the poore on Christmas eve following. 1664—allowed by the auditors. Signed, Henry Cornish, Minister.

Out of the receipts from the church goods, which sold for £17 : 7 ; 1 were paid, "the bricklayer for mending the walls on both sides the chancell, where the same stood; and, "for the *covenant* and a frame to putt it in to hang upp in ye church;" also, "five shillings to Thomas Howard, pewterer, for a new bason, cut square on one side, to baptize in, more than the old bason came to."*

And April 8, 1645, "it being agreed upon by the inhabitants, (not the vestry) on the choice of officers, that the blue velvet carpet, and taffitie blue curtains, that did formerly hang in the chancell, with the embroidered cushions, and two embroidered books, should be sold to the best advantage, and the money employed for the use and benefit of the church and parish." They were sold accordingly; and the following year an order was made, that "the railes that stood about the communion table, be sold to Major Walter Bigg."

In 1647 is this item. "Paid for lyning the honourable Lady Dudley's pew with green baise and other materials, two straw matts, and workmanship," £3 2 0

---

* It is evident on the whole, that the pomp and useless pageantry of the priesthood of this period, so remote from the primitive simplicity of christianity, was carried by Laud and others to a dangerous extreme, and mainly contributed to the spoliations complained of. Among the innovations of the clergy, Hume relates that Cozens, dean of Peterborough, would not suffer the communicants to break the sacramental bread with their fingers, a privilege on which the puritans strenously insisted; nor would he permit it to be cut with an ordinary knife, a consecrated one must perform that sacred office, never afterwards to be profaned by any vulgar service.

Parton considers this as an atonement to that lady, for the injustice of selling her gifts in her very presence, her house being adjoining the church.

1650. The fall of royalty being complete, there appears an order, for "putting out the king's arms," probably those painted in the body of the church, and an entry is made to the glazier "for taking down the king's arms," (which appear to have been beautifully executed in stained glass in the south window, and was given by Sir William Segar) and new glazing the windows;" which it appears was replaced by a sun dial; and it was ordered that (anno 1654) the organ loft, where confused music had hindered devotion, should be let as a seat. Hume further tells us, " that such was the zeal of Sir Robert Harley, under the order of the Commons to destroy all images, altars, and crucifixes, that he demolished all crosses in the streets and markets; and, from his abhorrence of that superstitious figure, he would not allow one piece of wood or stone to lye over another at right angles!"

During the year 1643, Strype informs us, Alderman Pennington, being Lord Mayor of London, he ordered all the saints to be omitted in the designation of the churches, and the parishes became unsainted, a divorce sanctioned by parliament. This continued until the restoration, 1660.

The joyful period of the restoration arrived, which was welcomed with such eagerness, that the ringers of this parish were paid for a merry peal of three days; and the kingdom became so intoxicated by the change, that nothing like a condition was exacted in favour of civil liberty, an omission much to be deplored, and which was productive of the worst consequences: so much do men run from one extreme to another.

In reference to our parish, the king's arms in the vestry and the window were restored on the following year, and all the parochial regulations reverted to their usual former channels. Various memorandums appear in the minutes, in 1657 £10 was collected towards repairs of the church. In 1664, a petition was presented to the bishop of London for erecting galleries; for the better accommodation of the nobility coming to church.

1670. The bishop's seal for erecting galleries was applied for, and repairs were effected to the gate and steps of the church, now become defective; and a brass branch was ordered, containing sixteen candlesticks, and an hour glass for the pulpit, which was a usual appendage at that day.

It would be useless to recite the particulars of the perpetual repairs required and practised upon this church, during the short term of ninety years, by which it is evident how badly this structure was erected. We have seen with what deficiency of foresight the hospital church was repaired, and a new steeple and bells added to it, at a considerable expense, a very few years prior to its being, from necessity, taken down and rebuilt; and we have seen that in the space of twelve years after this had been effected, decays and consequent repairs are announced in the vestry minutes, which were perpetuated during the short time of less than a century. In 1715 it was discovered that, notwithstanding the many reparations it had undergone, it had now arrived at a total state of decay, and was completely damp and unwholesome, from the accumulation of earth around it, the church being rendered low thereby, and beneath the level of the street. It was therefore determined by a resolution of the vestry, to take the opinion of the members of parliament *inhabiting the parish*, concerning the petitioning to have the church entirely rebuilt at the public charge. A paper was drawn up, intitled, " Reasons humbly offered for a bill to rebuild the parish church of St. Giles in the Fields, as one of the fifty new churches:" in which it was stated, "that it was built with bricks, and coined and coped with stone, was very old and ruinous, and upon a moderate computation, would cost £3,000 to put it into good repair and order. That the ground about it being higher than the floor, or body of the church, it lay lower than the street by eight feet at least, and thereby (and by the great number of burials within it) is become very damp and unwholesome, as well as inconvenient to the gentry and others, who were obliged to go down several steps to the church. That being built long since, it was ill-contrived for hearing, and in divers other respects; and that these inconveniences could only be remedied by an entire new building, and would remain still the same, though the church should be repaired by the inhabitants at the expense above mentioned; nor could it be thought proper (as was conceived) to lay out so great a sum in repairing a church under such circumstances." It was further urged, "that the church stood at the farthest end of that part of the town, and fronted St. Giles's High Street, which was the great thoroughfare for all persons who travelled the Oxford or Hampstead Roads; and a good church there, would be as great an ornament and as much exposed to view as any church which could be built in town. That St. Giles's being one of the out parishes, and very large, was so overburthened with poor, that the ex-

pense of maintaining and relieving them, a-mounted *communibus annis*, to £3,300 at least, though their allowance was very small in proportion to other parishes, and the poor's rate was constantly fifteen-pence in the pound, besides six-pence to the scavenger, and the rates to the highways, windows, and lamps."
It was allowed, "That there were several noblemen and gentlemen in the parish; but if the church was to be repaired, or re-built at the parish charge, the rate must be laid on all, by a pound-rate, according to the rents of the houses, which would also fall so heavy on the trading and meaner sort of people, that it must very much impoverish, if not ruin many of the most industrious part of the parish, the number of tradesmen and poor-inhabitants being above ten to one in proportion.

"The nobility and gentry, as was represented in 1711, by the then rector and vestry, upon an exact survey given to the commissioners for the new churches, in pursuance of an order from them to that purpose; and when the parish should be divided into two or more, on the building new churches, (one of which was then building) the inhabitants, who would in all probability be left to the old church, would be those that dwelt nearest to it, and they almost wholly tradesmen, or others of less substance; and then the expense of keeping so old and crazy a church in repair and decent order, and in due time of new building it, (which it must want in some years) being added to the other taxes of the parish, would be an unsupportable burthen to them, especially when charged with the loss which would happen by sinking the rents of the pews in the galleries, now taken and used by the nobility and gentry, who would then belong to other parishes and churches. That by making this one of the fifty new churches, the charge of purchasing a site for the church and churchyard, and also the maintainance for the minister, would be saved to the public, or if three or more of these churches were designed for the parish, (as was presumed) it would be very difficult, and even impossible, without giving extravagant prices, to find proper sites within this parish for more than two new churches; and if sites could be found, yet three churches in all were as many as were wanted, there being then but one church and two little chapels, and these sufficient. That this parish was already charged with a heavy quota to the land taxes, which obliges them every second or thirdy ear at furthest, to make a *re-assessment of six-pence in the pound above the common pound-rate intended by parliament*, although all the houses were taxed to the utmost of their rents and values, and no site for a new church and church-yard had, or could be bought in this parish, where there was *no waste or void ground*, without pulling down £200 a year in houses, which would still sink the land-tax, (as well as all other taxes) and raise the deficiencies and re-assessments."

I have quoted these *reasons* (some of which were futile enough) to elucidate the state and circumstances of the second church, the rates, &c. and also to bring into notice the then intention of dividing the district into three distinct parishes, on which I shall make some remarks hereafter.

By an order of the vestry dated two years later, (1717) these " Reasons" were ordered to be printed, and distributed among members of parliament and others who had interest with government; and in December the same year, it was agreed that Dr. Baker and Mr. Milner should prepare a petition to parliament, for appointing the church of this parish to be one of the fifty new churches. It recited principally the arguments contained in the " Reasons," and after encountering great opposition in the House of Lords, a Bill to the effect required passed into a law. The Duke of Newcastle and the Lord Chancellor, and other eminent parishioners, strenuously supported the Bill, and had afterwards the thanks of the parish voted to them for their exertions in its behalf. On the other hand, the Archbishop of York, and five bishops, with eleven temporal peers, protested strongly against the Bill.*

Such, then, is the history of the measures adopted preparatory to the erection of the present church, which one would imagine was not

---

* I here insert the Protest at length, it containing some historical information of that period.

1st. "Because it doth not appear to us, from any declaration in his Majesty's name to either house of parliament, that his royal leave was given for bringing in the said Bill, as it ought."

2nd. "Because this Bill, in our opinion, manifestly tends to defeat the ends of two acts of parliament for building fifty new churches, and yet at the same time asserts that the intention of the said acts would be hereby answered."

3rd. "Because this Bill further asserts, that the parish of St. Giles is in no condition to raise, or pay the sum of £3,000 and upwards for the repairs of its parish church, which we apprehend to be evidently false in fact; and if true, to be no reason for re-building the said church out of the fund given for building fifty new churches."

4th. "Because this Bill moreover asserts, that the said church, when re-built, and the church which is now building in the said parish, by virtue of the acts for building fifty new churches, will be sufficient for the inhabitants of the said parish; whereas, we are credibly informed, and upon the best calculation do believe, that there are about 40,000 souls in the said parish, and do think that three new churches will be barely sufficient for that number."

5th. "Because, if this precedent of re-building *old* churches out of the fund appointed for building *new* ones, should be followed, and the ends of the aforesaid acts should be thereby in any great measure defeated, we are apprehensive that many thousands of his Majesty's good subjects, in and about these populous cities, will be left unprovided for churches whereunto they may resort for the public worship of God, and will thereby remain destitute of the necessary means of being instructed in the true christian religion, as it is now professed in the Church of England, and established by the laws of this realm." (*See Parliamentary Reports.*)

of such urgent necessity as was represented by its not being carried into immediate effect. Eleven years longer the old church remained in its state of ruin, when in 1729 a proposal was stated by the churchwardens and vestry of St. Giles, to settle £350 yearly on the rector of the new parish of Bloomsbury, provided the commissioners under that act would build their church, or allow them a sufficient sum for that purpose.

This proposal was accepted, and a second act passed, by virtue of which the commissioners were empowered to grant the sum of £8,000 to be laid out in the said church, by trustees appointed (members of the vestry) for the management of the same.

In June, 1731, articles of agreement were entered into with Mr. Henry Flitcroft, architect, who contracted to take down, by or before the ensuing first of August, the old church and steeple, and to re-build on the same ground a new one, together with a substantial vestry room, in a complete manner, on or before December 25, 1733.

This was finally done, and the church was opened for divine service April 14, 1734, Doctor Galley being the then rector, and the sum of £8,436 : 19 : 6 was paid to the architect, as stated by receipt given.*

---
* This structure has been much criticised and admired by architects and competent judges. Ralph, whose taste has

The area of this church within the walls is said to be seventy feet in length, by sixty feet in width, exclusive of the recess for the altar. The roof is supported by Ionic pillars of Portland stone (of which the structure is built,) and there are vaults under the building. The steeple is 160 feet high, and consists of a rustic pedestal supporting a Doric order of pilasters, and over the clock is an octangular tower, with three-quarter Ionic columns, supporting a ballustrade with vases;—on this tower stands the spire, which is also octangular, and belled.

---

been celebrated, notwithstanding his fastidiousness, and who wrote in 1736, speaking of this church, says, "the new church of St. Giles is one of the most simple and elegant of the modern structures. It is raised at a very little expense, has very few ornaments, and little besides the propriety of its parts, and the harmony of the whole to excite attention, and to challenge applause, yet still it pleases, and justly too. The east end is both pleasing and majestic, and there is nothing in the west to object to, but the smallness of the doors, and the poverty of appearance that must necessarily follow. The steeple is light, airy, and genteel, argues a good deal of genius in the architect, and looks very well, both in comparison with the body of the church, and when it is considered as a building by itself in a distant prospect." He adds, "yet after all I have confessed in favour of this edifice, I cannot help again arraigning the superstition of situating churches due east and west, for in complaisance to this folly, the building before us has lost a great advantage it might have otherwise enjoyed. I mean the making the east end the front, and placing it in such a manner as to have ended the vista of what is called Broad St. Giles's; whereas, now, it is no where to be seen with ease to the eye, or so as justly to comprehend the symmetry and connexion of the whole."

By a very ingenious application of gas, the clock is illuminated every evening, so as to render the hours and minutes visible on the darkest nights, a convenience introduced in 1827, when its novelty and utility attracted crowds to visit it from the remotest parts of the metropolis.*

---

* The following is a correct list of the rectors of St. Giles in the Fields, from the first institution by Sir Wymonde Carew, to the present period, 1829, embracing a term of 282 years :—

1. 1547. Sir William Rowlandson, presented by Sir Wymonde Carew, in the first year of Edward VI.
2. 1571. Geoffery Evans, presented by Queen Elizabeth, November 8, and resigned in 1579.
3. 1579. William Steward, presented by Queen Elizabeth, August 3.
4. 1580. Nathaniel Baxter, presented by Queen Elizabeth, resigned in about a year.
5. 1591. Thomas Salisbury, presented by Queen Elizabeth, December 24.
6. 1592. Joseph Clarke, A. M. September 16.
7. Not known. Roger Manwaring, D. D.
8. ———— Gilbert Dillingham, died 1635. (Charles I.)
9. 1635. Brian Walton, A. M. (Charles I.) resigned.
10. 1636. William Heywood, S. T. P. (Charles I.)
11. 1641. Henry Cornish, till 1648.
12. 1648. Arthur Molyne Clerk.
13. 1651. Thomas Case, till the restoration, and was succeeded by Dr. Heywood again.
14. 1663. Robert Boreham, D. D. presented by Charles II.
15. 1673. John Sharp, A. M. January 3, presented by ditto.
16. 1691. John Scott, S. T. P. August 7. William and Mary.
17. 1695. William Haley Clerk. April 4.
18. 1715. William Baker, D. D. October 7. George I.
19. 1732. Henry Galley, D. D. December. George II.
20. 1769. John Smith, D. D. George III. Died August, 1778.

I should here notice what Parton says of the churchyard, a spot rendered somewhat interesting by its being part of the site of the Hospital.

"There is little doubt," he remarks, "but this was in ancient times the place of interment of the hospital, as well as the parish; but what was its precise extent does not appear. The first mention of it in the parish books occurs in 1628, where it was agreed in vestry, that, whereas for many years, till of late time, there were standing upon the churchyard glebe certain cottages, to the number of three tenements, out of which there did issue a yearly rent due unto the parson in the right of his rectory, to the value of six pounds ten shillings yearly. And the said parson having agreed, upon intreaty made to him, that the said three cottages should be demolished, as well because they were an annoyance to the churchyard, as an hindrance to the burial ground, of which latter the parish stood in great need; the said vestry should consider a recompense answerable to such annual rent, as the said parson should lose, by the said tenements being removed."

---

21. 1796. Right Reverend John Buckner, L. L. D. Bishop of Chichester.
22. 1824. Christopher Benson, A. M.
23. 1826. James Endel Tyler, B. D.

Thomas Magnus, immediately after the dissolution, is mentioned as parson, with Lord Lisle's licence to marry.

A succeeding vestry agreed to compensate Doctor Manwayring with £34 per annum, instead of the annual rent received, and on the condition of his performing some additional pastoral duties.

The old hospital wall in part remained till the above-named time, and it seems enclosed the north side of the churchyard; but having in two years after, from age, fallen in partly, and become dangerous, an order was made in 1630 "that the workmen should view the ruins of the churchyard wall, *lately fallen down*, and consider whether the rest of the wall was not likely to fall," and to make an estimate of the expense of taking it down, "and new building a *brick wall* round about the churchyard, with the building in, and enclosure of the piece of ground intended to be given by Mr. Speckart."* This does not, however, appear to have been done till 1639, from an entry which directs some paving to be done against the wall on the south side.

---

* Mr. Speckart was allowed, in return, a private entrance from his back premises that way to the church, which had been granted to Lady Dudley, and two other principal benefactors before. But to prevent the future claim as a right, an order was made in vestry 1637, that these four private doors should, on the death or removal of any of the parties, be stopped up. The Lady Dudley's gate was kept in repair, at the parish expense, according to a subsequent payment.

Soon after the restoration, the further enlargement of the churchyard became necessary, and after some difficulty, about a quarter of an acre more was added to it on the south side, purchased of Sir Richard Stiddolph, stated to be "for the sole benefit of the poor" in the conveyance, "and not anyways for the advantage, or benefit of the parson, or his successors." *Query. Has this been observed?*

The ground here conveyed, forms that part of the churchyard which is bounded by Compton Street in part, and Phœnix Street, which had formerly been part of the precinct, or enclosure for St. Giles's Hospital. The garden plot from which it was divided, was let afterwards to a gardener of the name of Brown, and was, from him, called Brown's Gardens.

The sexton having petitioned, in 1670, to be allowed to continue the lights he had made into the church-yard, from his additional building to his dwelling-house, it was agreed to, during pleasure, on condition that he gave, as an acknowledgment to the Rector and Churchwardens yearly, on the Tuesday se'nnight after Easter, *two fat capons, ready dressed.*

In consequence of a resolution of vestry, in 1686, for forming a substantial gate to the church, the Resurrection Gate, as it is called, was erected the following year and completed. Over this is the well-known curious piece of sculpture of the Resurrection, an ornament much admired and celebrated. The whole cost altogether £185 : 14s : 6d.*

In 1805, a new burial ground having been obtained and consecrated, situate at St. Pancras, except in particular cases, the burial of the poor and other inhabitants was discontinued here.†

---

* The " New View of London" (1708) says, " The churchyard is fenced with a good brick wall, and under a large compass pediment over the gate near the west end is a prodigious number of carved figures, being an emblem of the Resurrection, done in *relievo* very curiously, and erected in the year 1687." The composition is, with various alterations, taken from Michael Angelo's Last Judgment. The original gate stood eastward of its present site.

† Pennant, in his Account of London, page 157, observes as follows. " I have, in the church-yard of St. Giles, seen with horror, a great square pit with many rows of coffins piled one upon the other, all exposed to sight and smell; some of the piles were incomplete, expecting the mortality of the night. I turned away disgusted at the view, and scandalized at the want of police which so little regards the health of the living, as to permit so many putrid corpses, tacked between some slight boards, dispersing their dangerous effluvia over the capital. Notwithstanding a compliment paid to me in one of the public papers, of my having occasioned the abolition of the horrible practice, it still remains uncorrected in this great parish. The reform ought to have begun in the place just stigmatized."

Strype enumerates many of the Monuments in St. Giles's church and yard : we shall notice here only two remarkable ones. The oldest monument remaining in the church-yard in 1708, was dated anno 1611, and is thus described in the New View of London. " In the cemetery or church-yard, close to the wall on the south-side, and near the west-end, this inscription is on a tombstone :—

' Johannes Thornton, &c. In memory of his deare wife.'

A building, situate on the site where Dudley Court now stands, was, with a garden attached, purchased by Duchess Dudley in 1646, and was given for a perpetual mansion for the incumbent after three lives, whereof two were expired. Some time previous to 1722, it was probably taken down, Dudley Court having been then erected on the ground it had before occupied, and a committee of vestry was appointed to treat with the Rector, Dr. Baker, for purchasing the whole, to build a workhouse thereon. It was, there is little doubt, as well as Dudley House, which adjoined it, once part of the ancient hospital. The Rector of St. Giles, for the time being, is still entitled to receive the rents, &c. of Dudley Court, where this residence stood.

This lady is described in the English lines which follow, as having died in child-birth. The husband was the builder of, and gave the name to *Thornton's Alley*, which was probably his estate. The family was originally from Yorkshire, and from the following lines ' round the margent of the stone', had been parishioners as early as the hospital times:—

' Full south this stone four-foot doth lie,
His father, John, and grand-sire, Henry;
Thornton of Thornton, in Yorkshire bred,
Where lives the fame of Thornton's being dead.'

A stone in the church-yard against the east-end of the north aisle of the church has this inscription:—

' Neare this place lyes the body of Eleanor Stewart, who dyed the first day of May, 1725, aged 123 years and above 6 months. She lived in this parish near 60 years, and received £160 by a pension of 4s. a week, in the last 15 years of her life.' "

The Pound and Cage originally adjoined each other, and stood in the middle of High Street, from whence Parton informs us it was removed in 1656, to make way for the almshouses which were afterwards built there. "The Pound," he adds, "probably existed from a very early period, as a necessary appendage to the parish while a village, and abounding in pasture lands, though it is unnoticed in the books of the parish, till Lord Southampton's grant of the ground on which it stood for the almshouses, where it is described as occupying a space of 30-feet, which was to be the dimensions of the *new* Pound, therein directed to be removed to the end of Tottenham Court Road. The exact site of the Pound was the broad space where St. Giles High Street, Tottenham Court Road, and Oxford street meet, where it stood till within memory. Noticed for the profligacy of its inhabitants, the vicinity of this spot became proverbial: witness a couplet of an old song,

" At Newgate steps *Jack Chance* was found,
And bred up near *St. Giles's Pound*,"

It was finally removed about the the year 1765, since which the neighbourhood has experienced many improvements, particularly by the erection of the great Brewery of Messrs. Meux and Co.

The Cage appears to have been used as a prison, not merely of a temporary kind, but judging from the parish records, with little lenity.*

The Plague. St. Giles's parish has the melancholy celebrity of originating the plague of 1665, the most severe visitation of that malady that ever occurred in this country. It is on record that this dreadful scourge has extended its ravages to this country at five different periods within eighty years, namely, in 1592, when it destroyed 11,503 persons; in 1603, when it destroyed 36,269; in 1625, when 35,500 fell; and in 1636, 13,480 in London only; but the severity of the disease in 1665, was far more extensive, when no less than 97,306 of the inhabitants of London and its suburbs died of it, according to De Foe, in ten months.

In 1592 and 1625, this parish is named in the bills of mortality. In the former instance,

---

* The following entries are copied in proof of this:—

	s.	d.
1641. "Paid to a poor woman that was brought to bed in the cage	2	0
For a shroud for a poor woman that died in the cage...	2	6
1648. (July 9th.) To Ann Wyatt, in the cage, to relieve her and buy her a truss of straw...................	2	6
(July 12th.) Paid for a shroud for Ann Wyatt	2	6

The death of this latter unfortunate, three days after the relief is stated to have been afforded her, leaves too much reason to fear she died of want. The cause of the former's death, is, to say the least of it, doubtful.

there died of the plague 596, and the total number of burials was stated at 894. In 1625, the number stated which died of the plague was 947, and total of burials 1,333. No doubt can be entertained of nearly all these dying, in fact, of the plague.*

---

* A pest house, which had been fitted-up (1625) in Bloomsbury " for the nine out parishes adjoining London," among which was St. Giles in the Fields, was afterwards engaged by the parish on its own account, and there are entries in the minutes of relief sent there to the poor at various periods. This direful malady progressed more or less till 1648, during which time 13,581 persons in all died of it. The vestry appointed agreeably to the act *two examiners* to inspect the visited houses, as on former occasions. No assessment on its early appearance was made, the wealthy inhabitants having fled into the country to avoid the disease.

There was afterwards an order made to pay Mr. Pratt the churchwarden, monies advanced during the calamity in the following words:—" Whereas in the year 1640, it pleased Almighty God to visit divers of the poore people of this parish, with the infec'tion of the plague; and becanse divers of the gentry and p'sons of estate were then out of towne, there could not be an assessment made, and money collected amongst the p'shioners for the p'sent reliefe of the said infected, whereof Mr. William Pratt, &c. borrowed of Theodore Colley, Esq. £50; which sum appearing to have been faithfully disbursed to the said visited poor, it is ordered that the same be repaid."

1642. The entries indicate an increase in the virulence of the disease, as the dormant practice of shutting up the infected house, was then first resorted to, and the bodies were collected in carts, and unceremoniously thrown into pits or graves of large dimensions by torch light. The following entry had for its object the fastening in the infected, and to prevent access to, or coming from thereto, under severe penalties, excepting the

The plague of 1665 is well described by De Foe, mixed unfortunately, however, with romance. It is pretty well authenticated that it began its melancholy progress in St. Giles's parish, near the upper end of Drury Lane, where two men, said to be Frenchmen, died of it. He tells us, its havoc in this parish alone was truly frightful, amounting to 3,216 in one year, 1665. He concludes his book thus:—

> "A dreadful plague in London was,
> In the year sixty-five,
> Which swept an hundred thousand souls
> Away; yet I alive."

The following are parish entries in 1643, which are curious records of the time:—

	s.	d.
"To the bearers for carrying out of Crown-yard a woman that dyed of the plague	1	6

medical or other attendants, by permission of the watchman, who kept the key. There are other entries added:—

	£.	s.	d.
"1642. Paid for the two padlocks and hasps for visited houses	0	2	6
Paid Mr. Hyde for candles for the bearers	0	10	0
To the same for the *night cart* and cover the summe of	7	9	0
To Mr. Mann for links and candles for the night bearers	0	10	0"

The candles were to search such infected houses as did not return an answer to the cry of 'bring out your dead,' and it was not unusual to find the whole household had perished; the bodies were, in such cases or otherwise, collected in covered carts and taken to church-yards, fields, &c. and thrown into pits dug for the purpose at midnight, the persons doing this duty carrying links to light them, and generally smoking to prevent infection.

	s.	d.
Sent to a poor man shut up in Crown-yard of the plague	1	6
Paid for a booke, and two orders concerning the visited houses	1	6
Paid Mr. Hyde for padlocks and staples for a house	1	2
Paid the sexton for making ten graves and for links, as per bill	5	6
Paid and given Mr. Lyn the bedle, for a piece of good service for the pisshe, in conveying away of a visited household out of the pisshe to Lond' Pest House, forth of Mr. Higgons's house at Bloomsbury	1	6
Received of Mr. Hearle, Dr. Temple's gift, to be given to Mrs. Hockey, a minister's widow, shut up in the crnche-yard of the plague	10	0"

Dr. Mead and others have ascribed the origin of the plague of 1665 to the importation of some cotton from Turkey, which was saturated with the infection. Maitland, speaking of it at its height, says, " all the houses were shut-up, the streets deserted, and scarcely any thing to be seen thereon but grass growing, innumerable fires for purifying the infected air, coffins, pest carts, red crosses upon doors, with dismal aspect and woeful lamentations carrying their infants to the grave, and scarcely any other sounds to be heard than those occasionally emitted from the windows of ' Pray for us,' and the direful call of ' Bring out your dead,' with the piteous groans of departing souls, and melancholy knells for bodies ready for the grave."

"This plague," says Dr. Sydenham, "discovered its first malignity among the poorer sort of people in St. Giles in the Fields, towards the latter end of the year 1664." *(See Practical Method for the Cure of the Plague, 1665.)* Dr. Hodges and Sir Richard Manningham corroborated this idea in their works on the plague.

The following are a few of the entries of that period:—

"1665. (August) Ordered, that an additional rate be levied for the use of the visited poor, to the amount of £600; and that the inhabitants of the parish be valued accordingly."

Independent of this contribution by assessment, various sums were subscribed:—

	£	s.	d.
"Received of Mr. Williams, from the Earl of Clare, (gift money)	10	0	
Received of Mr. Justice Godfrey, (Sir Edmondbury) from the Lord Treasurer	50	0	0
Received of Earle Craven and the rest of the justices, towards the visited poore (at various times)	449	16	10
Earle Craven, towards the visited poore	40	3	0

The appointment of searchers, shutting-up of infected houses, &c. are thus noticed:—

	£	s.	d.
"1665. (August.) Paid the searchers for viewing the corpse of good-wife Phillips, who dyed of the plague	0	0	6
Laid out for good-man Phillips, and his children being shut-up and visited	0	5	0

Laid out for Lylla Lewis in 3' Crane Court, being shut-upp of the plague, and laid out for her, and for the nurse and burial 0 18 0

1666. (July.) Ordered, that the constables, &c, do take an especiall account of all inmates coming from other parishes, and to take security that they be not burdensome. And also to take care to prevent the spreading of the infection for the future, by a timely provision for them that are, or hereafter may happen to be visited."

I will conclude the subject by quoting two eminent writers on the plague at this period. " London might well be said to be all in tears, the mourners did not go about the streets indeed, for nobody put on black, or made a formal dress of mourning; it was, however, truly heard in the streets. The shrieks of women and children at the doors and windows of their houses, where their dearest relations were dying, or perhaps dead, were enough to pierce the stoutest hearts. At the west-end of the town, it was a surprising thing to see those streets which were usually thronged, now grown desolate, so that I have sometimes gone the length of a whole street, (I mean bye streets) and have seen nobody to direct me but *watchmen*, set at the doors of such houses as were shut-up: and one day, I particularly observed, that even in Holborn the people walked in the middle of the street, and not at the sides, not to mingle, as I supposed, with anybody that came out of infected houses, or meet with smells and scents from them."

" In the streets might be seen persons seized with the sickness, staggering like drunken men: here lay some dozing, and almost dead; there, others were met fatigued with excessive vomiting, as if they had drank poison: in the midst of the market, persons in full health fell suddenly down as if the contagion was there exposed to sale. It was not uncommon to see an inheritance pass to three heirs within the space of four days. The bearers were not sufficient to inter the dead," &c. *(See Dr. Hodgson's Journal of the Plague, and Dr. Hodges on the Plague.)*

Bloomsbury—Its Manor and Derivation—Progressive Extension—Abstract Statement of Buildings—Mr. Burton's vast Enterprise—Bedford and Foundling Estates noticed, &c.

The new and opulent parish of St. George, Bloomsbury, which now claims our attention, is well-known to have been abstracted from that of St. Giles in the Fields, and it still remains connected with it, being only distinct in respect to its ecclesiastical government, which we shall have occasion to notice as we proceed.

Maitland and others describe the district of this parish as anciently bearing the name of Lomesbury, and he speaks of the King's Mews being destroyed by fire in the reign of Henry VIII. But the more probable derivation of its name was from a lord of this manor in the reign of Henry III. William de Blemund, or Blemot. In 1216 and subsequently, he witnessed several hospital deeds, now extant, at which time it was called "Blemund's Land,"

and "Blemund's Fee;" since then, by an easy transition, it has acquired the modern names of Blemundsbury or Bloomsbury. This is somewhat confirmed by the circumstance of the Manors of St. Giles and Bloomsbury being originally divided by a great fosse or ditch, (as before mentioned), called Blemund's Ditch, which ran east and west at the back of the north side of Holborn. This William de Blemund had a yearly obit or anniversary service for his soul performed at the hospital of St. Giles, in consequence of a grant made for that purpose.

The Manor of Bloomsbury is bounded on the south, by the Manor of St. Giles; on the north, by the Prebend of Tottenhall; on the east by the Manor of Portpool, or Gray's Inn; and on the west by that of Mary-la-bonne.*

---

* The ancient natural division of the two, north and south, districts, which now form the joint parishes, was a road or highway running east and west on the site of Holborn and Broad Street, St. Giles, which was a great and principal thoroughfare.

This was built on and chiefly inhabited first on the north side, along which gradually arose a few scattered dwellings from its eastern extremity to the *Pittsunce Croft*, which was opposite the *Hospital.* These had gardens behind them reaching to the ditch which bounded the south side of *Blemundsbury* or *Bloomsbury*. In the midst of this principal street or highway was the common spring or conduit, which supplied the inhabitants with water; and near it, and exactly facing the north end of *Aldewych*, was a stone cross called *Aldewych Cross,* with a cottage and gardens adjoining. Ex-

The successor of the Blemund family was Sir William Belet, Knight, of Chigwell, who in the hospital deeds is said to be then (19th of Edward I. 1291) lord of the fee; but the intermediate owners from this period to its coming into the possession of the Southampton family are not known, nor does it appear material here to notice the lords of the manors of St. Giles.†

---

actly in a line easterly with the present street, Holborn, the road ran to the termination of the parish near Chancery Lane, near the " *Barram vetori Templi*," which gave it the designation of " St. Giles without the bars of the old Temple," and before the building of the Temple, " St. Giles without the bars of London." There were besides this three other principal roads or thoroughfares, viz. *Eldestrade*, or Old Street, (now Crown Street), leading from the north to Westminster; another lesser one, called *Le Lane* (now Monmouth Street); and a chief highway, the *Via De Aldewych* (Drury Lane), which, as has been shown, gave name to land on each side, and was of great antiquity. There were also other minor intersecting paths or ways, which had no distinguishing denomination in the old grants.

† By Indenture, dated 14th of James I. 1617, between Sir Henry Riche, Dame Isabella Riche, and Dame Dorothy Cope, sold to Phillip Gifford and Thomas Risley, Esqs. trustees for Henry Earl of Southampton, in consideration of the sum of £600 paid by the said most noble Henry Earl of Southampton, &c. by the description of, " all that the manor and dissolved hospital, commonly called the manor or dissolved hospital of St. Giles-in-the-Fields without the bars of London, in the county of Middlesex, with all their rights, members, and appurtenances; and all and singular messuages, mills, houses, edifices, structures, gardens, orchards, &c. situate in the villages, hamlets, parishes, and fields of St. Giles-in-the-Fields, St. Pancras, Kentish Town, Maribone, St. Martin's in-the-Fields, Holborne, and Paddington, in the county of Middlesex, or elsewhere in the same county; *except the*

The ancient plan before referred to, (anno 1570) exhibits almost a complete void in reference to houses in this now parish, all the space which is now Red Lion Street to a point where Dyot Street commenced is entirely vacant, and there only appears a cluster of about ten houses. In the distance, Southampton House is delineated, surrounded by extensive fields and enclosures, but no other vestige of a building till the eye is carried to the neighbourhood of the dissolved hospital. In this unbuilt state, Bloomsbury* is supposed to have continued till about 1623, when a neighbourhood began to form, as appears by the assessment for the new church, viz. street side of Bloomsbury, 19 houses; north side, 11; west side, 37; east side, 45;

---

tythes of a certain parcel of land called Bloomsbury, sold to one Samuel Knowles."

From Henry Earl of Southampton, the Manor of St. Giles, (together with that of Bloomsbury, which was before in the same family) descended to his son and heir, Thomas Wriothesly, fourth Earl of Southampton, and Lord Treasurer to Charles II. who held it till his death, 1668, when it became the property of his daughter and co-heiress, Lady Rachel Russell, the wife of the celebrated William Lord Russell, who by her marriage brought it into the Bedford family, the present holders of the Manor of St. Giles with Bloomsbury.

It may here be noticed, that the whole of its southern side, or half, is in the Manor of St. James, viz. from Crown Street west to Lincoln's-Inn Fields east; and in breadth, from the hospital walls and the line formed by St. Giles's Street and Holborn to Long Acre in part, and St. Clement's parish in the other part.

* It is called a certain parcel of land so late as 1617.

and Little Alley in Bloomsbury, 24 houses—total 136. Thus it stood, with little variation, till the end of Charles I.'s reign, being an advance of 26 years (1649), as may be seen in the parliamentary plan of that period, wherein little else but fields is shown, except the buildings enumerated, and two batteries for defence on the north side of Southampton House.

Great Russell Street was described in 1708, as "a very spacious and handsome street, between King Street, Bloomsbury, north east, and Tottenham Court Road west, extending in length 725 yards; and from Charing Cross north, it is 1,170 yards." Strype, in 1720, calls it "a very handsome, large, and well built street, and the best inhabited by the nobility and gentry, (especially on the north side, as having gardens behind the houses, and the prospect of pleasant fields up to Hampstead and Highgate) insomuch as this place is esteemed the most healthful in London.—In its passage it saluteth Southampton House, Montague House, and Thanet House;* all these seats of noblemen. But for stateliness of building and curious gardens, Montague House hath the pre-eminence, as indeed of all the houses within the cities of

---

* Thanet House, the residence of the Earls of that name, was situate opposite Dyot Street, and was subsequently divided into two spacious houses, one of which, during many years, was occupied by the late Alderman Coombe.

London and Westminster, and the adjacent parishes." Russell Street took its name from the ducal family of Russell, whose residence was near it; but Parton mentions, as a singular coincidence, a respectable family of that name who resided on this spot, and had several estates here, as far back as the reign of Henry III.

BLOOMSBURY SQUARE. This spacious square was first called Southampton Square, and the noble mansion which formed the north side, was also called Southampton House. The names of the rows forming the east, west, and south sides of the square, were called in 1720, Seymour Row, Allington Row, and Vernon Row. These three sides were erected in the character the square now exhibits, about the same time as Russell Street was built. The north side consists of ten modern houses, erected since 1800, with an opening into Bedford Place, all on the site of the former Southampton, (since, Bedford) House. The Earls of Chesterfield had a mansion here during many years; and other, of the higher classes, had residences in this square.* Its area contains about three acres and a half:

---

* We will here subjoin the critical notice given of this square, by an architect of great acknowledged taste and judgment. "Bloomsbury Square," he says, "is, at present, remarkable for nothing but its being a place capable of great improvements; there is not one tolerable house in it; and the area in the middle is almost as much neglected as the buildings. The ground on which the Duke of Bedford's house

BLOOMSBURY MARKET. This is said to be among the earliest erections on this part of the parish. Strype describes it as "a long place with two market-houses, the one for flesh and the other for fish, but of small account, by reason the market is of so little use and so ill served with provisions, insomuch that the inhabitants deal elsewhere." It still retains that character.

Maitland, in summing up what he calls the remarkables of Bloomsbury, says "that it contains a stately parish church, with the statue of George I. ridiculously placed on the top of its steeple; a magnificent square; a spacious market; and one of the parliament forts." Kingsgate Street bounds the parish, and stands to the east of Bloomsbury Square.

This street is only remarkable for the circumstance from which it derives its name. In the reign

---

stands, is, beyond dispute, one of the finest situations in Europe for a palace, and I am not a little grieved to see it so wretchedly mis-employed.—In the first place, it has the whole side of a square for a front, and the square itself would serve as a magnificent area before it. Then there is a grand street just opposite to it, which throws the prospect of it open to Holborn, and must excite the curiosity of every passenger to regard and admire it. Then behind, it has the advantage of most agreeable gardens, and a view of the country, which would make a retreat from town almost unnecessary; besides the opportunity of exhibiting another prospect of the building, which would enrich the landscape, and challenge new approbation."

of James I. it was a mere country lane, with a barred gate at its entrance (as may be seen in various old plans of London); which gate, from the king usually passing that way in his journey to Theobald's, received the denomination of "Kingsgate," and thence the street subsequently built on its site, was called at first "Kingsgate Road," and afterwards "Kingsgate Street;" and Theobald's Road, to which it leads, acquired its name from the same cause.*

Strype describes the other streets on this division of the parish briefly, as follows. King Street runs in a parallel direction with Kingsgate Street, but more to the west, and took its name from the King passing through it, or near it, to Theobald's; he tells us, that in his time it was "very long, running northward to the fields, and the side to the east best inhabited, having gardens at the back sides." It has been rebuilt since his time.

"SOUTHAMPTON STREET:—very spacious, with good houses, well inhabited and resorted unto by gentry for lodgings; which said street cometh out of Holborn, and fronts the square called Southampton Square."

---

* Pepys, in his Diary under the date of March 3, 1668—9, says "that the King and the Duke of York, when going to some foot and horse races at New-Market, left Whitehall at three in the morning, and had the misfortune to be overset, with the Duke of Monmouth, and the Prince (Rupert) at the King's-gate, in Holborne; and the King all dirty, but no hurt.—It was dark, and the torches did not, they say, light the coach as they ought to do."

"Duke Street cometh out of Great Russell Street, and passing by Little Russell Street and Castle Street, falls into St. Giles's through a narrow passage of a brewhouse." The vicinity of Duke Street, to the Ducal residences of Montague and Bedford Houses, very well accounts for its name; and Little, (like Great) Russell Street, was, no doubt, so called in compliment to the Russell family." "Silver Street, running from Southampton Street to the market place, is indifferent well built and inhabited. Then on the south of the market is Lion Street, but short, and gives an entrance into Holborn. Gilbert Street, which, with Little Russell Street, falls on the backside of Arlington Row, used for coach-houses and stables; these streets are but very ordinary. Castle Street hath on the east side Hart Street, a good broad Street, and on the west side Phœnix Street; both of which are but ordinary. Castle Yard is a small place near here, and also Brewer Street, both of little account; as is also Peter Street, a short avenue. Queen Street, now Museum Street, opposite to Montague House, is a good broad street, indifferently well built and inhabited. Bow Street, now Museum Street, comes out of Holborn and falls into Peter Street (also now Museum Street,) dividing Hart Street from Brewer Street (now Thorney Street,) both narrow and not over well inhabited Hyde Street is a tolerable good street, and is situated between Bloomsbury Market east and the meeting of Peter Street, Bow Street, and Brewer Street west." The above particulars, with what has been said before in treating on the division of this district, will be found a tolerably correct view of the buildings erected up to the period of 1720; when Strype published his survey of the cities of London and Westminster. The boundaries at that date comprised nearly all the old portion of the parish, extending to the north in a line with Great Russéll Street, taking an easterly direction from opposite Dyot Street, (now George Street) to King Street; thence a southerly direction, including Kingsgate Street and part of Eagle Street, to the north side of Holborn; from thence in a direct line to Dyot Street westerly, and ending with its termination on the east side, to the north side of Great Russell Street again.

Maitland, whose "History of London" was published in 1739, states the number of houses in Bloomsbury at 954, when the parish remained nearly stationary during the preceding twenty years, being an increase of 818 since 1623,—116 years. But a new and astonishing era commenced here in 1792, when an ingenious and enterprising architect, *James Burton*, *esquire,* began to erect a number of houses on the Foundling Hospital estate, partly in this parish, and partly in that of St. Pancras; and subsequently since from 1792, on the Duke of Bedford's estate, within the same parishes. *Baltimore House,* built towards the north-east of *Bedford House, by Lord Baltimore in* 1763, appears to have been the only erection since Strype's Survey, to these periods, with the exception of a *chimney-sweeper's cottage* still further north, and part of which is still to be seen in *Rhodes's Mews, Little Guilford Street.* In anno 1800 *Bedford House* was demolished entirely, which, with its offices and gardens, had been the site where the noble family of the Southamptons, and the illustrious Russells, had resided during more than 200 years, almost isolated. Hence commenced the formation of a fine uniform street, Bedford Place, consisting of forty houses, on the spot; also, the north side of Bloomsbury Square, Montague Street to the west, and one side of Southampton Row to the east.

Towards the north, an extensive piece of waste ground, denominated the Long Fields, was transformed into a magnificent square, with streets diverging therefrom in various directions; since which various squares have arisen on the Foundling, as also on the Bedford estate, some of which are in Bloomsbury parish, and shall be hereafter enumerated and noticed more particularly.

In the year 1739, (December) the governors of that charitable institution, the Foundling Hospital, purchased the estate adverted to of the Earl of Salisbury: it comprised fifty-six acres, for which they gave £7,000, the whole of which is now covered with streets and buildings of other descriptions. The annual produce of the ground-rents cannot but prove very considerable now; and in process of time, as the leases fall in, the income will be immense. The number of houses so built since 1792 to 1829, on this fifty-six acres, is 1082; of which number, 525 belong to St. George Bloomsbury.

To those who have lived to witness what has been effected in this enterprise of building, astonishment must take place of every other feeling, on viewing the prodigious efforts made chiefly by and through the influence and example of one individual, who cannot be named but with respect. Let it be remembered that this vast speculation of Mr. Burton's was begun and finished during a long disastrous war, most unfavourable to such an undertaking, yet he *sternly* persevered, and in spite of predictions to the contrary, succeeded and prospered to an extent far beyond his expectation.

The fields* where robberies and murders had been committed, the scene of depravity and wickedness the most hideous for centuries, became, chiefly under his auspices, rapidly metamorphosed into splendid squares and spacious streets; receptacles of civil life and polished society This pleasing transition, however, required firmness of nerve and energy of no common description, and these Mr. Burton eminently possessed. If he accumulated a fortune by the vast improvements of these estates, he well deserved it; and knowing, as I do, the probity of his conduct and character, I hope he will enjoy it in happiness during his future days.

Having lived in Bloomsbury during the long period of nearly thirty years, and being much connected with the buildings here for a considerable portion of that time, I may be considered competent to give a tolerable accurate statement of their progress; I have therefore taken some pains to collect such partioulars of them which come within my own knowledge, which I here present to my readers; presuming that very few, if any instances, can be adduced of a similar extension within the same period, and by private individuals.

---

* Called Long Fields, and by Strype, 1720, the Southampton Fields; no doubt they were then so named.

A complete List of Houses and Tenements built on the Foundling Hospital Estate since 1792, and on that of his Grace the Duke of Bedford since 1798, within the parish of St. George, Bloomsbury.

Abbey Place	17	Keppel Mews, South	35
Bloomsbury Square	10	Keppel Mews, North	42
Brunswick Square	12	Montague Place	35
Bedford Place	40	Montague Streets	36
Bedford Place, Upper	50	Montague Mews	13
Bernard Street	40	Marchmont Street	40
Brunswick Mews	21	Marchmont Place	20
Coram Street, Great	59	Rhodes Mews	9
Compton Street	9	Torrington Square	70
Coram Street, Little	33	Torrington Street	5
Coram Place	16	Torrington Street, Little	6
Chapel Place	21	Tavistock Mews	21
Colonnade	26	Russell Square	65
Everett Street	29	Russell Place	16
Guilford Street	14	Wilmot Street	27
Guilford Street, Little	33	Russell Mews	7
Hunter Street	37	Woburn Place	51
Hunter Mews	7	Woburn Mews	21
Henrietta Street	29	Woburn Mews, West	13
Henrietta Mews	23	Southampton Row, West	20
Kenton Street	41	Southampton Mews, Do.	39
Keppel Street	40		

Total 1198.*

---

* In James I.'s reign, 1623, Parton informs us, from the Parish Minutes, there were houses assessed in Bloomsbury 138
In George II.'s reign, 1732, Malcolm says, they had increased (in 113 years) to 900
In 1739 (same reign), Maitland makes them 954
In 1799, Malcolm (60 years afterwards) reduces them to 916
In 1829, It now contains, Michaelmas, 1829 1976

It will be seen here that the total increase from 1792 is 1198, of which extraordinary accumulation I have ascertained that no less than 663 of these were built by or for Mr. James Burton, within a period of eleven years only, namely, from 1792 to 1803!

But these form only a portion of what he performed, including St. Pancras parish: the whole number, if these are added, is 922, being an addition of 259 more.

Whilst on this subject, it may not prove uninteresting to insert here an Abstract taken from a printed paper, which in July, 1823, was handed to a company of builders, friends of Mr. Burton, assembled at a public dinner at the Freemasons' Tavern, when a piece of plate was given him as a testimonial of their affection and esteem.

The statement here annexed has been taken so accurately, that I can vouch for its correctness, which made me conclude that Malcolm is wrong in his calculation, especially as there does not appear to have been any houses pulled down, except a few in Dyot Street, a few years since, which would not suffice to make the apparent difference.

Unless the addition of stable tenements assessed with the houses attached to them, makes the statements correct, there would require 138 more houses to make the accounts agree.

The number of houses, about 20 of which have not been assessed, Michaelmas, 1829	1976
Being an increase since 1792	1198
Leaving the number at that period only	778
Difference as above mentioned	138
Being Malcolm's calculation, 1799	916

Abstract Statement of Buildings, erected by or for an Individual, from 1785 to 1823, both inclusive; exclusively of Buildings erected for others under his Superintendence.

ESTATES.	1st Rate.	2nd Rate.	3rd Rate.	4th Rate.	Total.	Estimated Rental including Ground Rents. £.	Estimated Gross Value. £.
Stamford, Bennett, and Brunswick Streets, Albion Streets, Newgate Gilspur Streets Eastcheap, Ty e Place, Crescen Place, New Bri Water Lane, O d Broad							
Clapham Common, from 1785 to 1792	17	24	15	14	70	7,420	90,300
e, from 1792 to 1802	29	169	172	226	596	36,540	296,700
from 1798 to 1803	132	43	8	153	336	32,240	299,400
Estate, from 1807 to 1816	4	146	284	189	623	21,194	309,600
Estate, from 1808 to 1814	1	—	143	67	211	10,120	78,800
1803 to 1807	3	—	4	20	27	1,500	25,000
t Street, &c. from 1816 to 1823	39	104	38	10	191	29,170	338,400
t's Park, from 1815 to 1823	76	21	14	76	189	25,060	317,100
re's Estate, from 1818 to 1823	10	3	116	4	133	9,060	93,600
					2366	172,300	1,848,900

RECAPITULATION.

The Number of Buildings so erected	2,366
Annual Rental estimated at	£172,300
Estimated Value	£1,848,900
Annual House and Window Duty	£45,120
Duties on the Materials, upwards	£150,000

And Residences for about 13,000, at Five and a Half (being the allowed Average) to each Building.

London, July, 1823.

Since this period, 1823, Mr. Burton has built many additional houses of magnitude in the Regent's Park, and, at an advanced stage of life, he is finally forming a new town near Hastings.

Note continued from page 147.

The discrepancy between the calculations of Maitland and Malcolm, 1739 and 1799, is very unaccountable, and shows how little the authority of writers, even of eminence, may be depended upon in many instances.

It is remarkable, that when it was in contemplation to form the New Road from the City to Paddington, anno 1756, the Duke of Bedford violently opposed it in parliament, on the ground of its being likely to deteriorate his property! The measure, however, was effected, and experience has shown how contrary has been the result; the advantage to that noble family has been, and will be, prodigious. All the Duke's estates in its neighbourhood have been since covered with houses, except a new square parrallel with Torrington Square, which is now in progress, intended to be named Rothsay Square.

Chapter V.

Bloomsbury—Formation of its Parish—Church and Public Buildings—Criticisms of Ralph and Walpole—Squares and Institutions—Historical notice of Resurrectionists—Places of Worship—List of Rectors—Population of the joint Parishes, &c.

Reverting again to my more immediate subject, Bloomsbury, I shall here notice the public edifices, squares, and streets, with whatever other objects are worthy of attention, beginning first with the Church, which constitutes it a parish.

An official return was made to parliament in 1710 (8th of Anne), which represented that the parish of St. Giles in the Fields contained 5,800 families and 34,800 inhabitants, whose places of worship were one church, three chapels, and one Presbyterian meeting-house. This disproportion suggested the propriety of dividing the district into two parishes, which was finally effected, January 8th, 1724, (10th of George I.) when the deed for setting out the new parish of Bloomsbury was enrolled in Chancery. (*For Acts relative to the Church, Minister, &c. see Appendix.*)

A piece of land was purchased of Lady Rachel Russell and the Duchess of Bedford, situate between Hart Street on the north side, and Little Russell Street on the south, comprising in the front and rear about $106\frac{1}{2}$-feet by about 165-feet in depth. This had been called Plough Yard, and here the new Church was erected prior to anno 1724, and on the 8th of January in that year, five of the commissioners by deed poll under their hands and seals, did declare and appoint, that the said Church should from and for ever after the enrollment of that deed, and the *consecration of the said Church*, be made a parish Church. And in the same deed was described, a certain portion of the parish of St. Giles-in-the-Fields as the limits of the new parish; but for some unknown cause, no provision was made for the Rector until the Act of the 3rd of George II. (*See Appendix.*)

The Church is situate on the site described, and stands in the unusual position of north and and south. It was built under the direction of an architect of the name of Hawksmore, at the estimated expense of £9,790, which Malcolm affirms was exceeded by only three pounds!

When viewed from the south side of Hart Street it has an imposing appearance, having a massive portico with columns of the Corinthian order. As a whole, however, it has not been held in much repute, and Walpole calls it a mass of absurdity.* It is dedicated to St. George the Martyr, in honor of King George I., and the tower is surmounted with a statue of him supported by square pyramids. Lions and unicorns adorn the steeple, ornamented with festoons, which have excited ridicule from the animals being injudiciously large, and

---

* " Nicholas Hawksmore, scholar of Wren, was the architect of St. George Bloomsbury; as also of St. Mary Wolnoth in London Street; Christ Church, Spitalfields; St. George, Middlesex; and St. Anne's, Limehouse. The statue of the king on Bloomsbury steeple is hugged by the royal supporters. A lion, a unicorn, and a king on such an eminence is very surprising;

> The things we know are neither rich nor rare,
> But wonder how the devil they got there."—*Walpole.*

The author of " a new Critical Review of the Public Buildings," before quoted, speaks of this structure as follows : " The new Church of St. George Bloomsbury, is built all of stone, is adorned with a pompous portico, can boast many other decorations, has been stinted in no expense; and yet upon the whole, is ridiculous and absurd even to a proverb. The reason is this, the builder mistook whim for genius, and ornament for taste : he has even erred so much, that the very portico does not seem to be in the middle of the Church, and as to the steeple, it is stuck in like a wen to the rest of the building; then the execrable conceit of setting up the king on the top of it excites nothing but laughter in the ignorant, and contempt in the judge: in short, it is a lasting reflection on the fame of the architect, and the understanding of those who employed him."

placed upon very small columns. The folowing epigram was written to satirise the bad taste of placing the statue on the apex of the tower:—

> " The king of Great Britain was reckoned before
>   The head of the church, by all Protestant people;
> His Bloomsbury subjects have made him still more,
>   For with them he now is the head of the steeple."*

Bloomsbury Church was not consecrated till 1730, 28th of January, although it was built six years earlier. Dr. Edward Vernon was the first appointed Rector, and the Rev. Mr. Knapper, Lecturer.

The living, which is in the gift of the crown, was at first valued at £400, including fees, dues, &c.; but now, after the lapse of a century, it must be much more lucrative, especially from the increased extent of the parish.

It is worthy of remark, that there has been only three rectors of this parish during the long period of nearly ninety-eight years!

1. Dr. Edward Vernon held the living till his death, which took place in March, 1761, having filled it thirty-one years.
2. Dr. Charles Tarrant succeeded him, being presented 2nd April, 1761. He was a noted pluralist,† and died 22nd February, 1791, having been Rector thirty years.

---

* Mr. Hucks, who was an eminent parishioner and vestryman, and whose name is mentioned in connection with the workhouse, &c. gave the above statue. Whether he conditioned it should be placed there, I have not learnt.

† He had numerous preferments during his life, amongst which he held the following at the time of his decease: Dean

3. Dr. Thomas Willis was next appointed in 1791, and died 5th November, 1827, after being Rector the longest of the three, namely thirty-six years.*

The Rev. John Lonsdale, the present Rector, was promoted here in February, 1828.

March 8th, 1730. The commissioners by another deed reciting in part the former, and stating that the Lord Bishop of London had on the preceding January 28th consecrated the new Church, which had now become a new parish, by the name of the Church and Parish of St. George, Bloomsbury; did nominate and elect, with his consent, certain persons therein named, as and for vestrymen of the new parish, together with the rector and churchwardens for the time being, being sufficient inhabitants, &c. These were in number thirty-six, besides the rector and churchwardens.*

---

of Peterborough, Subdean, Subchanter and Prebendary of Salisbury, Prebendary of Rochester, Rector of St. George Bloomsbury, Vicar of Wrotham in Kent, and Chaplain in in Ordinary his Majesty.

* Dr. Thomas Willis was the son of the Rev. Francis Willis, who had the merit of curing the mental malady of King George the Third, in 1789.

Dr. Willis, the Rector, was brought up at Queen's College, Cambridge, and took his degree of L.L.D. in 1791, and was presented to this living the same year by Lord Chancellor Thurlow, and became Prebendary and Treasurer of Rochester, and Vicar of Wateringbury in Kent, all of which he held when he died. *(See Gentleman's Magazine, &c.)*

* Among the names of the first vestrymen were, Wriothesley Duke of Bedford, Chief Justice Eyre, Baron Thompson, Sir James Hallet, Sir Conrad Springel, John Duke of Montague, Sir John Cope, Sir Henry Featherstone, Sir William

By the authority of the same act, 10th of Anne, the commissioners purchased in 1713, a piece of ground for a church-yard, described as part of sixteen acres of meadow ground, and abutting east partly upon the queen's highway leading from Gray's Inn to Highgate. This ground, situate on the north of the Foundling, is now surrounded with buildings, and no one would imagine a public highway had ever existed here, were it not for the above recital. It consists of about three acres, and was divided into two cemeteries, of an acre and a quarter each, being apportioned to St. George the Martyr in Queen Square, then called St. George's Square, which chapel was intended to be made a parochial Church, and the other portion to St. George's Parish, Bloomsbury; the remaining part, about half an acre, was reserved for a common passage to the said church-yards respectively.

Humphries, Sir Hans Sloane, and Mr. Serjeant Baynes, William Hucks the brewer, &c. The rest were mostly gentlemen and tradesmen of high respectability.

The parochial customs, uses, &c. of the old parish being communicated to, and continued to the new one, under the act, the number of vestrymen at present necessary to constitute a vestry is *thirteen* at the least.

Their first meeting took place nine days after their appointment, when they elected a vestry clerk, parish clerk, lecturer, sexton, six pew openers, three bearers in ordinary, and three bearers extraordinary.

At their second meeting, 24th of the same month, they settled the rents of the pews, appointed when prayers should be read, &c.

The freehold and inheritance of the new church-yard, with the mansion or dwelling house of the rector, are also by 10th of Anne, vested in such rector and his successors, who are declared to be seized thereof, as in his and their demesne as of fee in right of the church, in such manner as other rectors are seized of their respective churches and glebes.

There is a remarkable circumstance attached to this burial ground, which is the more worthy of notice on account of the horror excited recently by the Edinburgh murders.

On the 9th of October, 1777, the grave-diggers here and others were detected in the act of stealing a corpse from this ground for dissection, the only instance of this kind then ever known, and which, in consequence, involved a difficulty in the decision of the law, from its being the first indictment on record for such crimes.

John Holmes, the grave-digger of St. George, Bloomsbury, Robert Williams, his assistant, and Esther Donaldson, were tried under an indictment for a misdemeanour, before Sir J. Hawkins, Knight, chairman, at Guildhall, Westminster, 6th December, 1777, for stealing the dead body of Mrs. Jane Sainsbury, who died on the 9th October, same year, and was buried in the burial place of the said parish on the following Monday.

Mr. Howarth, counsel for the prosecution, stated the case to the jury with great exactness and proper comments on such species of inhumanity, observing, that by their verdict they would afford the court an opportunity of inflicting a punishment on men whose crimes were shocking to humanity.

Mr. Keys, counsellor for the prisoners, objected to the indictment, and contended, that if the offence was not felony, it was nothing, for it could not be a misdemeanour, and therefore not cognizable by that court, or contrary to any law whatever.

Sir J. Hawkins inquired of Mr. Howarth the reason for not indicting for a felony, as thereby the court was armed with power to punish as severely as such acts deserved.

Mr. Howarth explained this, by saying, that to constitute a felony there must be a felonious act of taking away property; and if the shroud or any other thing, such as the pillow, &c. or any part of it, had been stolen, it would have been a felony. In this case, he said, nothing of that kind had been done, the body was stolen only; and though, in their hurry of conveying away the deceased, they had torn off the shroud and left pieces behind in the churchyard, yet there being no intention of taking them away, it was no felony, and therefore only a misdemeanour.

Mr. Keys again insisted, that it was no misdemeanor; but Sir J. Hawkins very ably refuted him, showing, from the earliest ages, that the rights of sepulture in all countries and all religions were deemed sacred, and the violation of them as a species of sacrilege. He mentioned the time of the Romans as a period wherein the most sacred regard was held to burial places, and to the ashes of the dead; that it was dictated by intuitive religion, and an offence both under the public and the canon law, and particularly defined in all books of law, or otherwise, (and he said he had searched every book written on the subject with great care and attention), as a crime *contra bonos mores*; and expressed his surprise, that any man in the capacity of a lawyer could stand up and say it was not a misdemeanour, when it was an offence against decency and good manners. Sir J. Hawkins also reminded Mr. Keys, that if his objection was good, it was premature, for it should come as a motion for an arrest of judgment. The trial then went on.

Mr. Eustanston, who lives near the Foundling Hospital deposed, that going by that hospital, about eight o'clock in the evening, with some other gentlemen, they met the prisoner, Williams, with a sack on his back, and another person walking with him. Having some suspicion of a robbery, he stopped Williams, and asked him, what he had got there? to which he replied, " I don't know;" but that pulling the sack forcibly from his back, he begged to be let go, and said " he was a poor man just come from harvest." Mr. Eustantone then untied the sack, and to his astonishment, found the deceased body of a woman, her heels tied up tight behind her, her hands tied together behind, and cords round her neck, forcibly bending her head almost between her legs. The horror they were all in at such a sight, prevented them from securing the other person, who ran off; but they secured Williams, and took him to the round-house, where he was well known to be the assistant grave-digger to Holmes, and went by the name of Bobby. To make a more effectual discovery, the next day they, with Mr. Evans, a constable, applied to Holmes as he was digging in the burial ground, who on being asked, denied all knowledge of Bobby or Williams, or of any such a man; neither could he recollect if any body had been buried within the last few days, or, if there had, he could not tell where. However, by the appearance of the mould, they insisted on his running into the ground his long iron crow, and then they discovered a coffin, only six inches under ground, out of which the body had been taken. This appeared, on strict inquiry, to be the coffin of a Mrs. Guy, who had been buried on the preceding Wednesday, very deep. The gentlemen present, not yet satisfied, examined the ground further, and then discovered another coffin, out of which the body of Mrs. Jane Sainsbury had been stolen; and whilst this examination took place, Holmes was detected hiding in his pockets several small pieces of shroud, which lay contiguous to her grave.

Mr. Sainsbury was under the painful necessity of appearing in court, and swearing, that the body found on Williams was his deceased wife; and indeed, poor man! he seemed but too much afflicted in giving his evidence.

Mrs. Elizabeth Barret, who has the care of the other burial ground, proved, that Williams had been constantly employed by Holmes.

Mr. Evans, the constable, also produced several sacks, marked H. Ellis, found in Holmes' house; and this was brought as circumstantial evidence, as the sack in which Mrs. Sainsbury was tied, was also marked H. Ellis.

Sir John Hawkins summed up the evidence, and the jury directly found the two men guilty; but acquitted Esther Donaldson.

They were sentenced to six months imprisonment, and to be each severely whipped, twice, in the last week of their confinement, from Kingsgate Street to Dyot Street, St. Giles's, which is full half a mile; but the whipping was afterwards remitted.

From the Vestry Minutes, 1st April, 1731, the Duke of Bedford gave 100 guineas to the parish, to purchase plate for the communion table.

The commissioners had left the church without a pulpit, and a moveable one was now ordered, to try in what part of the church the minister could be best heard.

December 3rd, 1731. A rate of six-pence in the pound was made on Bloomsbury parish, to defray the charges incurred about the new church and burial ground.

A committee reported, that they had caused to be erected a gallery on the west side from north to south, at an expense of £140, which was paid by Mr. Milner, who would wait for re-payment thereof, with interest, until the rents of the pews in such gallery should be sufficient for that purpose.

In respect to its other public buildings, the British Museum must ever hold the pre-eminence; and as a great national establishment it is entitled to our notice, it being justly esteemed the glory of Bloomsbury, and the pride of our country.

Montague House, now the British Museum, was built previous to 1676, as we gather from Evelyn's Diary. "May 11, 1676," he says, "I went to see Mr. Montague's palace, near Bloomsbury, built by Mr. Hooke, a member of the Royal Society, after the French manner." In another place he says, "January 19, 1686. This night was burnt to the ground, my Lord Montague's palace in Bloomsbury, than which for paintings and furniture, there was nothing more glorious in England. This happened by the neglect of a servant airing, as they call it, some goods by the fire in a moist season; indeed, so wet and mild a season had scarce been seen in man's memory."

There is another account of this calamitous fire, rendered so interesting by the pen of Lady Rachel Russell in her Letters, that I cannot forbear inserting it. It is part of a letter addressed to Doctor Fitzwilliam, and is dated January 22, 1686 :—

"If you have heard of the dismal accident in this neighbourhood, you will easily believe Tuesday night was not a quiet one with us.

"About one o'clock in the night I heard a great noise in the square, so little ordinary, I called up a servant, and sent her down to hear the occasion; she brought up a very sad one, that Montague House was on fire, and it was so indeed; it burnt with so great violence, the house was consumed by five o'clock.

"The wind blew strong this way, so that we lay under fire a great part of the time, the sparks and flames covering the house, and filling the court. My boy awoke, and said he was almost suffocated with smoke, but being told the reason, would see it, and so was satisfied without fear; and took a strange bedfellow very willingly, Lady Devonshire's youngest boy, whom his nurse had brought wrapt up in a blanket. Thus we see what a day brings forth, and how momentary the things are we set our hearts upon!"

The present house was built on the former site, and on the same french plan, and by the same nobleman, the first Duke of Montague, who had been ambassador to the court of France.

The second Duke and Duchess of Montague resided in one of the wings only of this edifice until their house was finished at Whitehall. After which, it remained unoccupied until it was converted to its present valuable purpose.*

The British Museum had its origin in the circumstance of the celebrated naturalist and antiquarian, Sir Hans Sloane, in 1753, bequeathing to the public the invaluable collection of curiosities contained in his museum, on condition of his executors being paid £20,000.

---

* Montague House, when first built, was considered the most splendid private mansion in the metropolis. Ralph is certainly severe, however, on its architectural merits; whilst Lord Oxford says, in his anecdotes of paintings, "What it wants in grace and beauty, is compensated by the spaciousness and lofty magnificence of the apartments."

This was readily acceded to by parliament, as also a resolution for providing a general repository for the better reception of this and other collections.

One hundred thousand pounds was raised immediately by lottery for this noble purpose, and trustees from the most eminent persons in the kingdom were appointed to manage it.

A short time after the passing the act, and while the trustees were at a loss where to purchase, or build a repository for the occasion, an offer was made by the heiresses of the Montague family of their noble house and garden, which was purchased for £10,100, and £30,000 more was expended in necessary repairs, and conveniences for the establishment.

It was first opened in January, 1759, and contains at the present period, a wonderful collection of all that is curious in art and nature. Besides the museum of Sir Hans Sloane,* the Cottonian Library has been added, the Harleiañ Manuscripts, Sir William Hamilton's antique vases, &c. the Townleian, Elgin, and other marbles; Egyptian antiquities, Hatchet's and other minerals, &c. &c. and above all the splendid gift of the late King's library, given by his present Majesty, George IV. Some extensive additions have been made

---

* Sir Hans Sloane is said to have expended £50,000 on his collection.

to the original building for the reception of the Elgin marbles, &c. and also for the above library; and many expensive, yet praiseworthy improvements, have been made since its first establishment.

This library is said to consist of 185,000 volumes, and the room where they are now deposited is 300 feet in length, 42 wide, and 30 feet in height. The whole is elegantly fitted up, and supported by four massy columns of polished granite, which have a beautiful effect, and are greatly admired for the polish and noble style they exhibit. They are each in one ponderous stone, and in height about twenty-five feet, and in circumference at the base three feet six inches.

It is intended gradually to erect an entire new museum, of which the east wing, which contains the library, will form a part; it is altogether 500 feet in length, which includes a large hall to the south, where is deposited the numerous and invaluable collections of manuscripts of the museum. This hall is said to be eighty feet by seventy feet, except the two ends. The whole has been arranged under Mr. Smirke the architect.

The articles contained in this noble repository filled, some years ago, a catalogue of thirty-eight volumes in folio, and eight in quarto: we may notice a few of them.

Among them is a number of valuable and large collection of pamphlets, published in the reign of Charles I. given by his late Majesty; the entire library of Clayton Cracherode, Esquire, bequeathed in 1799; a Biographical collection, given by Sir William Musgrave; Garrick's collection of Old Plays; a fine series of coins of our Saxon Kings, by Mr. Tyssen; curiosities brought from the South Pacific Ocean by captain Cook and others; a number of antiquities obtained from Herculaneum, by Sir William Hamilton, &c. &c.

In the court are the Egyptian monuments, the most curious of which is a beautiful large sarcophagus of variegated marble, covered with hieroglyphics, and believed to have been used as the exterior coffin of Alexander the Great. In the hall are two Egyptian monuments of black marble also, covered with hieroglyphics, which belonged to the Mausoleum of Cleopatra; with some large pieces from the Giants' Causeway in Ireland, &c.

There is among the artificial curiosities, a model in wax of the Temple of the Sybil at Tivoli; a model in wax of Laocoon and his Sons; a Chinese junk; specimens of Raphael's china model of the famous Barbirini vase; a model of a Persee burial ground; many ingenious cuttings in paper, &c. &c.

The coins and medals of Sir Hans Sloane's collection alone consist of 20,000 and upwards, and there are many more; and the figures, especially on those of Greece, are exquisitely beautiful.

Here is the original Magna Charta of King John, written on a large roll of parchment, and part of the broad seal is preserved. It was damaged by the fire at the Cottonian Library at Westminster, in 1738. There is an immense number of manuscripts of high interest and value.

The Elgin marbles, for which £35,000 was given by grant of parliament in 1817, are the remaining relics of the ancient temple of Theseus and Minerva, the works of Phidias and Praxiteles, which Canova especially admired. It has, however, been truly observed, that it " requires the eye of a critic, the fire of an artist and a philosopher, and the zeal of an antiquarian to discover and appreciate the beauty and value of these Grecian remains."

This celebrated edifice, exclusive of its extensive offices, is 186 feet in length, and in height 57 feet to the top of the cornice.

By plans already made out, and approved of by the lords of the treasury and the trustees, it is intended to erect the new museum farther north, which will surround a quadrangular court, and occupy all the present garden.* The east wing is already built.†

THE RUSSELL INSTITUTION, Great Coram Street. This useful literary institution was originally built by Mr. Burton, in 1802, for an assembly room, and is the second building erected here for that purpose; the former one, when nearly completed on the same plan, having been entirely destroyed by fire in 1803. Concerts and assemblies were held here several times after the completion of the present structure, under the patronage of the present Duke and Duchess of Bedford, who honoured them with their presence; but eventually, these were discontinued, and the building remained useless for some time. At length, in 1808, it was converted to its present useful purpose, and has been conducted, generally, with spirit and economy. It contains a tolerably extensive library of valuable books, which the proprietors and subscribers have, with some exception, the privilege of perusing at their own houses. Periodical works of taste and literature, with

---

* See plan of Parish.

† On the west side a spacious building was erected under the architectural direction of G. Saunders, Esquire, for which £16,000 was voted in 1804, for the reception of the Townly marbles, Egyptian antiquities, &c. Attached to this is a temporary building by Mr. Smirke, in which the Elgin and Phigalean marbles are at present arranged and displayed. The whole of these are to be pulled down, and the west wing to be rebuilt to correspond with the east wing.

the morning and evening news-papers, are always to be found in the spacious and convenient reading rooms; and lectures on philosophy and science are often delivered in its theatre, fitted up for that purpose. The committees of management deserve great praise for the care they have exercised in the appropriation of its funds, whereby they have given permanency to this institution; whilst others, and especially the Surry, have been relinquished for want of similar prudence.

It is a large structure, and has a handsome portico entrance, with Grecian Doric columns, and is 112 feet in length by 55 feet in depth.

The number of original shares of this institution were five hundred, which was subsequently extended to seven hundred, at twenty-five guineas each; beside which, there are many annual subscribers at three guineas each, who are entitled to nearly all the privileges of proprietors. The building was purchased of Mr. Burton, and was vested in three trustees in 1808, who were the following respectable gentlemen:—

Sir Samuel Romilly, M.P.—William Dickenson, M.P.—and Mr. Serjeant Lens; they now consist of four, William Dickenson, Esquire, M.P.—Sir James Scarlett, M.P.—Honourable Mr. Justice Gaselee—and Mr. Serjeant Storks.

The present librarian is E. W. Brayley, esq. F. A. S. well known as the author of Londiniana, History of Middlesex, &c. &c.

The committee and managers comprise the names of twenty-four gentlemen of high literary attainments.

We may here notice the ROYAL COLLEGE OF SURGEONS, a fine building, situate on the south side of Lincoln's Inn Fields. The Surgeons were incorporated as one of the city companies, by Henry VIII. but in 1800 they received a royal charter, separating them from the Barbers, with whom they were before conjoined. The Surgeons' Hall in front exhibits a portico of the Ionic order. The museum is a large room with galleries; and here are deposited the collections of the celebrated Hunter, purchased by government, and committed to the care of this college. Mr. Hunter's object was to exhibit the gradations of nature from the simplest state of life, to the most perfect and complete of the animal creation. He had by force of genius carefully preserved in spirits, or in a dried state, the corresponding parts of animals' bodies, that the various links in the chain of a perfect being may be clearly understood. These preparations are mostly displayed in the gallery. Among the curious exhibitions may be seen, the embalmed wife of the noted Martin Van Butchell.

Among the contributors to the museum, Sir William Blizard presented 500 specimens of natural and deceased structure. Sir E. Home presented it with specimens of natural history, and also contributed to the library. The dissection of murderers, executed in London, is under the direction of the master and governor of this college. The museum may be seen, in parties, every Tuesday and Thursday (except in the months of May and June,) by previously leaving their names.

In taking more minute notice of the improvements in Bloomsbury,—RUSSELL SQUARE demands our attention. This has a magnificent appearance, and is built, as before observed, on what was called in Strype's time, 1720, the Southampton Fields, but subsequently the Long Fields. It is so extensive as to decide a common observer, that it vies in that respect with Lincoln's Inn Fields Square; nor is it far behind it when fairly compared. It has, from its first formation, been a favourite residence of the highest legal characters; and here merchants and bankers have seated themselves and families, the air and situation uniting to render it a pleasant retreat from the cares of business.

The following dimensions given of this square are accurate, by which it will be seen that its four sides are unequal.—

	Feet.	Inches.
North side contains	655	6
South ditto	665	3
West ditto	672	7
East ditto	667	1
Total	2661	5 ft. square.*

Lincoln's Inn Square has been already stated at about 2,800 feet.

If examined critically, there are several acknowledged circumstances in reference to the former square, which detracts from its beauty. The pleasure ground stands in a hollow declivity, which has many inconveniences, arising from the vast quantity of brick earth taken therefrom when the buildings were in progress, and which ought to have been replenished. The elevation of the north and west sides are greatly exalted above those of the east and south, which has a bad effect to the eye, and above all, renders the carriage pavement so unequal, that no art can prevent its overflowing

---

* Mr. Britton, who has published so many useful and elegant works on architecture, &c. has given the dimensions of several of the fashionable and modern squares as follows:—

Belgrave Square	684 feet, by	687
Eaton ditto	1637	371
Cadogan ditto	1450	370
Grosvenor ditto	654	654
Portman ditto	500	480
Bryanstone ditto	814	194
Montague ditto	820	156

with wet in various parts, at certain seasons of the year.*

---

* Baltimore House, since the formation of this square, has been divided into two splendid residences, after standing alone during forty years, comprising, with its gardens, a considerable portion of its east side.

Soon after its erection and occupation by Lord Baltimore, it acquired a celebrity dishonourable to that nobleman, by a criminal occurrence which made a considerable sensation throughout the kingdom at the period alluded to, and which, as connected with the history of Bloomsbury, we will here briefly notice.

Lord Baltimore married the daughter of the Duke of Bridgewater, but his unbounded attachment for women, rendered the nuptial connection a scene of unhappiness, he keeping agents for the infamous purpose of providing him with fresh faces in various parts of the metropolis.

Hearing, through one of these (a Mrs. Harvey,) in November, 1767, that a young female of the name of Woodcock, who kept a milliner's shop on Tower Hill, was handsome, and suited to his ignoble purpose, he went there several times under pretence of purchasing laced ruffles and sundry other articles, until at length she was conveyed into his lordship's carriage by Isaacs, a jew, who had become an accomplice with Mrs. Harvey in the vile conspiracy. Under pretence of taking her to a lady who would give her orders for millinery, these wretches drove her rapidly through the metropolis with the glasses drawn up, and it being dark, she was unaware of its being other than a hackney coach, until, at length, they arrived at the court yard of a house of magnitude and splendour.

She was now ushered, by Mrs. Harvey, through a suit of rooms elegantly furnished, when Lord Baltimore made his appearance, at which she became greatly alarmed on recollecting his calling upon her at Tower Hill.

Under pretext of his being steward to the lady she was to be introduced to, she became more composed on his promising to fetch her; and going out, he soon returned with Mrs. Griffinburgh, telling her she was the lady who had ordered the

After all, it has claims to admiration; and it obtained a great acquisition by the statue,

---

goods. This was another of his creatures, and she detained her, under various pretences, till a late hour, when she became importunate to depart.

Keeping up the character of a steward, he took her over several apartments to delay time, and afterwards insisted on her staying supper; and being alone with her, he took such indecent liberties as induced her to resent the insult, and when Doctor Griffinburgh, husband to the woman of that name, and Mrs. Harvey, came in to assist his lordship, she contested the matter with them all, and forced her way to the door, insisting upon going home.

At a late hour she was conducted to a bed-room, overwhelmed with distress, where she continued walking about till morning, lamenting her unhappy situation, the two women being in bed in the same room.

In the morning she was conducted to breakfast, but refused to eat, and demanded her liberty, weeping incessantly, whilst his lordship was vowing excessive love, and urging it as an excuse for detaining her; and whenever she went towards the window, to make her distress evident to the casual passenger, the women forced her away.

The details of his succeeding conduct are of the grossest description; soothing her and threatening her by turns, during several hours; and at length, under pretence of taking her to her father if she would dry her eyes and put on clean linen, supplied by Mrs. Griffinburgh; she was hurried into a coach and conveyed to Epsom, where his lordship had a seat, accompanied by the doctor and the two infamous women.

Here his wicked intentions were forcibly accomplished, the house being better adapted by its loneliness for his disgraceful purpose.

At length her friends attained a clue to her detention, after enduring the most painful anxiety at her absence, during about a fortnight, and a writ of Habeas Corpus being obtained, she was restored to her liberty. Lord Baltimore and his two female accomplices were tried at Kingston, March 26, 1768, and were acquitted through an informality in Miss Woodcock's deposition, arising, evidently, from the agitation of her mind.

The title has since become extinct.

erected on the south side, of the late Francis Duke of Bedford, who died so prematurely, and whose memory has been greatly lamented. This statue is of bronze, and stands just within the rails at the centre, and opposite Bedford Place, and seems to be looking towards the spot where his family mansion stood, whilst viewing, at the same time, the statue of his much loved friend, Charles James Fox, which is fixed in an opposite direction in Bloomsbury Square.

It is the work of Westmacott, on whom it reflects the highest credit, for elevating the character of Britain in chisel and allegorical statuary. The pedestal is of massy Scotch granite, and with the statue of his Grace (which is nine feet high,) measures twenty-seven feet in height. His Grace reposes one arm on a common plough, the left holding the gifts of Ceres, to mark his agricultural pursuits; whilst the four seasons are personified in the endearing semblance of children playing round his feet; and to the four corners are attached, bulls heads in very high relief. Herds of cattle are seen in recumbent postures, and rural subjects in *basso relievo*, representing the preparation for the ploughman's dinner, and the wife on her knees attending her culinary department, a youth sounding a horn, rustics, and a team of oxen. Reapers and gleaners are delineated in their various employ; and a young female in the centre, looks comely and graceful, as a village favourite. These enrichments, the four seasons, and the duke's statue, are all successfully cast in bronze, and are said to preserve the spirit of the original model.*

---

* Whilst on this part of my subject, it is natural to revert to a former period; when, in 1800, these fields lay waste and useless, until you approached some nursery grounds near the New Road to the north, and a piece of ground enclosed for the Toxopholite Society towards the north-west, near the back of Gower Street. The remainder was the resort of depraved wretches, whose amusements consisted chiefly in fighting pitched battles, and other disorderly sports, especially on the sabbath day. Often did I walk over this spot, to view, with delight, the former residence of the illustrious martyr of liberty, Lord William Russell; and I still retain it in my mind, having a perfect recollection of its venerable grandeur, as I surveyed it in the distance, shaded with the thick foliage of magnificent lime trees. The fine verdant lawn extended a considerable distance between these, and was guarded by a deep ravine to the north from the intrusive footsteps of the daring. Whilst in perfect safety were grazing, various breeds of foreign and other sheep, which, from their singular appearance, excited the gaze and admiration of the curious. All this, and much more, has disappeared, and nothing remains but the remembrance of them.

Tradition had given to the superstitious at that period, a legendary story from remote times, of two brothers who fought in this field so ferociously as to destroy each other; since which, their footsteps, formed from the vengeful struggle, were said to remain, with the indentations produced by their advancing and receding, nor could any grass or vegetable ever be produced where these forty footsteps were thus displayed. This extraordinary arena was said to be at the extreme termination of the north-east end of Upper Montague Street; and, profiting by the fiction, the Miss Porters have recently written and

BLOOMSBURY SQUARE we have already spoken of, but we advert to it again, principally, to notice the statue of the Right Honourable James Fox, which is here set up. Westmacott was the artist, and it has been much admired as a work executed in his best style. It is of colossal dimensions, being on a scale of nine feet in height, and is executed in bronze, and elevated upon a pedestal of granite, surmounting a spacious base formed of several steps, or gradations. The pedestal and statue is about seventeen feet in height, and the latter is placed in a

---

published an ingenious romance thereon, entitled, "Coming Out, or the Forty Footsteps."

At a later period, anno 1801, part of these fields became the scene of martial deeds, when we were menaced with invasion by Buonaparte. On this occasion Britons were aroused by the puny threats of the blustering foe, and a great portion of them flew everywhere to arms, and numerous volunteer corps sprung up, and formed in defence of their country. The loyalty and enterprize of Mr. James Burton would not allow him to be the last in a cause so laudable; and under his auspices a race of hardy mechanics, mostly under his employ and influence, united together for the same purpose, who were denominated "The Loyal British Artificers." At first these consisted of a phalanx of upwards of 1000, of which I became one, anxious, like them, to march in an attitude of resistance to the enemy, with Colonel Burton at our head, should he dare to violate our shores.

On these fields, still uncovered with buildings, and especially on the Toxopholite Ground, we regularly mustered for exercise, and here have I undergone excessive fatigue by going through the arduous manœuvres of a light company soldier, which I was not then unfitted for in bulk and size. We continued to form together as long as our services were thought useful and necessary.

N

sitting position, habited in a consular robe, the ample folds of which pass over the body, and, falling from the seat, gives breadth and effect to the whole. The likeness of Mr. Fox is well preserved, and the right hand is supporting Magna Charta, whilst the left is in repose. The head is inclined forward, expressive of attention, firmness, and complacency; whilst dignified serenity is depicted on his countenance.*

---

* It was in this square that the ruffian hand of lawless bigotry wreaked its vengeance against the great and venerable Lord Mansfield, in 1780. His lordship's elegant mansion was plundered and burnt to ashes, together with an invaluable collection of scarce manuscripts, notes on law cases, pictures, books, deeds, &c. The mob had been engaged in the work of destruction four days, without meeting with resistance; such was the intimidation and panic which prevailed in the metropolis at this juncture. Hence, however, a small body of the military opposed it, headed by a civil magistrate, who read the Riot Act, and afterwards ordered the detachment to fire, by which six men and one woman were killed, and several other persons wounded. Many of the mob, having made their way into his lordship's cellars, suffered from intoxication. The case of the female who was killed on this occasion was most pitiable. She lived servant to a Mr. Dubois in the square, and was going towards the street door, when she was killed by a ball which passed through it into the passage. Several bullets, also, entered the parlour window at the same time, yet no other person was hurt, though several were in the room.

This occurrence having taken place nearly forty-nine years ago, it may not prove uninteresting to mention, that the mansion of Lord Mansfield stood on the site of three houses since erected, on the north-east corner of this square, which now includes one in Bloomsbury Place.

TORRINGTON SQUARE is also on the Duke of Bedford's estate, and is lately in a state of completion. It contains seventy houses of a moderate size, and is so pleasantly situate on an elevated healthy spot, as to have been filled with occupants, as fast as it progressed in building. Its form is rectangular, or what is called, improperly, a long square; and it has proved a very successful speculation to its very industrious and worthy builder, Mr. Sims.

BRUNSWICK SQUARE is entirely on the Foundling Hospital estate, and contains only twelve houses in Bloomsbury Parish, the remaining thirty-eight being in that of Pancras. Its east side is formed by the west front of the hospital and its gardens, which building was erected in 1734, under the direction of Mr. Gibbs, an architect. The square is smaller than many others in the metropolis, but elegant and pleasant, and from its near approach to the city, it has always been most respectably inhabited by merchants and others.

Among the principal streets newly formed in this parish, we may enumerate that part of Guildford Street leading into Russell Square on the east side; Keppel Street leading into the west side; Bedford Place, which connects itself with Bloomsbury Square, and enters Russell Square in a northern direction; Upper Bedford Place on the opposite side, which connects itself to the north, with **Tavistock Square** (in Pancras parish), and Russell Square to the south; Montague Place, which runs in a parallel line with Keppel Street toward the south forming a junction with Bedford Square and Russell Square; west and east Montague Streets, which take a direction from the southwest corner of Russell Square into Great Russell Street in a south line, and on the opposite side of the square in a northern line into a new square now forming, to be called Rothsay Square. At the east side of Russell Square, Bernard Street forms a junction with Brunswick Square, and in a northerly direction from the commencement of this street is Woburn Place, a fine street which leads again into Tavistock Square. Great Coram Street opens itself out of Woburn Place, nearly at the centre of the east side, leading into Brunswick Square; and, finally, Southampton Row, (the west side only of which is new), takes a contrary direction from that of Woburn Place on the south, leading into King Street and Holborn.*

---

* An eccentrical lady formerly resided on the east side of this row, whose death and other particulars were announced as follows:—" Died, 16th January, 1792, at her house, Southampton Row, Bloomsbury, Mrs. Griggs. Her executors found in her house eighty-six living and twenty-eight dead cats. A black servant has been left £150 per annum, for the maintenance of himself and the surviving grimalkins

These are the principal streets and avenues erected since 1802, but there are others connected with them, and intermediate, which are both respectable and ornamental.

In contemplating this vast accumulation of houses, and particularly when reviewing them as forming a small portion of what have been built within a few years in the metropolis, astonishment cannot but be excited to an extreme degree.

Our former monarchs, Elizabeth and James, who issued proclamations to restrain the extension of their capital, as involving evils of the greatest magnitude, would indeed be surprised

---

The lady was single, and died worth £30,000. Mrs. Griggs, on the death of her sister, a short time ago, had an addition to her fortune; she set up her coach, and went out almost every day airing, but suffered no male servant to sleep in her house. Her maids being tired frequently of their attendance on such a numerous household, she was induced at last to take a black woman to attend and feed them. This black woman had lived servant to Mrs. Griggs many years, and had a handsome annuity given her to take care of the cats. She also left some annuities for life to several friends (relatives she had none.) The residue of her paternal estates to be applied to the benefit of poor widows and maidens of sixty years of age—the widows of seamen and their daughters to be preferred."

In Aikin's Life of Howard, page 159, we have another instance of a person of the name of Norris of Hackney, who from the multitude of cats assembled under his roof, acquired the name of Cat Norris. The attachment of Mahometans to cats is well known; amidst their disregard to the human species in the hospitals, Mr. Howard found an Asylum for Cats. *(See Annual Register and Gentleman's Magazine.)*

could they behold what has been effected within the last 200 years, and without the baneful results they so much deprecated. Sir William Petty ascribed much of the increase in his time to the general introduction of brick buildings by the Earl of Arundel, by which the growth of London, both in extent and beauty, was prodigious.* From 1600 it doubled every forty years, so that in 1680 it contained four times as many inhabitants as at the beginning of the century. What would this eminent calculator say now?

In a collection of Epigrams written by Thomas Freeman, a native of Gloucester, and published in 1614, 4to. under the title of " Rub

---

" In the 17th of Edward IV. Sir Ralph Jocelyne, the Lord Mayor, obtained an Act of Common Council for repairing the city wall betwixt Aldgate and Aldersgate. For ' the more furtherance of the worke,' also as Stowe records, 'he caused the Morefielde to be searched for clay, and willed *bricke* to be made and *brent* there, and likewise caused chalke to be brought out of Kente, and to be *brent* in lime in the same Morefielde." This, says Mr. Brayley, is one of the earliest notices of the use of brick in London that occurs, though soon afterwards the larger houses were began to be built principally with this material. *(See Beauties of England and Wales, 10th vol. part 2, page 33.)*

We learn from Matthew Paris, that in the reign of Edward III. William de Trumpington, Abbot of St. Albans, bought a house, or rather a court of houses, in London, as extensive as a great palace, with chapel, stable, garden, a well, &c. for one hundred marks, (1314), to which he added fifty marks more for improvements. *Matt. Paris, page 125-6.*

and a Great Cast," are the following lines called " London's Progresse."

All the prophetical annunciations of this effusion, except the union of Hoxton with Highgate, have already been accomplished ; and by the forming of a new road, a few years ago, across the enclosed fields from the Haberdasher's Hospital to Lower Holloway, and by the progressive increase of buildings up Highgate Hill, the whole prediction is in a rapid course of fulfilment.

" Why how now, Babell, whilt thou build ?
The old Holborne, Charing-Cross, the Strand,
Are going to St. Giles's-in-the-Field :
St. Katerine, she takes Wapping by the hand,
And Hogsdon will to Hy-gate ere't be long.
London has got a great way from the streame,
I think she means to go to Islington,
To eat a dish of strawberries and creame.
The city's sure in progresse, I surmise,
Or going to revell it in some disorder
Without the walls, without the liberties,
Where she needs feare nor Mayor nor Recorder.
Well, say she do, 'twere pretty, yet 'tis pity,
A Middlesex Bailiff should arrest the citty."

Brayley's Londiniana.

The earliest places of worship we know of, exclusive of the churches, are the three following :—

1. The private Chapel of Southampton House is mentioned in an entry in the churchwardens book literally as follows :—

"1699. Received of the r. honble the Countess of Southton, money given in her Chapel at the Holy Communion £8."*

2. Joseph Read's PRESBYTERIAN CHAPEL, which was situate in Dyot Street, and was built for him about 1672. He was born at Kidderminster, and was in great esteem with the celebrated Baxter, and was one of the ejected ministers with him, having had the living of Whitley in Worcestershire. He was taken up under the Conventicle Act in 1677, and endured much persecution, but was restored to his people, who were numerous, on the accession of James II. It was afterwards used as a Chapel of Ease to St. Giles's Church from 1684 till 1708, at a rental of £30. No vestige of it now remains.

3. GREAT QUEEN STREET CHAPEL. In 1692, an inquiry was set on foot to ascertain what number of pews would be taken by the

---

* The Countess of Southampton mentioned here was the second wife of the Lord Treasurer Southampton, and appears to have survived him some years, and to have resided at Southampton House, Bloomsbury Square. She was the Lady Leigh, daughter of Francis Leigh, Lord Dunesmore, created Earl of Chichester, 20th Charles I. and the mother (by Lord Southampton) of his second daughter, Elizabeth Wriothesley (who was co-heiress with his other daughter, Lady Rachel Russell, by his first Countess, Rachel de Massay.) This Elizabeth, the daughter, married first Joceline Percy, the eleventh and last Earl of Northumberland, and afterwards to Ralph Earl, and in 1706, Duke of Montague, the founder of Montague House, by which means the ducal families of Bedford and Montague became nearly related.

gentry of Lincoln's Inn Fields and its vicinity, in case a new chapel should be erected in that neighbourhood. Subscriptions were solicited in 1704 for the purpose, and in 1706 a treaty was entered into, which afterwards broke off, for purchasing one lately erected by one William Raguley (Baguely) according to Strype, who adds, that he, pretending to be a minister of the church of England, preached here without licence or authority, consecrated the Holy Sacrament, and administered the same. Wherefore the Bishops of London and Peterborough caused two declarations to be read therein, which eventually silenced him. On the site where this stood has been built a large elegant Chapel, at a considerable expense, for the use of the Wesleyan Methodists, which is well attended, and often crowded to excess.

Besides these we may enumerate, in St. Giles's parish, the dissenting Chapels in Gate Street, in Little Wild Street, in West Street, in Dudley Court, Eglise Suisse Chapel near Moor Street, and the Catholic Chapel in Duke Street, Lincoln's Inn Fields. A new Church is now erecting in Little Queen Street.

BEDFORD CHAPEL is the only ecclesiastical establishment in the parish of Bloomsbury, exclusive of the Church. It is situate in Charlotte Street, on the west side, and was first opened for divine worship in 1771, and it is well attended by respectable inhabitants.

The Rev. Dr. John Trusler was the first clergyman, and a party in the lease granted by John, Duke of Bedford, of the ground on which it is built, and it has been in much repute for eminent preachers, among whom was the unfortunate Dr. Dodd.

There is also a Baptist Chapel in Eagle Street, and another of the same persuasion in Keppel Street; and these, with the Church, comprise all the places of worship in Bloomsbury. It is however in contemplation to build an ecclesiastical Chapel in Rothsay Square.

Considering the extent and population of these parishes, it is a remarkable circumstance how few places of worship they contain, and especially in reference to Bloomsbury.

We have little means of acquiring a knowledge of the population of this district at an early period of its history. The grants of land and tenements to the hospital, added to the occupants under that institution in various parts of it, is the only datum to calculate upon in modern times.

It is supposed, from records extant, that the grantees of estates, in which the hospital had a property in the two manors of St. Giles and Bloomsbury, in the commencement of the fourteenth century, (Henry V.) amounted to somewhat more than a hundred. To these were to be added the hospital inmates, and those who were tenants, or holders of estates, in which it had no interest. In this view the whole population has been estimated at this period at about one thousand persons.

About 150 years afterwards, namely, in the reign of Edward VI. the *houseling people* was stated at 305, *(see page 45)* which, if it means only those old enough and qualified to receive the sacrament, we have no means of guessing the probable number of inhabitants. Parton tells us, that the transfer of the hospital operated much to the detriment of the village; consequently, we may presume that it had not greatly increased, if at all, during several reigns, nor does the neighbourhood seem to have augmented to any great extent until about anno 1600.

The restrictions on building, doubtless, had an influence at successive periods on the local population, but as the restraints ceased, it increased rapidly in the suburb villages, among which that of St. Giles stood prominent, and it has been seen that, in 1711, a vast augmentation had been made.

The statement, by order of parliament, gave to the parish 2,999 housekeepers, whereof 269 were gentlemen, 923 tradesmen, and 807 of a poorer class, making about seven persons to each house, the total being about 21,000 inhabitants.

The following is the most correct account of the population, at different periods, that I have been able to collect, including the number of houses where anything like certainty could be obtained.

1360. Edward III.'s reign, according to conjecture, 1000 inhabitants.

1550. Edward VI.'s reign, 305 houseling people. Number of inhabitants doubtful.

1623. James I's reign, 879 houses, 2000 inhabitants. *(See pages 94 and 100.)*

1680. Charles II.'s reign, 2,000 houses, probably 10,000 inhabitants.

1711. Queen Anne's reign, 2,999 houses, 21,000 inhabitants.*

1801. George III.'s reign, 3861 houses, census 36,502 inhabitants

1811. George III.'s reign, 4,871 houses, census 48,536 inhabitants.

1821. George III.'s reign, 4914 houses, census 51,793 inhabitants

The census is now taken every ten years, the last in 1821, but certainly not with precision. In 1811 the number of houses is stated too high, or how does it happen that they have increased only to 4996 to this period, 1829, about seventeen years?

---

* The Archbishop of York affirmed in his protest, that the number amounted to 40,000, which appears to be an excessive calculation, it giving nearly fourteen to each house; a criterion totally inconsistent.

It seems also strange that in 1711, the number of inhabitants should be in the ratio of seven to each house, whilst in 1801 they are taken at nearly nine and a half. In 1811 the ratio is more than ten to each house (ten would give 48,280.)

The census of 1821 gives us, upon the whole number of houses more than ten and a half to each.

Among the discrepancies which I cannot here reconcile, may be noticed the statement submitted by the Rectors and Mr. L. Hansard, to Messrs. Easterby, Tuely, and Taylor, on the tenth of July last (1829,) which reduces the number of assessed houses from 4,996 to 4,936, this being the period most essential to our views of parochial policy, and subject to our future strictures and remarks. The following is the statement alluded to :—

Number of houses	Rental, £20 & under.	£20 to £50	£30 to £50	£50 to £100	100 and £150	150 & upwds.
in St. Giles's	2,980	781	673	827	443	93	63
In St. George	1,956	409	212	403	576	217	139
Total*	4,936	1190	885	1230	1019	310	202

* Of all the subjects comprised in Political Economy, population seems the least understood, and it is really amusing to notice the clashing opinions of philosophers who have written upon it. Malthus has advanced an opinion, that mankind increases in geometrical proportion, as the numbers 1, 2, 4, 8, 16, &c; whilst subsistence cannot increase faster than the numbers 1, 2, 3, 4, 5, &c. which is arithmetical proportion. Hence he infers that the whole population of a state may be doubled every twenty-five years, a conclusion totally at

The following statement, taken from the census of 1821, will show that the the united parishes of St. Giles in the Fields and Blooms-bury, by comparison, is only inferior to the two largest parishes in the metropolis, Mary-labonne and St. Pancras, in population:—

Mary-la-bonne	96,340
Pancras	71,838
St. Giles and Bloomsbury	51,793

---

variance with experience, and yet he has obtained many disciples and excited much alarm. Nothing is so easy as the instituting calculations on any assumed hypothesis; and thus Wallace amused himself in exhibiting the geometric increase of mankind in the antediluvian world.

It has been argued against Malthus, that by an inverse ratio food increases beyond the people by a transcendant geometry, and that the food of man may be doubled a thousand times in every twenty-five years. A herring has 40,000 eggs, a cod fish ten times that number; and as to animals, in 1788, two bulls and three cows strayed away in New South Wales, which, in seven years, increased to 1000.

As to the increase of grain, it is incredible; M. P. Knetezmar, Counsellor of State to the King of Prussia, has given astonishing proofs of this from experiments he made; and let it be remembered, that men live on fish, flesh, and grain. Ensor considers the geometrical and arithmetical ratios of Malthus jargon, and he contends that that nation whose people live longest, will be most numerously inhabited; yet Blumenback calculates, that not more than seventy-three in a thousand die of old age. Bolingbroke insisted, that the increase of inhabitants is always advantageous to any state; Swift argued, that the people constitute the undoubted riches of a country; Sir James Stewart, that the increase of numbers in a state shows youth and vigour; Dagge and Paley, that population is *nationally* superior to every other advantage; and Mr. Bentham, in the language of Monsieur Dumont, considers it " la force et la richesse d'une nation."

Chapter VI.

Historical Sketches of Pauperism—Resort of Irish Poor to St. Giles's—Curious Items of Relief—Depravity of Mendicants—Monastic Support—Poor Laws—Legislative Difficulties—Parish Officers—St. Giles's Workhouse; &c. &c.

Parton tells us, " that in remote times, St. Giles's parish contained no greater proportion of poor than other parishes of a similar extent and population; the introduction of Irish mendicants and other poor of that description, for which it afterwards became so noted, is not to be traced farther back than the time of Queen Elizabeth."

Strype remarks, " that when London began to increase in population, there was observed to be a confluence here out of the countries of such persons as were of the poorer sorts of trades and occupations; who, because they could not exercise them within the jurisdiction of the city, followed them within the *suburbs;* therefore the queen, as well as forbidding the further erection of new buildings, ordered all persons within three miles of any of the gates of the city to forbear from letting or settling, or suffering any more than one family only to be placed in one house."

Other proclamations of a similar import were issued, and in one of them, dated 1583, it was set forth " that great multitudes of people were brought to inhabit in small rooms, whereof a great part were seen very poor, yea, such as must live by begging or worse means, and they heaped up together in one house or small tenement; wherefore, for offences of this sort, namely, of increase of many indwellers, or as they be commonly called *inmates* or *undersetters*, which had been suffered within the last seven years, the proper officers were to see the same redrest."

A subsequent proclamation stated, " that there did haunt and repair a great multitude of wandering persons, many of whom were from *Ireland*, with whom were also many other like vagrants, and persons of that nation ; many of whom haunted about the court under pretence of suits, &c. and who mixed with disbanded soldiers from the low countries, and other impostors, did infest the city by day as common beggars, or did commit at night robberies and outrages" These were ordered, as before, to be suppressed.

It has been inferred that these complaints applied particularly to St. Giles's parish, from its immediate vicinity to the court, only a few fields then intervening, and this conclusion has been confirmed by the following extracts from Stowe's Survey:—" by the care of Fleetwood, the recorder, and other magistrates acting under these proclamations, there were few rogues in goal; and Westminster and the Duchy of Lancaster, St. Giles's, High Holborn, St. John Street, and Islington, *great harbours for such misdemeaned persons*, were never so well or quiet, for rogue, nor masterless man dared now once appear in these parts."

Rogue and beggar were, in those days, synonimous terms, as the following anecdote from the same useful writer will exemplify. " Upon occasion of a great parcel of rogues encompassing the queen (Elizabeth), while riding out one evening towards Islington, to take the air, (which seemed to put her into some disturbance) notice was given to Fleetwood, the recorder, who did that night send out warrants into these quarters and in Westminster and the Duchy; and in the morning he went out himself, and took seventy-four rogues, some of whom were blind, and yet great usurers and very rich, who were all examined together at Bridewell, and received there substantial payment." *(Strype's Stowe.)*

But the evil thus curbed was far from being suppressed, for we learn that James I. found it expedient also to issue out proclamations against inmates and multitudes of dwellers in straight rooms and places about the metropolis, and commanding that *newly-raised* dwellings should be pulled down, to prevent the too great influx of strangers and others. Such are the causes from which may be dated the original settlement of a numerous body of poor in this parish; that is to say, its being near the court, and its being a convenient suburb village for loose and idle persons to harbour in.

Neither Irish poor nor aliens are mentioned by name in the parish books until 1640, at which time the earliest churchwardens' accounts commenced, but they were included, no doubt, under the general designation of *inmates, undersetters, new comers, &c.* The vestry minutes contain some curious entries on these subjects, a few of which Mr. Parton has favoured us with:—

" Ordered, that the beadles do attend every Sunday, to give an account of *inmates*, and who take them in, and to take up all *idle persons*. And on pain of neglect, for the first offence, to lose their arrears of salary; and for the second offence, to be turned out, and to be incapable of being rechosen."

" 1630. On consideration of the statute, 43rd of Elizabeth, which directs the raising of a stock to set the poor to work; and that the churchwardens and collectors of the poor should once every month resort to church, and there, on the Sabbath day in the afternoon, take some good order for the relief of the poor, it was admitted ' that the relief of the poor is much lesse than it would be, if so many *new comers* into the parish did not find entertainment, as they doe, being most of them *dwellers,* or *inmates,* or *lodgers ;*' and it was ordered, ' that the constables and their deputys should give notice to the churchwardens and collectors every month, of all manner of persons likely to become any way chargeable to the parish, as well of such lately come, also the name of their landlords, in order that they might be dealt with according to law."

" 1637. To prevent the great influx of poor people into this parish, ordered, that the beadles do present every fortnight, on the Sunday, the names of all *new comers, undersetters, inmates, divided tenements, persons that have families in cellars,* and other abuses."

"This" says Parton, " is the first mention of *cellars* as places of residence, and for which the parish afterwards became so noted, that the expression of ' *a cellar in St. Giles's*' used to designate the lowest poverty, became afterwards proverbial, and is still used, though most of these subterranean dwellings are now gone. The term *cellar-mates,* mentioned in the next entries, proves the increase of persons so lodged."

" Ordered, that special chardge be given to the constables, beadles, &c. to search diligently for women great with child, that they be either removed, or good security got by the churchwardens in discovering and avoiding *inmates, sellermates, and new comers.*"

The receipts and expenditure on account of poor, mention the Irish expressly and repeatedly by name, and from the number of entries of them, it may be inferred that they then began to abound in the parish :—

	s.	d.
1640. Paid to a poore Irishman and to a prisoner come over from Dunkirk	1	0
Paid to John Brewer, a poore man travelling into Ireland	1	
Paid to John Read, a poore distressed man from Ireland	1	
Paid to an old soldier, pressed out of this parish, to convey him to his own countrie, having lost all he had in Ireland	2	6
Paid for a shroude for an Irishman that died at Brickils	2	6

Mr. Parton supposes this person died of the plague, which was then raging.

The following entries are curious, as illustrative of the poor's relief previous to the establishment of a workhouse in St. Giles's parish.

	s.	d.
1640. Paid to poore *Slater*, in Queen Street, and his sick children	2	6
1641. Paid to a poore woman, brought to bed of two children, in the back lane	2	0
For a shroude for a poore child that dyed in Rider's Buildings	1	6
1642. To *Mrs. Mabbs*, a poet's wife, her husband being dead	1	
1647. Paid and given to *Goody Parit*, to buy her boy ij. shirts (Charles, his father, is a waterman at Chuswick) and he is to keepe him at £20. a year from Christmas)	3	
1648. Gave to the *Lady Pigot*, in Lincoln's-Inn Fields, poore and deserving relief	2	6

		s.	d.
1670.	Given to the *Lady Thornbury*, being poor and indigent..	10	0
1640.	Paid to Mr. Hibbs's daughter, with childe and like to starve...	1	
1641.	To oulde *Goodman Street* and oulde *Goody Malthus*, very poore................................		
1645.	To *Mother Cole* and *Mother Johnson*, xijd. a piece	2	0
1646.	To *William Burnett*, in a *seller* (cellar) in Ragged Staff Yard, being poore and verie sicke	1	6
1648.	To *Goody Sherlock*, in Maidenhead-Field, lent our lynnen wheel and gave her money to bye flax	1	0
	To *Goody Paret*, in Bore's-head Alley, in Queen Street, lent and gave as above..................	1	0

There are entries for casual relief to foreigners and others, some of them as follows :—

		£.	s.	d.
1640.	Gave to *Signor Lifcatha*, a distressed Grecian			
1642.	To *Lazhie Milchitaire*, of Chimaica in Armenia, to passe him to his owne countrie, and to redeeme his sonnes in slavarie under the Turkes	0	5	0
1654.*	Paid towards the relief of the marriners, maimed soldiers, widowes and orphans of such as have died in the service of parliament..	4	11	0
1666.	Collected at severall times toward the reliefe of the poor sufferers burnt out by the late dreadful fire of London	25	8	4

* It was in this year, as the parish records informs us, that Oliver Cromwell gave £40 to the parish, to buy coals for the poor.

	£.	s.	d.
1670. Total of money collected this year from the parishioners, towards the redemption of slaves	164	15	9

" 1679. By an order of special sessions, for the relief of casual poor, a paymaster was directed to be appointed annually, who was only to pay by the authority of a note from two overseers, which was to express the name and place of abode of the party relieved; to be examined at the next Sunday meeting."

	£.	s.
1640. Paid to a poore gentleman undone by the burning of a cittie in Ireland, having licence from the lords to collect....	0	3	0
Paid to Mr. Smith, his goods cast away coming from Ireland	0	1	6
1642. Paid to foure Irishwomen and to foure poore women that came out of Ireland, passing to their own countrie	0	1	6
Paid to two porters for carrying two loads of cloathes to be sent into Ireland	0	3	0
Paid to a poor Irish minister	0	2	0
Paid to John Waters, his wife and two children, being very sicke, that came oute of Ireland	0	1	0

The troubles in Ireland obliged vast numbers of the natives to take refuge in England, and the following items probably were for relief in consequence:—

1647. Paid and given one Heycock, a plundered Irish	0	0	6
Paid and given a plundered *Irish* minister's wife	0	1	0
Paid to poore plundered *Irish*	0	2	0
Paid and given to James Burges, a plundered *Irish*, per certificate		2	0
Paid and given Mrs. Renzi, a plundered *Irish*	0	1	0

Many other cases occur about the same period, but after 1648, the *Irish* are seldom mentioned by name, probably from being incorporated with other poor. Numbers of fresh comers, however, arrived, as appears by the appointment of an assistant beadle in 1653, whose express business it was to search out and report such to the parish officers, as also by an entry afterwards, as follows:—

"1659. Agreed on, that there be a meeting of vestry the first Tuesday in every month, to acquaint themselves from the constables and beadles, of inmates and other persons come into this parish, and likely to become chargeable to the same."

The following vestry minute, no doubt, is applicable to the French refugees and other foreigners.

"1675. Whereas the charges of the poore do daily increase by the frequent resort of poore people *from several countries and places*, for want of due care to prevent the same; it is, ordered, that Giles Hanson be elected an assistant beadle, with a salary of £40 a year, to find out and notice all new comers, inmates, &c.; and that a coat and badge be provided for him, that he be the better known in his office."

In 1679, 1680, 1690, and 1692, orders to search out new comers were again repeated, and the answer of the churchwardens to the commissioners for building the new churches, anno 1710 states, "that a great number of the inhabitants of St. Giles's are *French Protestants*." Hogarth admirably satirised, at a later period, their dress and other peculiarities in his "Four Times of the Day."

There are some farther curious entries in the parish accounts, some of which we will copy:—

	£.	s.	d.
1640. Gave to *Tottenham-court Meg*, being verie sicke	0	1	0
1642. Paid and given to *Guy*, a poore fellow	0	1	0
Given to the *Ballad-singing Cobler*	0	1	0
1646. Gave to old *Friz-wig*	0	6	0
1657. Paid the collectors for a shroude for *oulde Guy the Poet*	0	2	6

These were probably well known beggars of that day, judging of them from the familiar way in which they are mentioned. Again:—

	£.	s.	d.
1657. Paid for a lodging for *distracted Bess*	0	0	6
Paid for a shift for *mad Bess*	0	3	6
1658. Paid a year's rent for *mad Bess*	1	4	6
1642. Paid to one Thomas, a traveller	0	0	6
To a poor woman and her children, almost starved	0	1	0
To *William Long*, almost starved, and to Charles Powell, xijd. a piece	0	2	0
1645. For a shroude for *Hunter's child*, the blind beggar man	0	1	
1646. Paid and given to a poor wretch, name forgot	0	1	0
Given to *old Osborne*, a troublesome fellow	0	1	3
Paid to *Shotton* the lame glazier, to carry him towards Bath	0	3	0
1647. To *old Osborne* and his blind wife	0	0	6
To the old *Mud Wall Maker*	0	0	6

Parton observes, "the lame glazier and the old mud wall maker were probably not mendicants but distressed artizans."

The general corruption of manners among the lower orders, owing to the continual influx of poor in this district, is noticed by Hogarth in his prints: the scene of his "Harlot's Progress" is laid in Drury Lane; Tom Nero, in the "Four Stages of Cruelty" is a St. Giles's charity-boy, and is shown, with other vicious boys tormenting a dog near the church. His "Gin Street" is situate in St. Giles's; and in a night cellar, in the same parish, the "Idle Apprentice" is supposed to be taken up for robbery and murder. Fielding also strictly agrees with the truth of these representations, in a pamphlet published a few years afterwards, where he mentions to have had it as information from Mr. Welch, then High Constable of Holborn, "that in the parish of St. Giles's, there were great numbers of idle persons and vagabonds, who have their lodging there for two pence a night. That in the above parish and in St. Georges's Bloomsbury, one woman alone occupies seven of these houses, all properly accommodated with miserable beds, from the cellar to the garret, for such two-penny lodgers. That in these beds, several of which are in the same room, men and women, often strangers to each other, lie promiscuously, the price of a double bed being no more than three pence, as an encouragement for them to lie together. That as these places are adapted to whoredom, so are they no less provided with drunkenness, gin being sold in them all at a *penny* a quartern, so that the smallest sum of money serves for intoxication. That in the execution of search-warrants, Mr. Welch rarely finds less than twenty of these houses open for the receipt of all comers at the latest hours; and that in one of these houses, and that not a large one he hath numbered fifty-eight persons of both sexes, the stench of whom was so intolerable that it soon compelled him to quit the place."

Such was the revolting picture of these parishes about eighty years ago, applicable, however, chiefly to St. Giles's; and to show that its features have not greatly improved, I will here detail the evidence of Mr. Sampson Stevenson, a parishioner, who was a fellow overseer with me in 1814, given before a Committee of the House of Commons, 27th June, 1815, The Right Hon. George Rose, in the chair:—

"What is your business? I am an Ironmonmonger, and live at No. 11, King Street, Seven Dials.

Have you served any office in the parish? I was one of the overseers last year.

Have you had any opportunity of making observations on the characters of beggars? A great deal, not only before I was an officer, but having been led, by being one, to look into the matter, I have made a great many observations, because there was a house which those people used, not more than eight yards from my own house. Complaint being made against it, the nuisance was done away.

Have you had an opportunity of making particular inquiry into the particular character of individual beggars? I have, in fact, I made inquiry, not only of the landlord, but of some of those who seemed to be of a superior class, or petition writers, that was before I was overseer. A year or two ago this house lost its licence; it not only encouraged those kind of people, but people guilty of felonies and so on. This threw them into another quarter, and they made their residence at a public house called the Fountain, King Street, Seven Dials, where they assembled not only at night, but in a morning before they started on their daily occupations, as they express it. I have seen them come in. As it is a house, the landlord of which is very respectable and has a family, I have gone into the bar on purpose to see their goings on, which is very near the tap room: they come at night, perhaps individuals, and likewise those sailors, or pretended sailors, in a body; but those that go out one and two together, come also; those who are sailors never take any thing on their backs like knapsacks, for they only beg or extort money, but the others beg clothing or any thing they can get, and always have a knapsack to put it in. They will come laden with shoes and other habiliments, which being near Monmouth Street, the place where they translate old shoes into new ones, they sell, and likewise the clothing. I have heard them say they have made three or four shillings a day in begging shoes, for sometimes they got shoes that really were very good ones, and their mode of exciting charity is invariably to go bare-foot, and scarify their feet and heels with something or other to make the blood, as it were, to flow. I have seen them in that situation many times, and thus they sally out to their different stations, but invariably changing their routes each day, for one is scarcely ever seen in the same direction two days together, but another takes his situation. I have seen them myself, I never saw them outside, but I have seen them pull out sums of money and share among themselves, both collectively, and those who go out two or three together.

Victuals I do not think I ever saw brought into that place, for I rather think they throw it away when they get it; mostly shoes and clothes, and such things as that, which they sell immediately. They stop as long as the house they use is open, and get violently drunk and quarrel with each other, and very frequently fight;

after that they are not allowed to remain, if they were, the licence would be stopped ; and very likely there are other houses in St. Giles's where they spend the other part of the night, if they have any money left.

What is their general character? They are people that are initiated in this mode of begging, one teaches another these modes of extortion, for I can call it nothing else, and they are of the worst characters; characters whose blasphemy it is almost impossible to repeat. They will follow you in a street for a length of space, and if they do not receive money, they give a great torrent of abuse, even although all the time you may hear them.

Do you know any individual character? I know several I have taken notice of. There is one whose real name I do not know, but he goes by the name of Granne Manoo; he is a man, I believe, who is scarcely out of goal three months in the year, for he is so abusive and vile a character, he is very frequently in goal for his abuse and mendicity; he is young enough to have gone to sea, but I believe he has been ruptured, consequently they will not take him. I have seen him scratch his legs about the ancles to make them bleed, and he never goes out with shoes. That is the man who collects the greatest quantity of shoes and other habiliments, for he goes so naked as to make it almost too disgusting for any person to see him in that situation. Another man I have known upon the town these fifteen or twenty years; he was as nimble as any man can be. I have seen him fencing with the other people, and jumping about as you would see a man that was practiced in the pugilistic art. He goes generally without a hat, with a waistcoat with his arms thrust through, and his arms bare, with a canvas bag at his back; he begins generally by singing some sort of a song, for he has the voice of a decent ballad singer; he takes primroses or something in his hand, and generally goes limping or crawling in such a way, that any one would suppose he could not step one foot after the other. I have also seen him, if a Bow-street officer or beadle came in sight, walk off the ground as quick as most people.

There is a man who has had a very genteel education, and has been in the medical line, an Irishman; that man writes a most beautiful hand, and he gets his livelihood chiefly by writing petitions for those kind of people of various descriptions, whether truth or falsehood, I know not; but I have seen him write them, for which he gets sixpence or a shilling.

Do you know whether they change their beats? I have seen them come out from twenty to thirty of them, out of the bottom of a street they call Dyot Street (now George Street) they branch out five or six together, one one way, and one another; invariably, before they get to any great distance, they go into a liquor shop, and if one among them has saved (and it is rare but one of them saves some of the wreck of his fortune over night) he sets them off with a pint or half a pint of gin before they set out, then they trust to the day for raising the necessary contributions for their subsistence for the evening. They have all their divisions, the town is quartered into sections and divisions, and they go part one way and part another. In regard to the mendicity of people begging with children, I can give a little information upon that. There is one person of an acute nature, who is practiced in the art of begging, will collect three, four, or five children, from different parents of the lower class of people, and will give sixpence or even more to those parents per day for those children, to go begging with; they go in gangs, and make a very great noise, setting the children crying in order to extort charity from the people. I had an opportunity whilst I was in office to see many of these things. They will have the audacity sometimes to come to the board for relief, which we have four days in the week. There is a great deal of money given away in St. Giles. They will, if necessary, swear they are all their own children, and being generally of Irish parents, (wherever the tree falls it must lie) consequently they get some relief till we can make proper inquiry; but in a very short time they are found out, for we usually send to the place they come from; but the landlords and landladies are so cunning, they would willingly swear that the children belong to them. But we have people of their own class, to whom we are obliged to apply, and by giving them something, we detect the impositions we are liable to. A great many cases were before me last year as a parish officer; there was one where a woman had been in the habit of receiving five shillings per week, and at last a woman from her own country came forward and taxed her, that three of the children were not her own. We never saw them again, but they went into other parishes, such as Mary-la-bonne and St. Andrew's Holborn, and sought relief there; they know we cannot remove them. We have had other persons whose families were their own, and when they have a habit of begging and get a good deal of money, they will not go to work, and we have complaints from around Bedford and Bloomsbury Squares of those persons being nuisances.

When the parties have come to the board, we offered them the house to come into with the wife and children; 'No, I expect my husband home soon, and I will not accept of going in.' In those cases we get rid of them, but we invariably offer them the house, and when they will not accept it we stop the relief.

How do they usually spend their evenings? When they have done their work, which is towards evening, they get into a public-house, and call for gin, rum, beer, &c. whatever they like; and very frequently they have some very comfortable food; perhaps they will go to an eating-house, and get ham, beef, &c. I never saw a worthy person beg, they are ashamed of it. These people send out one of their crew to one of these eating-houses, and have ham, &c. brought, with knives and forks, and eat very heartily with the property they had procured, but I never saw any of them eat broken victuals or articles given them, they either sell it or throw it away. I have never seen one instance of their bringing it to the public-house of rendezvous.*

---

* The following instances of vagrancy are taken from the public papers:—

" A Professional Beggar—At Mary-la-bonne Office, John Driscold, an old mendicant, who has for a long time infested the streets of the metropolis, was charged with begging and annoying every person he met whose appearance was respectable, and even following fashionable women into shops. In his pockets was found a small sum of money, some ham sandwiches, and an invitation ticket, signed, ' Car Durre, Chairman,' in which the ' favour of his company is requested on Monday evening next, at seven o'clock, at the Robin Hood, in Church Street, St. Giles's', for the purpose of taking supper with

Have they not taken it to their families?' No, it is seldom they go to them till they have been to the public-house; in fact, they most of them have no lodging; there are houses where there are forty or fifty of them, like a goal; the porter stands at the door and takes the money; for three-pence they have each clean straw, or something like it; for those who pay fourpence, there is something more decent; and for six-pence, they have a bed. They are all locked up for the night lest they should take

---

others in his line of calling or profession. Mr. Rawlinson said, he supposed that an alderman in chains would grace the beggars festival board, but he would prevent the prisoner forming one of the party on Monday, and sent him to the house of correction for fourteen days."—*Bell's Life in London*, 12th *July*, 1829.

A set of mendicants now infest the metropolis, and rouse the feelings of the public by writing an exaggerated account of their distresses upon the pavements. It would appear that they succeed in obtaining more by these practices than by industrious habits, if the following statement be correct:—

"Francis Fisher was, on Monday, taken before the magistrates, when it was said that he belonged to a gang of forty Pavement Chalkers, who in the evening change their dress, and with their ladies, enjoy themselves over a good supper, brandy and water, cigars, &c. That in the winter time, when their situations appear most distressing, they often succeed in procuring from passengers as much as ten shillings per diem; and the average earnings of these fellows is calculated at ten shillings per day by an intelligent officer of police. This would make £20 a day for the forty, and no less than £7,300 a year. He was, however, known as an old offender, and the magistrate sent him to the tread-mill for fourteen days."—*Examiner*, 12th *July*, 1829.

the property, and in the morning there is a general muster below. I have asked country paupers, who have come for relief, how they have been entertained; they said, very badly when they have gone there. The men go and examine all the places to see that all is free from felony, and then they are let out into the street, just as you would open the door of a goal, forty or fifty of them come out together, and at night come in again. They have no settled habitation but the places to which they resort; and there are many of these houses in St. Giles's. They live constantly in a state of mendicity, it is their daily business, and on Sundays the same. They would not work; they are constant beggars, and they get more money by begging than many hard-working industrious men do at their work; in hard frosty mornings you may see some perhaps beg for work, but not at other times. Children beg at the instigation of their parents, and they are sent as early as possible; they can extort relief, and are distributed about. They perhaps take a broom, and if they do not bring home more or less, according to their size, they are beaten for it. A family of children is the greatest resource of such persons.

When beggars do not get enough for their subsistence, I believe they have a fund amongst them, for I never saw an application made for relief, their being brought into the house to be taken care of, or to be any way relieved. If they were Irish, they would be afraid to apply, for fear of removal to their own country, it being a constant practice to send them home as soon as possible, There is a Mrs. M'Carthy, who keeps a better sort of lodging-house than those already described, being more for strangers on their travel; I never heard of her harbouring such people as I have been describing.

Do you know what the largest sums are that have been gained by beggars? That I have been unable to ascertain, but I have heard them brag of getting six, seven, and eight shillings a day or more, according to their luck, as they call it, and if one gets more than the other, they divide it with the rest.

Are there many of the paupers lodging in this way parishioners of St. Giles? No, that is an evil in St. Giles's; there are so many low Irish, that of £30,000 a year collected by poor rates, £20,000 goes to the low Irish. I cannot speak of the number residing here who live by mendicity, they ebb and flow; in the summer they branch out when the town is thin, perhaps to watering places, or elsewhere; they are birds of passage. The Irish have a settlement anywhere, they tell us so to our face, and that they have as much right to a settlement in St. Giles as we have ourselves."

In treating of the laws and other matters relative to the poor, it will be necessary to revert to the early periods of our history, to trace their origin and their progress.

Early records inform us, that the poor, until the reign of Henry VIII. subsisted by the charity of private benevolence entirely. "For although," says Blackstone, "by the common law the poor were to be sustained by parsons, rectors of the church, and the parishioners; so that none of them die for default of sustenance, and though by the statutes 12th of Richard II. chap. 7, and 19th Henry VII. cap. 12, the poor are directed to abide in the cities or towns wherein they were born, or such wherein they had dwelt for three years (which seem to be the first rudiments of parish settlements) yet till the statute of 26th of Henry VIII. cap. 26, I find no compulsory method chalked out for this purpose; but the poor seem to have been left to such relief as the humanity of their neighbours would afford them."

"The monasteries were in particular their principal resource, and among the bad effects which attended the monastic institutions, it was not perhaps one of the least (though frequently esteemed quite otherwise) that they supported and fed a very numerous and a very idle poor, whose sustenance depended upon what was daily contributed in alms at the gates of the religious houses. But upon the total dissolution of these, the inconvenience of thus encouraging the poor in the habits of indolence and beggary, was quickly felt throughout the kingdom, and abundance of statutes were made in the reign of Henry VIII. for providing for the poor and impotent; which the preambles to some of them recite, had, of late years, strangely increased. These poor were principally of two sorts—sick and impotent, and therefore unable to work; idle and sturdy, and therefore able, but not willing to exercise any honest employment. To provide in some measure for both of these in and about the metropolis, his son Edward VI. founded three royal hospitals, Christ's and St. Thomas's, for the use and relief of the impotent through infancy or sickness; and Bridewell, for the punishment and employment of the vigorous and the idle. But these were far from being sufficient for the care of the poor throughout the kingdom at large, and therefore after many other fruitless experiments, by statute of 43rd of Elizabeth, chap. 2, overseers of the poor were appointed in every parish."

He then adds, " that these officers are to be substantial housekeepers, according to the spirit of the act, to be elected annually every Easter; that their duty was to raise competent sums for the necessary relief of the poor, impotent, old, blind, and others unable to work; and secondly, to provide work for such as are able and cannot get employment otherwise." *The latter duty,"* he justly remarks, " *is now most shamefully neglected*. The act in question empowers the overseers to make and levy rates upon their respective parishes, which has been subsequently enforced and explained by various statutes."

The two leading objects of the Act of 43rd of Elizabeth (as before observed,) was to relieve the impotent poor, and them only, and to find employment for such as were able to work; but Blackstone contends, " that accumulating the latter class into a workhouse for the purpose of employment, is not calculated to produce the most beneficial effects;" but he recommends them "to have employment at their own houses, to prevent the sober and industrious being placed on a level in their earnings with the idle and dissolute."

It has been contended by others, that the Act in question was, in principle, understood very indistinctly by the legislatures of that day; it not being in the power of the churchwardens and overseers, to whom the charge was confided, to make effectual provision for full and free employment of the poor, however authorised by law, and aided with the support of magisterial power. It does not seem to have occurred to the wise counsellors of Elizabeth, how inefficient the powers of these men would ultimately prove, in finding work for those who could not themselves find it. The shameful neglect Blackstone complains of must, therefore, be understood with some qualification, and not in the abstract.

Of all the legislative measures which have engrossed public attention, the poor laws have involved difficulties of the greatest magnitude, and this is strongly evinced by the multifarious form they have assumed. I have been at some pains to ascertain from the statute book, as a matter of curiosity, their number, and find they amount to no less than seventy-three public Acts, viz.—

	Cap.		Cap.
18 Elizabeth	3	6 George II.	31
43 ditto	2	12 ditto	29
7 James I.	4	13 ditto	18
13 & 14 Charles II.	12	16 ditto	13
1 James II.	17	17 ditto	3
3 Wm. & Mary	1	17 ditto	37
8 & 9 Wm. III.	30	17 ditto	38
9 & 10 ditto	11	9 George III.	37
2 & 3 Anne	6	13 ditto	82
4 ditto	19	20 ditto	36
8 ditto	9	22 ditto	83
12 ditto	18	23 ditto	23
6 George I.	3	30 ditto	49
9 ditto	7	33 ditto	35
3 George II.	29	33 ditto	54
5 ditto	19	35 ditto	101

	Cap.		Cap.
36 George III	10	53 George III	113
36 ditto	23	54 ditto	91
41 ditto	9	54 ditto	107
41 ditto	23	54 ditto	170
42 ditto	74	55 ditto	137
43 ditto	47	56 ditto	129
43 ditto	61	56 ditto	139
43 ditto	110	58 ditto	47
45 ditto	54	58 ditto	69
48 ditto	96	59 ditto	12
49 ditto	68	59 ditto	50
49 ditto	124	59 ditto	85
50 ditto	49	59 ditto	95
50 ditto	50	59 ditto	127
50 ditto	51	1 George IV.	36
50 ditto	52	1 & 2 ditto	32
51 ditto	79	1 & 2 ditto	56
51 ditto	80	5 ditto	71
52 ditto	73	6 ditto	57
52 ditto	160	5 ditto	83
53 ditto	21		

These Acts, when added to the numerous local ones, which have been thought necessary to regulate the poor, are proofs of the perplexed state of the subject and seem to confirm the conclusion of Blackstone, that "the further any subsequent plans for maintaining the poor have departed from that of the 43rd of Elizabeth, the more impracticable, and even pernicious, such visionary attempts have proved."*

---

* The laws of our ancestors were extremely harsh against what were termed "strong beggars, and persons whole and mighty in body." An Act of the first of Edward VI. visited

Every session of parliament develops some new scheme in reference to the poor laws, whereby the pressure of the rates might be alleviated, and a better and more practicable system prevail; but these have been generally abandoned as soon as proposed, and little has been effected beyond the conviction of the subject being bounded by insuperable difficulties.

Want of employment for the industrious is the medium of engendering poverty; when that fails, no resource remains but public benevolence, which ought never to be withheld from the deserving artizan, and needy applicant. Could this demoralizing evil find a remedy in new fields of industry, we should have little to combat but idleness, imposture, and low profligacy. The impotent, the helpless, and the aged, a prey to destitution, are the legitimate claimants on the parish funds; and although they are a numerous class, it would sink the aggregate to comparative insignificance, could we find a means of disposing of the others.

The present mode of assessment for the relief of the poor, is confessedly managed with great irregularity. It had its origin at an early period

---

the offence of vagrancy, with the barbarous penalties of slavery, mutilation, and death. These severities were somewhat softened before the expiration of that short reign it is true, but a milder system was not wholly adopted, till after the beginning of the last century.

of our history, when the poor were partly subsisted by the contributions of the church, and the alms of the charitable. They were allowed to beg within certain districts, and the people were exhorted to be liberal and bountiful towards them, that is, the impotent, decrepit, indigent, and needy poor. Statutes in the reign of Edward VI. were directed to the same object, till at length, by the fifth of Elizabeth, cap. 3, upon the exhortation of the priest, bishop, and justices, proving fruitless in exciting many to benevolence; they and the churchwardens were empowered to assess such persons according to their discretion, for a weekly contribution. This compulsory measure was afterwards matured and incorporated in the celebrated Act of the forty-third of that queen, and has, from that period, been the operative law on this important subject.

The parliamentary reports state, that no means can be resorted to, to ascertain the amount of the assessments for the poor during the seventeenth and eighteenth centuries. The preamble of 13th and 14th, chap. 2, states, " the necessity, number, and continual increase of the poor to be very great and exceeding burthensome;" and in the year 1699, King William thus expresses himself in a speech from the throne: " the increase of the poor is become a burthen to the kingdom; and their loose and idle life does in some measure contribute to that depravity of manners which is complained of, I fear with too much reason, whether the ground of this evil be from defects in the laws already made, or in the execution of them, deserves your consideration."

Complaints of a similar kind have been made at different intervals, and it seems very singular that no authentic accounts were ever called for under legislative sanction till 1776. The following are the successive results:—

1776. The whole sum raised for the poor was	£1,720,316
Expended on ditto	1,556,804
1783-4-5. Average sum raised was	2,167,749
Expended on ditto	2,004,238
1803. Sum raised for ditto	5,348,205
Expended on ditto	4,267,965
1815. Sum raised for ditto	7,068,999
Expended on ditto	5,072,028

The excess above the sum applied to the poor was expended, according to the returns, in church rates, county rates, highways, and militia.

In order to obtain a correct and enlarged view of the state of the poor in England, committees of inquiry were appointed by parliament, who reported in 1818, that their opinion was in favour of the principle of the law of 43rd of Elizabeth, the main object of which was, first, to provide funds for the support of the real poor; and secondly, to furnish means of employment for those destitute of work, yet able to labour. But they condemned the administration of the churchwardens and overseers, who under the eye of the local magistrate had become so little discriminative, as to have raised the number of paupers for the years 1813, 1814, and 1815, to 940,626, being above nine in the hundred of the whole population. For these no less a sum than £6,132,719 were annually expended in maintenance, besides other sums for connected rates and expenses, forming a total of upwards of eight millions sterling, entailing a burden yearly of more than sixteen shillings a head on the whole population of England and Wales.

Lord Malmsbury stated that, that annual sum had not decreased, in a motion he brought forward on the 16th of April, 1828, for a revision of the poor laws, and he complained of £1,360,000 of this amount, levied solely as poor rates, being annually applied to other indefinite purposes, calling loudly for inquiry and correction. We shall see as we advance, how far the censure is applicable to the district we are treating of.*

---

* From the parliamentary returns, it appears that the gross sums raised in England and Wales under the general head of poor rates during the year 1828, amounted to £7,715,000, of which £1,370,000 was for other purposes than the relief of the poor, and £6,300,000 expended for that object. There is an average diminution of expense, as compared with the year preceding, of about two per cent. throughout the country, which is, at least, a satisfactory circumstance, considering the increased price of corn.

Churchwardens and overseers are incorporated with the act of Elizabeth, and so often adverted to, as to require some definite notice with other appendant officers, before we enter more minutely into the appropriation of the funds, &c. of these parishes.

The institution of churchwardens is of ancient date, probably in the time of Henry VII. as the duties are set forth in a visitation made in 1498. They are therein enjoined "*to be well chosen every yere, aftyr the manner of the chirch,*" and to make "*every yere a ful and playne accompte of the receptys and paymentys by them during their wardeynshype; and also to render compte at the tyme of chisyne other wardeynes of the landys, tenementys, juellys, and money longyng to holy chirche.*" For this purpose, "*a ful and clyere inventory of the goodys and landys*" entrusted to their care, was to be furnished by them to their successors, on their quitting office; that it might be seen "*that the chirch goodys were wel kept, and that no landys nor tenementys were let to certayne persones, frendys, or kinnes-folke, for lesse somme than they be worth yerely,*" &c. They were also to see that "*good provyson was made for the prestyes and clarkys that ben retayned for the chyrche, that none of them attended in foul and unclenly surplisys,*" and generally they were to look to "*the due mayntenying of Gody'e servyce.*"

Blackstone defines the office and its duties as follows:—" Churchwardens are the guardians or keepers of the church, and representatives of the body of the parish. They are sometimes appointed by the minister and sometimes by the parish, sometimes by both together, as custom directs. They are taken in favour of the church, to be for some purposes a kind of corporation at the common law; that is, they are enabled by that name to have a property in goods and chattels, and to bring actions for them, for the use and profit of the parish, yet they may not waste the church goods, but may be removed by the parish, and then called to account by action at the common law: but there is no method of calling them to account, but by first removing them; for none can legally do it, but those who are put in their place. As to lands or other real property, as the church, church-yard, &c. they have no sort of interest therein; but if any damage is done thereto, the parson only, or vicar, shall have the action. Their office is also to repair the church, and to make rates and levies for that purpose; but these are recoverable only in the ecclesiastical court. They are also joined with the overseers in the care and maintenance of the poor.* They are to levy a shilling forfeiture

---

* Churchwardens are appointed overseers by 43rd of Elizabeth, chap: 2. ' They were anciently the sole overseers of the poor.—*Nolan on Poor Laws.*

on all such as do not repair to church on Sundays and holidays, (Statute 1 Elizabeth, chap. 2.) and are empowered to keep all persons orderly whilst there; to which end it has been held, that a churchwarden may justify the pulling off a man's hat, without being guilty of either an assault or trespass. There are also a multitude of other petty parochial powers committed to their charge by divers acts of parliament."

The churchwardens since the division of these parishes are four, two for each. They are elected on Easter Tuesday, at the separate vestry rooms, by the suffrages of the inhabitant householders who pay poor rates.* This elective privilege, as regards St. Giles's parish, was decided in the Court of Exchequer, in 1670.†

---

* Mr. Marriot, (Master of the Workhouse) in 1729, left a sum of money to buy *gowns* for the use of the churchwardens, if they would wear them, which we do not find, however, that they ever did.

† The following account is derived from the minutes of vestry, detailing the particulars of the transaction:—

"November 15th. 1669. At a vestry held according to *ancient custom* of the said parish, John Hooker was elected and chosen churchwarden, in the stead of John Andrews, late gone out of the parish, by the general consent of the said vestry and all other of the said inhabitants then present: signed by about thirty-three persons."

After this election appeared the following notice, signed by two magistrates and the rector:—

"*Middlesex to wit.* We, whose names are under-written, do declare that the meeting of the vestry at St. Giles in the

Sidesmen or synodsmen, as they were anciently called, were, according to Burn, divers creditable persons summoned by the bishops out of every parish to give evidence at their episcopal synods of any existing disorders of the clergy and people.

In the days of superstition they had the

Fields, in the county of Middlesex, was an unlawful meeting, and to the disturbance of the quiet of the inhabitants of the said parish, and contrary to the intent of the greater number of the members of the said vestry, and contempt of his majesty's government, they having been commanded in his majesty's name by two of his majesty's justices of the peace, for the said county to depart in peace, and not to act in a tumultuous way against the known laws of the land.

THOMAS LAKE.
J. MOYLE.
ROBERT BOREMAN, *Rector*.

" February 8th, 1670. The vestrymen ordered the verdict for the election of churchwardens to be entered in their book as follows:—

" The reason why the following exemption was transmitted into this book for the choice of churchwardens was as followeth:—that Dr. Robert Boreman, Rector of the said parish, pretending the right, according to the canons of the church, to the election of one of the churchwardens to be in him without the consent of the parishioners, and they not allowing thereof, (it being contrary to the right and custom of this parish time out of mind), did elect and choose both the churchwardens; wherefore Mr. Thomas Furth being appointed by the said Doctor as churchwarden, in opposition to Mr. John Andrews, who was chosen by the parishioners 13th of April, 1669, did cite him, the said John Andrews, into the Spiritual Court, from which he had his appeal to his majesty's Court of Exchequer, where he obtained a verdict, which is here transcribed, to the end that the parishioners for the future may know their right in election, and it is necessary the same be read every Easter Tuesday in every year to the inhabitants in vestry before their election."

power of searching out heretics and other irregular persons, whom they presented officially to the bishops of their several districts. In more modern times, sidesmen are the mere attendants of the churchwardens, " to carry up the wine at the communion, that the bearers and other mean persons be not employed in so high an office." They were also, with the churchwardens (the parson consenting thereto) " to collect the dutyes for burialls, and to pay the parson and clarke their dues out of the same; also to go along with the clarke, each in his turne, to assist him in taking the names, for the purpose of collecting the Easter offerings."

They consist of two to each parish, and are chosen by the past wardens, with the approbation of the vestry (by a regulation, 1617.) They are considered candidates for the office of churchwarden, and have been usually so appointed.

Overseers of the poor appear to derive their name and office from the 43rd of Elizabeth, the particulars whereof, duties, &c. have been already stated in page 214; they were formerly called " collectors of the poor," in this parish, till after 1620, at which time four were elected and appointed by minute of vestry, to be renewed annually. In 1631 they are termed " overseers."

A regulation was made in 1638 by the vestry, restricting the overseers from receiving any sums of the inhabitants of the parish of St. Giles, other than what they were rated at in a book confirmed by his majesty's justices of the peace, and also they were to pay the pensions of the poor according to such book. Other monies they were to pay over to the churchwardens, according to a former order; and if they refused to perform such order, " the disposing of such monies should not be allowed upon their accounts." This shows how at an early period the power and authority of these officers was abridged, and in 1649 £3 : 12 : 6. was disallowed them by the vestry. " so much having been paid by them without the knowledge of the churchwardens."

This regulation, and the consequent arbitrary enforcement of it, was a palpable infringement of the rights of the overseers, whose office and duties were by law distinct from such interference. It would be curious to know how resolutely it was opposed at that remote period, which it probably was, however, unsuccessfully.*

---

* In 1673, *six* overseers were appointed; in 1678, *seven* ditto; in 1680, *eight* were appointed; and in 1682 they were increased to *nine*; they were still further increased to *eleven* in 1690; reduced to *nine* again in 1691; and in 1693 were once more raised to *eleven*; their number at present is, for the two parishes, *twelve*, by act of 14th George III.

The office and duties of Constable, Headborough, Beadles, Watchmen, &c. is sufficiently understood without entering into minute particulars thereon.

SEXTON. The first mention of the sexton, by name, in the existing parish records, is during the plague year, 1668; but it is no doubt an office the most ancient.

A particular account was delivered by a vestry order, 1683, of the profits attached to this office, and they were estimated at £135 : 17 : 6. per annum. Several payments were in consequence directed to be paid out of this money, to the amount of £55 annually, and four additional pew openers ordered to be kept from it. *(See the sexton's curious tenure, page 122.)*

PARISH and VESTRY CLERKS. Anno 1623, Charles Robinson, parish clerk, was this year chosen clerk of the works in building the new church. His duties are specified in the vestry minute, 1638, and it seems his office combined with it that of vestry clerk,* and he was " directed not to collect his wages in vestry, but to go to the sev'ral houses of the p'isshioners to receive the same, unless they please to pay

---

* The first mention of vestry clerk on minutes is dated 1630, when an order was given to summon the vestrymen who were to be fined for non-attendance.—*Parton.*

him." His name occurs in the parish Doomsday Book, *(see page* 98.)

1640. The sum of 3s. 6d. is entered as paid to " Mr. Smyth the scrivenor, for writing some parish business," which makes it probable that payments were only made, at first, for business done.

1657. Mr. Robinson, the parish clerk, is this year mentioned as being paid for copying of bonds and indentures. Other entries also for writing parish business occur afterwards.

1666. Mr. Stanislaus Bowes is now first mentioned as writing parish business, and he afterwards signs himself, " vestry clerk." *This is the first appointment to that office.*

Robert Mayes succeeded Bowes, and died before 1686.

John Reynaulds was appointed vestry clerk January 1686, in the room of Robert Mayes, deceased. He compiled an alphabetical list of vestry orders, still remaining, for which he was paid in 1690.

John Arden was chosen in the room of John Reynaulds, deceased, September 24th, 1710. In 1721, he accepted the sextonship on the decease of George Hoskins, for which he vacated the more respectable (but probably then less lucrative) office before mentioned. He appears to have continued in the latter office till his death, which happened in 1726.[*]

Thomas Powell succeeded, on the resignation of John Arden. He is stated to have been chosen " *during pleasure only ;*" but, notwithstanding, held it until his death, 1724.

Daniel Bolton was chosen on the decease of Thomas Powell, with a condition to have " £80 per annum as usual." This

---

[*] The vestry minutes collected by him, and called Arden's Extracts, were produced as evidence on the trial, 22nd July, 1829, Rogers *versus* Tyler.

is the first instance of the vestry clerk's salary being mentioned. Mr. Bolton continued in office until anno 1757, when he died. He left his family in some degree in want, and the parish generously allowed his daughters a decent pension during several years.

Humphrey Elmes, who had been clerk to Mr. Bowes, was chosen " in the stead of his late master," at an increased salary, (for which he agreed to include certain extra parish business.)

He was succeeded by Mr. Herbert Robertson.

Mr. William Robertson was, in 1790, appointed vestry clerk, in conjunction with the former-mentioned Robertson, 27th August, 1800: he is stated to be vestry clerk, and heir at law of the late Mr. Herbert Robertson. He died in 1814, and

Mr. John Parton, who had been, in effect, vestry clerk, many years previously, was appointed his successor. He had at one time no less than fourteen appointments. He died in September, 1822, and was succeeded by

Mr. Earle, who continued in office till October 4th, 1826, when he was suspended for converting the parish funds to his own use, and finally dismissed.

Mr. D. W. Robinson was appointed, (October, 1826), at a salary for himself and clerks of £1050 a year, and lost his appointment by the decision of the Court of King's Bench, 22nd July, 1829.*

The WORKHOUSE. The parish of St. Giles, in common with many others, seems first to have used a general Workhouse, which is mentioned in the following entry:—

---

* Since this event three clerks, at a weekly salary, attend at the workhouse, and are found amply sufficient to transact the whole of the parochial business. This will be productive of a considerable saving to the joint parishes, inasmuch as their collective salaries amount to only £6 : 17 : 0. per week, being little more than £300 a year.

" 1662. Paid and expended agoing to Hixes Hall, (Hicks's Hall,) for to petition for the Corporation and Workhouse" £0 8 0

The " Corporation," here mentioned, was a union of several parishes to erect a Workhouse for their poor; in which business St. Giles's took the lead, by first collecting money, petitioning, &c. as appears by several other entries.

" 1663. Paid in collecting the money for the Workhouse bookes and going to the Workhouse, by order of warrant" £2 10 0

The funds necessary for establishing a suitable building were tardily raised, from some obstacles we are unacquainted with now, and six years elapsed, when the vestry minutes inform us of an indictment being laid against the collector.

" 1669. Paid and expended in defending the accomptant against an indictment, for not collecting the money assessed for the Workhouse, he not being able to do the same; and the parish having formerly paid the sum of £996, or thereabouts, and little or no benefit accrued" £30 16 9

The same year, also, a charge of £6 12s. is booked for " defending the overseers" in the same business, and the matter not appearing to terminate very satisfactorily to the parish in a court of law, a petition was presented to parliament on the subject. These disputes afterwards subsided, and the Workhouse in question, (if the different entries refer to the same building) became peopled, as per following minute :—

" January. Ordered, that a committee be appointed to treat with the adjacent parishes, who were comprehended in the late Act of Parliament, concerning the Workhouse, in order to their contributing towards the fees and expenses for, paid p'curing the said act."

" 1649. Whereas the p'isshioners of the p'ish of St. Giles-in-the-Fields have been at the very great charge of p'curing or obtaining an Act of Parliament to passe, concerning a certain *Workhouse,* near *Clerkenwell Green,* built at the cost and charges of the in'itants of the parish of Stepney, al's Stebenheth, have agreed to pay to the ch'w'd'ns of this p'ish the sume of £35 for and towards the same. Ordered, that such sum of £35 be accepted, &c."

Having procured an asylum for their aged and impotent poor (for the above appears to have been provided for that purpose, rather than for labour) it remained to purchase or erect a second place, which might be properly called a Workhouse.

" 1674. Ordered, that the Churchwardene should treat with the landlord of a certaine tenement, in order to the taking of the same for to set the poore ou *worke.*"

The churchwardens the following week reported, that in pursuance of the last vestry order, they have taken " a certain tenement in *Browne's Gardens,* to sett the poore on work;" which was approved of by vestry. It was afterwards fitted-up and prepared for the reception of paupers by Robert Freshfield, carpenter, and in 1675, it was " Ordered, that the churchwardens do buy formes and tables for the Workhouse, necessary for the employment and use of the said house, for setting the poor on worke ;" and it was further ordered, " that the poor on the establishment, like the pensioners, do wear *brass badges.*"

In 1680, probably in consequence of the building of the Seven Dials, it was found necessary (the Workhouse being on that account to be pulled down) to seek out for another situation, and an order of vestry directed, " that certaine houses neare Whetstone should be enquired for to accommodate the poor with habitations."

1717. There seems from the vestry minutes to have been a design about this time to erect a new Workhouse ; a treaty was on foot with a Mr. Innocent, which eventually proved abortive, and the churchwardens had directions to enquire for some convenient houses for the "sicke poore ;" and a committee met at Joe's Coffee-house, Bloomsbury Market, " to view the houses in Coal Yard, for an hospitall."

These not answering the purpose, another committee was appointed to make inquiry about a piece of ground in *Tottenham Court Road,* for the same purpose, but this also ended in nothing. When, in 1721, the subject of a parochial Workhouse was again revived, and a treaty entered into with Dr. Baker, the rector, for the purchase of Dudley Court, (where the parsonage-house stood, and which had probably been pulled down and abandoned) for a Workhouse. This negotiation did not succeed; and, finally, a piece of ground, called *Vinegar Yard*, was purchased for the sum of £2,252 10s. for a burial ground, hospital, and workhouse.

A case was circulated soliciting pecuniary assistance, stating that the poor to be relieved amounted to upwards of 840 persons, at an expense of above £4000 a year, and that a piece of ground was now purchased, near Bowle Yard, for the purposes above mentioned, and that a proposal had been submitted to vestry by a Mr. Matthew Marriot, for employing the able, and maintaining the impotent poor, similar to an approved plan practised at Tring, Berkhamstead, Luton, &c.

But to execute the plans in question, a large house, or houses, must be built by the parish, sufficient for the reception of all such persons as were relieved; where they were to be one family, supplied with meat, drink, and lodging, and employed in such work as they were capable of, to be clothed when wanting, and lodged in a cleanly manner, and the produce of their labour sold for the benefit of the parish, &c. &c.

This appeal was successful, and the vestry signified to Mr. Marriot that his proposal was accepted; the deeds of purchase were prepared; Mr. Hucks (the brewer,) was appointed treasurer for the subscriptions, and a committee agreed to sit weekly during the progress of the building.

In 1724, March 30th, the then committee reported, that in pursuance of the order of vestry, they had caused the brewhouse to be pulled down for enlarging the burial ground, and they recommended the same to be fenced with a proper brick wall, &c.

That for an hospital they were of opinion, that "a long room, one pair of staires, in the old building, at the east end, would make a convenient one for the women, &c. and for the Workhouse, they stated, that two rooms under the hospital would be proper for this use, with certain alterations, &c. &c."

These buildings and alterations were finished before March, 1725, and on the 2nd of that month an additional rate was ordered to be made for the relief of the poor, " to make good the monies laid out in building and furnishing the Workhouse, and buying stock to set the poor to work." The following sums are in the churchwardens' accounts :—

1726. Purchase Money, as before stated.. ..£2,252 10 0
Paid towards building the Workhouse,
this year 1,461 16 4
Towards furnishing the same with all necessaries..................................... 423 5 0

Original cost.........£4,133 11 4*

1727. The present Infirmary was erected upon the site of Kempe's house and yard, the accommodations proving insufficient. The expense was £531 7s. 10d. and the part of the house fitted-up before for Infirmaries, was converted into wards for the convalescent poor and those able to work.

1728. The further sum was laid out this year of £680 7s. on account of repairs and additional buildings. Matthew Marriot was the first master, and was appointed April 23rd, 1724.

This building has necessarily undergone many alterations since its erection, and a considerable

---

* When it was in contemplation to build the Workhouse, the following was the state of the poor:—

162 all above 70 years of age...£750	
126 Parents over burthened with children	600
183 Children, parents dead or run away	800
70 sick at parish nurses	600
300 Men lame, blind, mad, &c. various ages...........1,200	
Incident charges, as surgeons, apothecaries, bills, clothes for hospitals, &c. at least...................................	250
	£4,200

addition was made to it in 1808, by building a school-house for the infant poor. As a whole, it is not very eligible as an asylum for the paupers; added to which, it is in a gradual state of decay, and must be rebuilt at no distant period. It contains on an average not less than from 800 to 900 inmates, which is however but a small proportion to the number constantly relieved, at an expense of nearly £40,000 ! !

HESTON ESTABLISHMENT. By an act of 7th George III. cap. 39, entitled " An Act for the better regulation of Parish Poor Children of the several Parishes therein mentioned, within the Bills of Mortality," provision was made to keep those under six years old at nurse in the country, within the distance of not less than three miles, and those under two years to be not less than five miles distant, &c.* It

---

* A clause in this Act provides, " that five noblemen, or gentlemen, inhabitants of each parish, shall, within fourteen days after the 1st day of July, 1767, be appointed and chosen under the denomination of *Guardians of the Parish Poor Children;* two or more to be chosen out of the select vestry, or out of the governors, directors, or managers of the poor of each parish ; and, where there is no select vestry, the said five guardians are to be elected by the inhabitants of each parish on some day in Easter week, by the said inhabitants of each parish, having a right to assemble in vestry ; and if there be no nobleman or gentleman, or not a sufficient number who will accept the office, then the same shall be chosen out of the principal and most respectable inhabitants. The first guardians to continue in office till the year 1770, and all future guardians to remain in office three years. Churchwardens and

has been the practice ever since this act has continued in force, to send the children of these parishes to cottagers and others at Enfield,

---

Overseers are declared to be ineligible. The said guardians to have singly or collectively free access to visit the said children, and if they discover the health of any of them in danger from neglect, to report the same to the vestry, or parish officers, and should they not take measures to remedy the evil, the said guardians are empowered to obtain redress of a magistrate."

There are other useful and humane clauses, most essential to the well being of this helpless class of paupers, but strange to say, the act has been entirely disregarded as far as it applies to the appointment of guardians for these united parishes until 1828, *(see list of vestrymen.)*

On this shameful omission, Mr. Thiselton, who served the office of overseer of Bloomsbury in 1810, makes the following judicious remarks in a sensible and useful pamphlet, published in 1812:—

" Had this act been attended to, it would not have fallen to the lot of three of the late overseers to discover seven young children locked up in a room at the top of the school, as naked as they were born, with the exception of an old bed-gown, confined with the itch, four of whom had been confined there upwards of six weeks, while three had not been there so many days. Upon the above being discovered, the school-mistress was sent for into the room, who pretended not to know any thing of the subject; upon which the apothecary was consulted, who stated, he did not consider children afflicted with the itch, required his attendance; and in short, these poor infants were locked up in the above place, without the knowledge or consent of any one officer of the establishment, or indeed of any one, except the nurse in whose ward such children were placed."

Suffice it to say, that such a gross dereliction of public duty was discovered by Messrs. Savage, Davis, and Thiselton; and the school-mistress, ashamed to meet the charge, resigned her situation.

Finchley, Hendon, &c. where they have been distributed in various numbers, at a weekly sum per head.

The many evils of this system, such as the privation of necessary food, and inattention to the morals and health of these helpless infants, had excited the humane attention of the officers, who, in the discharge of their duty, were in the habit of visiting them; and it had long been in contemplation to have an establishment where they could be taken care of collectively under one roof.

In 1827 such an asylum was obtained at Heston, where the children were safely lodged; but the measure encountered much opposition whilst the arrangements for so laudable a purpose were pending: however, I believe all parties are now satisfied of the utility of the change thus effected. In point of economy, much advantage will accrue to the parishes eventually by this new system, but much persevering vigilance is necessary to counteract mis-management and consequent evils; and I here quote the report of our worthy churchwarden, Mr. Mills, to illustrate this fact:—

" 20th July, 1829. Mr. Rogers and myself went this day to visit the Heston establishment, which we found a princely one." (Formerly a mansion occupied by — Frazer, Esq. a county magistrate.) " There are 259 children here, and we found no less than thirty-nine of them afflicted with the itch to a miserable degree. Several had scrophulous disorders; others the opthalmia, some of whom were blind. All the servants were healthy; and the food used was of the best quality, the best bread, meat, cheese, &c. and the best Carolina rice. The beds were remarkably clean, as were the rooms, and all was creditable except the prevalence of the diseases alluded to."

Subsequently, they enjoined more attention on the medical attendants, by which means health has been almost entirely restored to these distressed children, who, but for this humane interference, would have fallen a prey to neglect.

The annual expense of this etablishment, (to which we shall again revert) is stated at about £3000.

Chapter VII.

Public Charities—Almshouses—Shelton's and other Schools—Parish Estates—Mal-appropriations—Strictures on Vestry Refutation, &c. &c.

THE public institutions of charity and benevolence of the united parishes, come next under our notice, and in priority the almshouses claim our first attention.

ALMSHOUSES. The origin of these asylums for poor widows is derived from a grant of land by the Earl of Southampton in 1656, on which they were built This was in Broad Street, nearly at the north end of Monmouth and King Streets, where they stood until 1782, at which period they were pulled down to widen those avenues.

Strype informs us of there being in his time, " an almshouse in St. Giles, not far from the church, in the middle of the street, which hath this inscription, ' Saint Giles's Almshouse, anno domino 1656.' This ground was granted

R

to this parish by the right honourable the Earl of Southampton, for the term of 500 years, for the only sole use of Almshouses for aged widows, and for no other use, whereupon there was built these five Almshouses, and enclosed within the bounds of the same ground, which fabrick was erected at the costs of the said parrish the year above written."

Maitland, speaking of them, 1739, says, " they seemed to have yielded but a small income, for each of the inmates have only an allowance of £2 : 8 : 0, and twelve bushells of coals yearly; and at Christmas and Whitsuntide, out of Lady Dudley's gift, twenty shillings each." The whole expense in building them, &c. was £296 : 12 : 10.

In 1782, when it was in contemplation to remove these Almshouses, some difficulties arose as to the tenure of them, which rendered it necessary to have the opinion of counsel. The case was submitted to the Attorney General of that day, who was Sir Lloyd Kenyon. It stated, that they were situate in the middle of the street, rendering the adjoining passages narrow and inconvenient, and that they were in a ruinous state of decay. That " the vestry, *(which is select,)* was desirous to take them down, and lay the ground into the highway for public accommodation." It then stated, that the Duke of Bedford, as heir to the late Lord Southampton, was lord of the manor, and that his trustees, he being a minor, would give their consent to the ground becoming part of the highway. That the vestry intended building the Almshouses in a suitable situation, and to continue the payments of the women, but they had doubts whether they could carry their intentions into effect without endangering the forfeiture of the bequests, unless by an act of parliament.

The Attorney General answered, " I am of opinion that the vestry may carry their intention into execution without risking a reversion of the charitable donations. The gifts do not contain any condition as to the place where the Almshouses shall be situated; and therefore I have no doubt but the income of the several funds will be properly applicable to the almshouse people, although the Almshouses shall be removed to another situation."

The vestry clerk, Robertson, had directions forthwith to purchase a piece of ground, and a most singular situation was selected on the north side of Lewknor's Lane, for which £500 was given. Here the new Almshouses were erected on a spot both close and unhealthy, surrounded with buildings of the lowest description; and it is a fact, that very few of the parishioners have any knowledge of the existence of this charity, such is the obscurity in which it is involved.

The endowments to these Almshouses have increased, but they have been grossly mismanaged, as may be seen in a printed report (of 1827) circulated cautiously by the Almshouse and Audit Committee, appointed by the select vestry from their own body. We shall make a few extracts in a compressed form from that document, as illustrative of this fact, after stating the funds and their application to this charity, as set forth in the fourteenth report of the commissioners of charities.

"ESTATES:—	Per Ann.		
	£.	s.	d.
Premises at Rainham, Essex, Danver's gift..........	20	0	0
Houses in Prince's-street, Drury-lane, Holford's gift	60	0	0
Bailey's rent-charge, Turnstile, Holborn	3	10	0
Houses in Elbow-lane, Duchess of Dudley's gift ...	69	0	0
Houses in Charles Street, Drury Lane	18	0	0

FUNDED PROPERTY:—	Stock.		
Gift of Messrs. William and Henry Shakespeare, stock in 3 per Cent. Consols	1,500	0	0
Gift of Martha Gregory	666	13	4
Surplus of a soup subscription entered into in 1800-1801..........	915	0	11
Subscription of the inhabitants in aid of the fund in 1815.........	2,850	0	0
Produce of unclaimed dividends on part of a soup fund in 1810	21	11	5
Produce of William Wodden's gift, being an investment in lieu of a rent-charge on the Hampshire Hog	100	0	0
	£6,053	5	8
Annual dividends or interest thereof	181	11	10
Total Annual Income......	£351	19	10

APPLICATION.

	£.	s.	d.
Each of the twenty almswomen receive, by quarterly payments, an annual stipend of £16. of which £7. 2s. is considered as paid from the rents, and £8. 18. from the dividends, making a total per annum of	320		
There is also paid, by quarterly payments, to twenty female out-pensioners, called ticket-women, being old decayed housekeepers of one or other of the united parishes, appointed as vacancies occur in the list by the churchwardens...	29	4	0
	£349	4	0

The distributions of these sums, as settled by the vestry, are eight times a year, as may be seen in extracts from the churchwardens' accounts, 1824 and 1825, they being intrusted with the payments.

ACCOUNTS AS TO PAST TIMES.

The preceding statement of the income and its application is derived from the Fourteenth Report of the Commissioners of Charities, but it is not correct; the rent of part of the premises in Prince's-street is omitted, which, at the date of the Commissioners Report, was let for £20. The vaults under the almshouses should likewise be borne in remembrance, as expected to yield rent at the expiration of the first seven years of the present letting; and the legacy of £100. by the late Thomas Leverton, Esq. is an addition to the funded property. At the close of this Report is a correct statement of the improved revenue in future applicable to this charity.

In the minutes of vestry several entries exist showing the state of the funds at the time of such entries. *But previous* to 1815 no book of accounts or other documents can be found detailing the receipts and disbursements of this fund. In that year, in consequence of a representation of the committee in 1814, of the inadequate state of the income, an appeal was made to the benevolence of the inhabitants, and a considerable sum was raised by subscription. After investing to the amount of £562, £20. was carried forward to the cash account; several other subscriptions, afterwards made, are entered on the receipt side, and a few disbursements on the pay side; *the account then abruptly terminates, without any subsequent entries of receipts or dividends, or disbursements of them, from 1815 to the present time.*

From the preceding statement it appears, that the fund appropriated to the support of the almswomen has not been adequate to the expenditure charged on it; and it must not be forgotten, that it was to render this adequacy complete, that the benevolence of the parishioners was called upon in 1815, and which shewed itself by the liberal contributions that were then made, as they hoped to relieve the wants and add to the comforts of the pennyless and friendless widow, *(preventing the necessity of recourse to the poor's rates,)* and thereby render this fund effective of the pious intentions of those who by will had bequeathed estates or money for that charitable purpose, but which, from change of circumstances, had become inefficient for their designs.

How the rents have been collected there is no means of ascertaining; and no accounts are in existence showing any application of the receipts; and little information can be obtained from any oral source to supply this want. The churchwardens have been the channels or almoners through which and by whom the payments have been made to the almswomen, *but they have had no knowledge from what source the money ought to have been derived, and were scarcely aware that it came out of the poor's rate; and, if they had any idea of the kind, it was under the belief of its being repaid from the proper funds. Such, indeed, has been* *the successful endeavour to keep all in ignorance,* that few have had any knowledge of the circumstances detailed in this Report, till their minds were recently directed to enquiry and consideration.*

The sums for a great part of the expenditure have for the last two years and upwards been *surreptitiously drawn out of the poor's rates. The first trace that can be found of this practice is in 1822, when the present system of auditing the parochial accounts commenced.* By these it is ascertained, that from 1822 to 1826 the sum of £700. 2s. has been paid into the hands of the churchwardens for the time being, for distribution to the almswomen.

As the funds have been sufficient for the expenditure, rents and money to this amount must have been misapplied to some other purpose, and this sum irregularly drawn out of the poor's rate to supply the deficiency.

The existence of such an abuse for so long a time, and after the liberality of the parishioners had been called upon to aid an impoverished fund, is lamentable in the extreme. *Although the officer charged with collecting the rents is culpable for his abuse of the confidence reposed in him, yet the continuance of the misapplication must be ascribed to the want of a systematic mode of account, and a vigilant superintendence of the disposition of the funds according to the intention of the donors and directions of the Vestry."*

There cannot be a greater proof of the inutility of a self-elected vestry than is here exhibited. Can we imagine that any body of

---

* It is stated by Mr. Stable, that he knew the late Mr. Parton was in the habit of advancing the requisite sum from his own money; and a book, showing these advances, used to be produced by him at the meetings of the committee. An entry occurs in the account of Shelton's School of a payment by the clerk into that fund of £5. 6s. being a poundage received for collecting the rents given to the almswomen; and a similar entry occurs in the Vestry Minutes of 20th December, 1814.

men under the controul of the parishioners would have been so totally reckless of these charitable donations? The answer is obvious, and we see at once that the candid exposition here adduced would never have been resorted to, had not the Commissioners' Report made its appearance, which rendered longer concealment impossible. But for this the funds appropriated to the poor would have been put in requisition as usual, to cloke the carelessness of these pretended guardians of the parish.

The report goes on to prescribe a future plan to obviate the like recurrence. The accounts henceforth are to be kept with accuracy, and to be audited quarterly; the vestry clerk is not to have the receipt of the rents, nor to be charged with the custody of any money; the funds applicable to this charity are to be lodged in the hands of a banker, and only to be drawn out by prescribed signatures; and, finally, the sum of £200 is proposed to be advanced from the poor's rate to commence opening an account, to be replaced when the Almshouse revenue will admit of it.

Something in the nature of an apology is next offered for abstracting money from the poor's rate, for defraying the repairs and the expense of coals for this charity, on the ground of its revenue being barely sufficient for its other purposes.* The committee are, however, quite in the dark as to the length of time this custom has existed: all this and much more has been left, no doubt, by their predecessors to chance and accident, for want of the salutary controul of the parishioners.

Mr. Rogers, in a placard issued in 1828, makes the following remarks:—" The rents arising from property left for the support of Almshouses, have, there is good reason to believe, been most shamefully misappropriated, while the money to pay the almswomen has been illegally and surreptitiously drawn out of the poor rates. From the year 1822 to 1826, £700. 2s. 0. is admitted to have been taken in this way. Only one book concerning this fund was produced by the vestry agent; that book purported to be the minute-book of the Almshouse Committee from the year 1804 to 1815, and contained apparently regular entries of the proceedings of that committee during the whole of that period. Some circumstances in the nature of the entries caused an examination of the water-mark of the paper, when it was found that the paper itself was not manu-

---

* 15th, August, 1829. Application was made to the churchwardens and overseers to supply the almswomen with *coals* as usual, but they firmly refused compliance, determined that the poor's fund should be applied solely to its legitimate object.

factured until the year 1814. It may be in the recollection of many, that in the years 1814-15, an appeal was made to the inhabitants at large for subscriptions for the support of the almswomen, when nearly £2000 was very liberally subscribed for that purpose. It would have been well if the inhabitants had then ascertained what it was that made the subscription necessary, and what accounts there were of the ancient funds."*

---

* With a view to fair dealing, I will here copy some remarks made on this statement in a pamphlet entitled, "A refutation of charges against the Select Vestry." page 29. "The partial misappropriation of the rents of the property forming part of the Almshouse Fund has not been concealed by the vestry from the parishioners. The losses formed part of the former vestry clerk's defalcations; but there is no ground for the insinuation of any existing abuse in the *ancient funds* that rendered necessary the subscription in 1814-15, a necessity arising from their total inadequacy. And what is to be inferred from the discovery that the water-mark of the paper is 1814? The book does not pretend to have been written at a more ancient date; it is labelled 1814, being a general transcript of accounts of the funds made out in that year, not a document purporting to be of ancient date, written on paper of subsequent fabrication, which is meant by the insinuation.

The present improved state of the funds merits approbation, and the prospect thereby afforded of, in time, benefiting the condition of the objects of this benevolent institution, invites the support of the inhabitants, and shews that the vestry is not so negligent of their duty, so unworthy of good opinion, so swayed by sordid self-interest, or reckless of character, as their accusers would exhibit them.——It must be here observed, that it is from such documents, and those relating every circumstance with undisguised plainness, that the opponents of the vestry have culled the particulars of their accusations against the vestry, not from obscure and imperfect records.

SHELTON's SCHOOL.—In the year 1661, being the year after the restoration, Mr. William Shelton purchased a piece of ground, with certain erections thereon, for the sum of £458 10s. situate on the south side of Parker's Lane, which runs east and west, between Drury Lane, and Little Queen Street, containing in front next the said lane and its rear one hundred and five feet, and in depth fifty feet or thereabout.

This purchase, described as having been lately in the occupation of the Dutch Ambassador, he devised 4th of July, 1672, with all the houses,

---

They have discovered nothing, all has been displayed before the eye of the inquirer. What has been good the vestry has confirmed; where evils have existed, remedies have been applied to their correction. It is said that this shews that unsoundness of constitution prevailed, it is replied, that it equally shows a self-existing power to work its restoration to health, and the vestry neither delayed the reformation, nor required the stimulus of popular outcry."

This laboured account of the suspicious transaction of the water-mark, is, to say the least of it, very unsatisfactory. By their own shewing, no book of accounts or document detailing the receipts and disbursements could be found previous to 1815, (see page 246), and yet a book is here manufactured for the occasion with minutes from 1804! Was not the conclusion of Mr. Rogers very natural; and has not the vestry writer made the matter worse in thus attempting to repel the charge? If the constitution of the vestry is worth any thing it would not have carelessly suffered such acknowledged irregularities and especially the loss of £700 2s. (more than two years allowance to these poor women) which was surreptitiously abstracted from its funds.

These gentlemen, however, on the principle of the trite proverb always assume credit to themselves for "shutting the stable door when the steed is stolen."

messuages, lands, and tenements, to certain trustees and their successors, who, from the rents and profits thereof, were directed to lay out on Michaelmas-day, yearly, the following sums:—

	£.	s.	d.
"For twenty gowns for twenty poor old men and women of St. Giles	15	0	0
The like for ten gowns for St. Martin's	7	10	0
The like for five gowns for Covent Garden	3	15	0
To provide an able and fit schoolmaster to teach and instruct in learning, in the school and room he had appropriated for that purpose in Parker's-lane, fifty children of the poorest sort, thirty-five whereof to be of St. Giles, ten of St. Martin's, and five of Covent Garden, and to pay him per annum	20	0	0
To provide him a gown yearly of the value of	1	0	0
To provide a coat yearly for each of the scholars, at 6s. each	15	0	0
(The aforesaid gowns and coats all to be of a green colour)			
To lay in two chaldron of coals in the summer yearly, for a fire for the scholars in the winter	0	0	0
To pay his heir at law per annum	10	0	0
And the remainder or surplusage to be applied in binding out some of the scholars apprentice	0	0	0
The annual sum expressly appropriated (exclusive of two chaldron of coals) being"	£72	5	0

In the will, which was regularly proved 23rd December, 1668, there was a proviso, that Mr. Shelton's widow should, during her life, receive the rents, and elect the school-master and scholars, and also, exclusively purchase the gowns and coats. She dying, 1681, the trusts of the will devolved on the rector and churchwardens of St. Giles, under the superintendance of the vestry.

The premises consisted at that time of coach-houses and stables in the occupation of Lord Halifax, and of several small old houses, let out to paupers and poor people, at rents amounting, from £50 to £60 a year.

1687. The heir at law agreed to accept £7 10s., as his portion of the rents; in 1700, the whole premises were let upon lease to two persons at £34 per annum; and afterwards, the buildings being decayed, the whole were let for long terms, at ground rents, amounting to £25 10s. per annum. In 1763, Mr. Reid the schoolmaster died, and a considerable sum being due to the churchwardens, and the rents being quite inadequate to fulfil the intention of the testator, the school was discontinued. The gowns for the same reason were not provided more than twice.

1766. Mr. Richard Remnant, churchwarden, laid out the sum of £76 10s. monies accumulated to that time from this estate, in the purchase of £83 6 : 3 three per cent. consols, it being determined so to dispose of the rents regularly as to accumulate, and thereby to re-commence the school at a future period according to the testator's will, and trustees were afterwards appointed to carry this determination into effect.

The receipts and payments, under these arrangements, were audited annually until some time in 1815, when the following results where stated :—

	£. s.
Part of the estate, 62-feet in front, and the whole depth, is now occupied by Messrs. Cutler and Co. Ironmongers, as work-shops, at a net rent of This was let for a long term to Robert Cox and others, and will expire in 1843.	27 0 0
The residue of the estate, being 43-feet in front, has been let to John Bromley also, as workshops, for 61 years, which expired Midsummer 1815	8 10 0
The three per-cent consols accumulated in about 50 years, £6,758 4s, 5d.	202 14 9
Produce ..,............ .... £238	4 9
N. B. The rent charge of £10 had not been claimed for 70 years and more. Dividends in hand, and due January 1816, amounting to £228 8s. 10. Upon these facts, and upon the fair calculation of Bromley's premises letting for an additional £12, making in all £21 a year	12 10 0
The income would then be,......£250	14 9
Calculating on erecting or purchasing a school-room, and a residence for the master, requiring the sale of as much stock as will lessen the annual dividend	50 0 0
There will then remain to fulfil the will of the donor £200	14 9

By the directions of such will, the following matters are to be annually provided :—

	£. s. d. Prices specified in Will.	£. s. d. Estimated Expense in 1815.
Thirty-five gowns for old men & women	26 5 0	36 15 0
Salary and gown for schoolmaster	21 0 0	42 0 0
Fifty coats for scholars	15 0 0	35 0 0
Coals and candles	0 0 0	30 0 0
Heir at law of donor	10 0 0	0 0 0
Books and stationery	0 0 0	20 0 0
Water rent & other incidental expenses	0 0 0	15 0 0
Estimated annual expense of school		178 15 0
Estimated surplus of rents and dividends		21 19 9
		£200 14 9

The gown meant by the devisor was probably a warm loose woollen wrapper, open in front and fastened round the waist with a girdle, which in his time was worn by men as well as women.

The estimate is made on a supposition that they are to be supplied with strong warm coats, and the women with stuff gowns."

Founded upon these calculations, the vestry appointed a committee to look out a proper place for re-establishing the school; and eventually, premises in Lloyd's Court were selected and taken down, and a new building was there erected for that purpose; the whole expense of which, including surveyor's bill, agreements, insurance, &c. amounted to £1,163 : 10 : 1

December 4, 1816, a report was made in vestry, stating in substance, "that the committee had taken the ground alluded to, for sixty-one years from the preceding Midsummer, at a net rent of forty pounds; on which the school was built, and conducted under regulations agreeable to the tenets of the Church of England, and conformable to the wishes of the testator; and that the Paving Committee had agreed to give for the ground not so appropriated, for the whole term, forty pounds per annum.

	£	s.	d.
"That the said trust estate at present consists of the hereditaments in Parker's Lane, originally devised by Mr. Shelton, and which are let on building leases, at net annual ground rents amounting to...	48	0	
And £6,300 three per cent. consolidated annuities, producing an annual interest or dividend of	189	0	0
	£237	0	0

That it appears to the committee by the following estimate, the funds of the charity are sufficient for all the purposes specified by the donor, and for providing each of the scholars annually with one suit of clothes instead of a coat, mentioned in his Will.

			£	s.	d.
Thirty-five gowns and coats, for thirty-five old men and women...........................			36	15	0
One coat for the master			3	0	0
His salary			80	0	0
Coals, candles, water rent, insurance, and incidents			25	0	0
Books and stationery			15	0	0
One coat for each scholar of similar make	s.	d.			
to the school of Christ's Hospital......	12	0			
Breeches, 4s. 6d.; cap, 10d.; girdle, 9d.;	6	1			
Shoes and stockings	7	6			
Shirt, from 4s. to 5s.; say	4	5			
Fifty suits, each at £1	10	0	75	0	0
			£234	15	0

Mr. L. G. Hansard produced and read the following extracts, which were ordered to be entered upon the Minutes, and are as follow :—

"That on the 8th of June, 1826, evidence was given by Frederick Augustus Earle, (then clerk to the late Mr. Parton,) and now the vestry clerk of these parishes, before a committee of the House of Commons, appointed to enquire into the education of the lower orders of the metropolis, and ordered by the House of Commons to be printed on the 19th of June in the same year.

"That Shelton's School was conducted till the year 1763, when, it being greatly indebted to the parish, and the income reduced to £25 10s. it was discontinued; the rents from that time have been laid out in the funds to accumulate, under the direction of the vestry, and the account has been annually audited.

"The old premises are now let, from Lady-day last, at £48 a year, and the consols now standing in the trustees' names' with the accumulation, amount to £7,212 : 8 : 9.

"That the appointment of the trustees is in the vestry: the trustees named under the will were the minister and churchwardens, but the vestry has the management of this."

"That the commissioners appointed pursuant to Act 58 George III, cap. 91, to enquire concerning charities, in their second report to parliament, dated 5th July, 1819, and ordered to be printed on the same day, after reciting the facts already detailed on the minutes of this vestry, state, " that fifty boys are now educated in this school, according to the mode of instruction adopted in the National Schools; and are fully clothed once a year. They are selected from the parishes, and in the proportion specified in the founder's will, except that the children directed to be taken from the parish of St. Giles are now taken from the united parishes of St. Giles and St. George Bloomsbury ; this, among other privileges originally possessed by the parish of St. Giles, having, since the creation of Bloomsbury into a parish, been extended to the united parishes. They are appointed by a committee of a joint vestry."

And in concluding their report on this object, the commissioners state.—

"We have looked with some degree of jealousy into the management of the funds of a charity which appear to have been wholly suspended for a period of no less than fifty-three years; but we find, that during that time the accounts were regularly audited every year, and the accruing income added to the accumulating capital; nor does it seem that the period of suspension could have been materially abridged, without running the risk of the charity being put into activity, with funds inadequate to the full accomplishment of its objects."

In the report (page 4), of the committee of estates, &c. belonging to the joint parishes, dated December 11, 1826, is the following extraordinary statement. " The rents, amounting to £48. should be appropriated to the support of Shelton's School; and the commissioners of charities have been led to suppose this to be the fact; but the treasurer of the school, during five years that he has held the office, has received only twenty-one pounds annually, ignorant that the charity was annually defrauded of twenty-seven pounds, which sum has been received by the late vestry clerk, but carried to no account. In the accounts of the Shelton's School revenues, the whole rent is regularly entered as received up to Michaelmas 1821, when the late Mr. Parton's account closed. To this period the accounts of the charity are signed as audited.

Mr. Waddell then commenced the treasurership; but there is no subsequent entry of the twenty-seven pounds, nor are there any signatures affixed to the accounts indicating their examination. On reference to the receipts of the tenants, it appears that Mr. Earle has received the rents for the last six years, amounting to £162. This sum is unaccounted for by him."

It is impossible to read the above, without feeling surprise at the carelessness of the committee appointed to manage the school, and especially the treasurer, who was interested in keeping an accurate account. It surely was his duty to render, at least, an annual statement of receipts and expenditure, with vouchers, which would have completely precluded the collector from this mal-appropriation.

The following is an abstract account of the estates, rent-charges, annuities, and funded property, belonging to the charities, &c. of these parishes, which is inserted here for the future guide of every parishioner, and for want of which, at an earlier period, several estates and bequests have been entirely lost.

How acquired.	Date.	Description.

I.—PAROCHIAL ESTATES:

1. Parochial Funds	1723	Premises in Bowl-yard or Vinegar-yard, St. Giles, held by trustees, members of the Vestry, in fee
2. ditto	1792	Premises in Short's Gardens, held in fee
3. ditto	1821	Additional premises in the same place, ditto
	1803	ditto ditto
4. ditto	1806	Premises in Broad-street, St. Giles, held on lease of 99 Years, of Jane Cecil
ditto	1824	Land at Whitton, in the parish of Isleworth; held by trustees in fee
ditto	1783	Premises in the Coal-yard and Sword-bearer's-alley; held by trustees in fee
	1816	Premises in Lloyd's-court; lease from Sir Robert Clifton to seven vestrymen, dated 1816, for 61 years
8. Shelton's Will	1672	Premises in Parker's-street; devised to the Minister and Churchwardens, in trust, part let to Mr. Cutler, on lease for dated , and expires in 1843, at £27 0 0 p. ann. part let to Mr. Wood, expires in 1877, at 21 0 0 ditto

II. ANNUITIES and FUNDED PROPERTY:

1. Stephen Skydmore or Scudamore	1584	A payment by the Vintners' Company; a gift for fuel
2. Elisabeth Cummings	1735	Legacy of £200, the interest to be distributed in bread. Invested in South Sea annuities, in the name of the Accountant-general, payable to the Minister and Churchwardens
3. Margaret Boswell	1720	Legacy of £100 South Sea stock; interest to be given to ten poor sick families. Invested in the name of the Rector and Churchwardens
4. Frances Batt	1736	Legacy of £100. Invested in South Sea stock, in the names of the Rector and Churchwardens
5. Sir William Oosey	1672	Gift of £50 ⎫ said to be carried to the joint
6. The Hon. Robt. Bertie	1679	Gift of £50 ⎬ stock or poor rates of the parish.
7. Henry Carter	1676	Gift of £50 ⎭ [see 14th Rep. p. 191.]
8. Thomas Edwards	1791	Legacy of £500 for bread. Invested in the names of Peter Ladgate, Charles Stable, and John Waddell, in the 3 per cent. consols
	—	Stock in the 3 per cent. consols, stated to be the accumulation of invested rents during the suspension of Shelton's school; standing in the names of Dr. Willis and John Vaillant, Esq.
10. William Atkinson	—	A rent-charge of £1 on the Bull's Head public-house, in Lewknor's Lane
11. Unknown	1822	Gift of £90 navy 5 per cents. standing in the names of the Right Rev. John Buckner, lord bishop of Chichester, George Brettingham and Charles Stable. To be distributed to poor Irish women in childbed, living in St. Giles's parish. Now new 4 per cents.
12. Thomas Leverton	1825	A reversion at the death of Mrs. Leverton of £5000 3 per cent. consols, in trust for paying five widows £25 each
13. same	—	A legacy of £100 invested in 3 per cent. consols, in the names of John Vaillant and Charles Stable

Rents receivable.	Rents outgoing.	Appropriation.
£. s. d.	£. s.	
—	—	
—	—	The Workhouse.
—	—	
—	162 0 0	School attached to the Workhouse.
—	—	Intended for building an Infant Nursing establishment.
—	—	Watch-house, Round-house, and Engine-house.
let to Paving board for £40 per ann.	40 0 0	Shelton's school.
40 0 0	—	ditto.

Amount of Stock.	Annual Dividend, or Receipt.	
£. s. d.	£. s. d.	
—	—	
203 6 0	6 2 0	stated in the 14th Rep. p. 191, to form a bread fund, and at p. 191, to be distributed in twenty-four two-penny loaves twice a week, on Wednesdays and Saturdays, to the twenty almswomen, and four to distressed inhabitants selected by the churchwardens.
133 6 8	4 0 0	
100 0 0	0	
lost	lost	
554 4 3	16 12 6	25 three-penny loaves distributed to as many poor persons of the parish of St. Giles.
6,300 0 0	189 0 0	Shelton's school.
—	0	Premises in dilapidation; twenty-five years of the annuity in arrear.
94 10 0	4 2 9	according to the terms of the gift.
—	—	not in operation.
115 0	3 6 0	almshouses.

The Charity Schools of the united parishes are situate in Museum Street (formerly Queen Street), extending into Bloomsbury church-yard. These had their origin in a bequest from the Rev. Edward Leach, in 1734, of two houses in Plumtree Street, formerly called Newton's Houses, and were given in trust under his will for the education of poor children of the parish, whose parents were not able to pay.

They were instituted in 1805, and are open to the children of both parishes, consisting of 160 boys, 100 of whom are clothed, and 60 girls, who are both clothed and boarded. The master's salary is £80, with lodging; the ushers £40; and the mistress has £30 a year, with board and lodging.

By a statement made by the trustees in 1826, the funds for this foundation were highly flourishing: the following is an epitome:—

	£.	s.	d.
"Subscriptions, donations, and legacies of Sir Henry Featherstone and family, from 1705 to Christmas 1746, 41 years............................	1627	18	0
Perpetual benefactions, including donations, on admitting an additional number of girls, amount to	8568	10	5

These sums are funded, the dividends being applied to the annual expenditure.

| Annual subscriptions .... | 804 | 6 | 0 |

To which must be added, produce of three annual charity sermons and collections at anniversary dinners—amount uncertain.

Mr. Thomas Cook, on his examination before the Education Committee of the House of

Commons, stated, that the charity had several legacies in reversion, one of which amounting to £150 had already fallen in, and that the trustees, after expending about £2000 annually in the support of the school, had a surplus which enabled them during several successive years to vest several hundred pounds in the funds. When they were in contemplation to add 25 girls to the former establishment of 35, to board on the foundation, they went from house to house in the joint parishes, and were successful, by which means their funds had accumulated and flourished. The 60 girls cost them in board, clothing, &c. about £690 a year.

It is highly gratifying to know that 5,456 children had, up to 1826, been received into these schools, by which many of the evils arising from idle habits and street associations have been greatly lessened. No less than 2,887 boys had then been apprenticed and put to service therefrom, and 1,413 girls disposed of in like manner.

These Schools are well conducted, great regard being paid to the health, morals, and cleanliness of the children. The boys are taught reading, writing, and arithmetic; and the girls, added to the two former branches, are taught needle-work and housewifery. The order and regularity of this establishment is attributable in a great degree to the assiduity of the late Mr. Davis, who gratuitously devoted a great portion of his time and attention to promote the objects for which it was founded.

There are several other Charity Schools, among which may be enumerated the Bedford Chapel School in which 130 children are educated and partly clothed, supported by voluntary annual subscriptions and donations. There are others instituted and supported by the congregations of Eagle Street, Gate Street, Great Queen Street, and West Street Chapels, &c.

The Irish Free Schools in George Street were established in 1813 by and under the auspices of His Grace the Duke of Bedford, Sir Digby Mackworth, Bart., the Rev. J. Ivimey, Mr. Clerk of Bury Place, and many other benevolent gentlemen. They were founded for the purpose of affording instruction and clothing to the children of the poor Irish Catholics and others, without interfering with their creed. About 200 were thus taken from the streets, where they were exposed to depravity in the extreme; but, strange to say, this laudable institution met with the greatest opposition from the catholic priesthood, and the Rev. Mr. Gandolphy preached against it on the following Sunday, which produced an effect beyond what he intended. A mob assembled about the Schoolhouse and broke the windows; and the master,

Mr. Finigan, stated before the Committee of the House of Commons, that he and his wife were pelted with mud, and his child so beaten as to become a cripple. After this the number of children decreased from 230 to 38; but the schools gradually progressed, so that in six weeks after they arose to the full number again. The opposition has however been so incessant, as to prevent the Schools from flourishing to much extent.

ST. PATRICK'S SCHOOL. That branch of it applicable to female children is established in Denmark Street, where about 200 are educated in the Catholic principles on the Lancasterian plan. This charity school has much increased under the management of an excellent school-mistress, who undertakes the tuition without fee or reward: and there is another Catholic School in Wild Street.

THE LYING-IN HOSPITAL in Brownlow Street for married women, is an establishment instituted in the year 1749, where ample comforts are provided for such as are fit objects of this charity, which has been always well supported by voluntary contributions.

THE BLOOMSBURY DISPENSARY and other charitable institutions, to which we can only allude, are instances of that benevolence for which our district, in common with the British public, is so justly famed.

Some other charitable bequests will come conveniently under our more immediate notice, subjoined to biographical sketches of the donors.

Among the parochial bequests there is a remarkable one of William Baynbrigge, Esq. in 1672. He gave £300 to build a south gallery in St. Giles's Church, the rents and profits of which arising from the seats were to be given to the poor of that parish. When the church was about to be re-built, a clause was inserted in the Act of 4th George I. at the instance of Colonel Baynbrigge, his descendant, to secure this intention of his ancestor. It appears, that for some time the profits were disposed of as devised; since which they have been, during many years, otherwise appropriated.

This matter was taken up very properly by some of the overseers appointed in 1828, who complained, in a printed paper issued by them, that the Vestry had refused them access to the minutes of 1672, and the necessary accounts, to enable them to enforce the intention of the donor. Dated St. Giles's and St. George's Workhouse, 9th March, 1829, and signed by George Sams, Charles Yardley, Joseph Crane, and Daniel Bailey.

CHAPTER VIII.

Vestry defined — Legal Decisions thereon — St. Giles's Select Vestry—Bishop of London's Mandate—Churchwardens—Their Answer to Bishop Juxon's Articles—Minutes of Vestry Proceedings—Bloomsbury Vestry, under 10th of Anne —Maitland's Account—Dissensions with the Mother Parish, &c. &c.

AT this juncture, when so much interest has been excited respecting the powers, constitution, and legality of Select Vestries, it cannot be thought irrelevant to enter into a minute inquiry on the subject, which I shall endeavour to perform with the impartiality it deserves. This inquiry is indeed the more necessary in reference to our district, because, although a triumphant decision had seemed to set the question at rest, we are menaced with another appeal to the Court of King's Bench, to reverse the verdict already obtained*

---

* " On the trial of the cause in the Court of King's Bench, the jury gave a verdict against the Select Vestry, but in direct contradiction of the decision of the judge, who pointed out the powers contained in the Acts of Parliament, from which the joint vestry derived the authority under which it 'acted.

"A Vestry, properly speaking, is the assembly of the whole parish, met together in some convenient place, for the dispatch of the business and affairs of the parish; and this meeting being commonly held in the vestry-room adjoining or belonging to the church, it thence takes its name of Vestry, as the place itself does from the parson's vestments, which are usually kept there.* *(See Shaw's Parish Guide, edition,* 1743.

It was originally the right of every parishioner, who paid assessments, to claim a place in the Vestry; but where parishes are large, to prevent confusion, they have delegated that power to the best and most substantial amongst themselves, to represent and act for them. *(See more on the subject in Dalton's Justice, Burn's Ecclesiastical Law, &c.)*

Under such circumstances, the Vestry consider it a duty to itself and the parish to apply for a new trial; not that it is prompted by a desire to retain power, or by a pertinacity in clinging to authority, but by a determination to justify itself from the imputation of usurping the parochial government, and to show that the powers which it exercised were conferred by law. *(See " Refutation of Charges against the Select Vestry,"* page 47.)

* The Select Vestries originated from the practice of choosing a certain number yearly to manage the affairs of the parish for that year, which, by degrees, became a fixed method; and the parishioners lost, not only their right to concur in the public management, but also the right of electing the managers; and such a custom has been judged valid." (*Gibs,* 219.)

A Vestry, to be legal, must be founded on prescription, by election of the parishioners, or by Act of Parliament. It follows, therefore, that where none of these exist, validity cannot be pleaded, and it becomes an assumption in the most odious form.

The indolence and ignorance of our ancestors, have entailed the evil of select vestries upon their posterity; and the supineness which they evinced is but too prevalent at this day, or the usurped power which oppresses the present generation, would no longer be the subject of dissension and complaint.

"Reason," according to Coke, "is the foundation of law;"—can it be reasonable, then, that a few individuals, self-elected and self-appointed, should rule a parish with uncontrouled power? Is it reasonable that a body, so constituted, should perpetuate themselves without reference to the changes which the great innovator, Time, produces, without responsibility, and without restraint? Vestries had their foundation in the monastic ages of superstition, when faith was implicit and superstition had unbounded sway. Is nothing due to a more enlightened period, and are we never to be divested of the Gothic fetters which have so long enchained us?

It matters not, in my estimation, whether a Select Vestry be so by assumption or prescription, it is totally at variance with the imprescriptable rights of Englishmen; and I am, therefore, at war with it: it is contrary to the constitution, and I abhor it.

Well has it been remarked, that "no body of men in the state possess the right of taking money from our pockets, without rendering an account; neither have members of parliament the power of electing themselves, and rendering themselves permanent: it was reserved for Select Vestries to enjoy these exclusive privileges, so long as the people quietly submit to be the victims of their tyranny and assumed power."

"Ignorance is the mother of error," and it is this that has fostered and perpetuated the evils of Select Vestries, it never being the intention of the legislature to invest men with the unlimited power they have assumed in dispensing the hard-earned money of their fellow parishioners, as it suits their purpose, setting accountability at utter defiance. The King cannot raise money without the concurrence of the Lords and Commons; but, more omnipotent than royalty, these oppressors, in the shape of Select Vestries, assess and distress at pleasure, contemning the presumption of those who dare attempt to penetrate into the recesses of concealment in which they veil themselves. It has been said, with some appearance of plausibility, that the individuals who compose Select Vestries are highly respectable men—men, who would not lend themselves to any act of a dishonourable tendency. The premises, but not the consequences of such a proposition, are admissible; because the evidence of experience assures us, that when men become invested with power, it necessarily degenerates, and debases the human mind. Place any body of men in an irresponsible situation, and they become reckless of any other interests but their own; "such is the frailty flesh is heir to." But, on the other hand, how often does it happen that men of the greatest worth, who would shrink from the taint of baseness, are placed in the vestry lists, who have no opportunity of becoming effective, not being able, from various impediments, to attend the meetings. In respect to the parishes under our notice, it is well known that several judges, and men who fill eminent stations, have their names thus enrolled; they serve to grace and ornament the list, by adding to its dignity; whilst their high and laborious situations preclude them from becoming more than a dead letter, in usefulness to the parish. In short, it is a truth not to be controverted, that a few individuals (with difficulty assembled), have managed the vast concerns of this extensive district, and with what ability, the evidence of facts will best illustrate.

Parton informs us, that "the management of this parish (St. Giles), is entrusted to a Vestry which is select by prescription, and consists of the rector, churchwardens, and thirty-six other persons, being resident householders therein." He adds, "its existence and powers are confirmed by Episcopal Mandate, April 27, 1628; which contains the various regulations, as to the constitution, qualifications, and government, and by which they were empowered 'to doe and exercise all things belonging to vestriemen, for the good and benefit of their church and parish.' The nature of the parish business they had to direct, their mode of managing it, and other particulars, are subsequently set forth in an answer to the Bishop's Mandate, dated 1628. Vacancies, in case of death or removal, are filled up by the surviving, or continuing members." Such is the flippant account of the Vestry by its former clerk, a man of considerable research; and from his office, which he held during many years, necessarily competent to have given most useful and authentic information on a subject so important. It would, on the contrary, seem as if he viewed the "constitution" and "nature" of *his Vestry* so doubtfully, that he thought it most prudent to abandon dilating upon it with breathless precipitation.

"Prescription, or immemorial custom, has been long ascertained by the law to commence from the reign of Richard I. and any custom may be destroyed by evidence of its non-existence in any part of the long period from his days (1199,) to the present." "This rule was adopted when, by the statute of Westminster (3 Edward I. cap. 30,) the reign of Richard I. was made the time of limitation in a writ of right. But since, by statute 32 Henry VIII. (1541.) cap. 2, this period (in a writ of right,) hath been very rationally reduced to sixty years. It seems unaccountable, that the date of legal prescription, or memory, should still continue to be reckoned from an era so very antiquated." *Blackstone's Commentaries, vol. 2, p. 31.*

"A custom that there should be a Select Vestry of an indefinite number of persons, continued by election of new members made by itself, and not by the parishioners, is valid in law. But it seems that it must be part of such custom, that there should always be a reasonable number, and that the reasonableness of the number must decide with reference to long-established usage, and to the population of the parish, *such a custom having existed from time immemorial in a parish.*" *(Golding versus Fenn, 7th Barnwell and Cresswell's Reports, 765.)*

"In the second year of William and Mary, a Select Vestry, at Masham, in Yorkshire, was established by prescription, as was St. Mary at Hill, London, in 1735, in banco regius.

St. Saviour's and St. Olave's, Southwark, Select Vestries, on the other hand, for want of proof of prescription, were set aside." *(See Shaw's Parish Guide.)*

St. Martin's in the Fields. There are two remarkable decisions in this parish, worthy of recording, as a proof, if any were wanting, to show what trifling quibbles in law are sufficient to overturn justice.

The first parochial book extant of parish records here, is dated 1576, at which period there was no vestry. But in 1660, it is on record, that there was a Select Vestry, chosen by the parishioners at large, as all vestries ought to be; and, in 1662, a Select Vestry of this parish was confirmed by Gilbert Bishop of London, and on the same principle it was again confirmed by another Bishop of London, (Henchman) in 1672. The present Select Vestry was established in its now existing form, by the Act of 10th of Anne.

In 1791 the parishioners applied to the Court of King's Bench to be relieved from the despotism of this "select," when the parties agreed it should be tried on a feigned issue, and the point being mooted, the question was—whether from time immemorial a select vestry had existed in the parish? Lord Kenyon said, that unless this could be shewn to have been always fixed, there could be no legal custom; and the jury found, that there had been a select vestry, consisting of forty-nine persons.

A verdict in favour of the "select" consequently followed, and the parishioners were unsuccessful.

In 1823, thirty-two years after the above decision, the parish books were inspected in consequence of some proceedings in the Court of King's Bench, when it was found there had not been a "select vestry" consisting of a fixed number of forty-nine, but that it varied at different times, and had never consisted of so many, and in fact, it never amounted to more than twenty-two. This discovery shewed that the jury had given their verdict under erroneous information, which so firmly seated the "select," that they continued to exercise their illegal powers, levying rates, and performing all their parochial functions up to that period 1823. The Court of King's Bench was again applied to, and another feigned issue was tried before the present chief justice, Lord Tenterden, and it was a very strange thing it was not allowed to stand on the same terms as it was when tried before Lord Kenyon. The chief justice, for reasons best known to himself, altered it, by striking out the words "a certain number," and left it to be tried by inserting instead, "whether a body of parishioners had acted as a select vestry."

As it was clear that a set of parishioners, though not "a certain number," as had been laid down by Lord Kenyon, had acted as a "select vestry," a verdict was given as before, in favour of them, and against the parishioners, and the vestry continued in uncontrouled power.

The existence of a vestry pre-supposes the existence of a parish; now, it appears exceedingly doubtful whether St. Giles was one till after the dissolution of its hospital, as has been argued already at length. *(See page* 82.)

It is probable that one of the earliest vestries was that mentioned to have been held in 1617, *(see page* 91), and that it was appointed by the parishioners at large, according to the legitimate mode of former periods; and it has been shewn, that when it was in contemplation to build the second church in 1623, "the parishioners" met in open vestry, it being more suited to the importance of the subject. *(See page* 97.)

From the vestry minutes, (although Parton conceals the fact,) we learn that no less than eighty-four names were prefixed to this important document, with the addition of the rector himself. Here we have a clear and unequivocal proof that the individuals, composing the then vestry, in number twenty-one exclusive of the rector, as stated in the first vestry book, who no doubt were elected by the parish, considered themselves not invested with sufficient authority, on important occasions like this, to act alone. They therefore resorted to the only proper and legal means, where open vestries exist, by calling their constituents together, to confer on the best means of raising the sums required, by rating themselves for that purpose. This was a genuine specimen of a constitutional open vestry, which even the rector Manwayring, with all his high political notions, disdained not to assemble with; and one is surprised at the sweeping anathema pronounced upon it by Parton, which is both disingenuous and dishonest—disingenuous, because his argument as to the illegality of this meeting is not founded on truth—and dishonest, because it was advanced for a selfish purpose.

After the church was rebuilt, the celebrated parish record, Doomsday Book, contains a list of vestrymen then increased to thirty, besides the rector.

That these composed the whole of the vestrymen at that period is obvious, because, in a book specially intended to commemorate the whole of the names of the benefactors who contributed towards the building, it is more than probable the vestrymen would be all included.

Here again Mr. Parton exhibits his unfaithfulness as an historian, by concealing all the names, except those of Dr. Manwayring and Sir Wm.

Seager, neither does he state the number they consisted of. He knew how necessary it was for a legal vestry, immemorially constituted, to be regularly uniform; and as the number had arisen in two years from twenty-two to thirty, exclusive of the rector, and subsequently as at the present year to thirty-nine, it was prudent to exercise silence, that neither his official situation, or the persons from whom he derived it, might be placed in jeopardy. It is well known that in the compiling the work alluded to, he was greatly assisted by a man of great talent and research; and, as rumours will circulate, it is said, that in his inquiries he learnt sufficient to invalidate the existence of the select vestry, on which discovery it became necessary to suppress the unwelcome information.

This is corroborated by the further circumstance of his concealing from us the particulars of the " episcopal mandate" which " confirmed," as he states, " the existence and powers" of the " vestry select by prescription," and " which contains the various regulations as to their constitution, qualifications, and government."

It was very natural for Mr. Parton to have favoured the parishioners with a copy of this episcopal mandate, on which he places such emphasis; especially, as he is minute to a fault in many instances in trifling details, and matters of little interest. He was too good a casuist to introduce a document, which, in shewing the flimsiness of his argument, would at once undermine the superstructure of a select vestry, founded on rottenness. A copy of this mandate, obtained from the office of the Court of Faculty, Doctors' Commons, is in my possession, and I had intended to introduce it verbatim, but the late decision renders it unnecessary. I shall content myself with inserting the substance of it.

The mandate in question is dated April 1628, and recites, that he, the Bishop of London, (George Mountain), had been applied to by two parishioners, Abraham Speckart, Esq. and Robert Hope, one of the new churchwardens, to appoint a certain number, namely, twenty-five, of the better and more ancient sort of the parishioners of St. Giles in the Fields, to act as vestrymen for the said parish. Under the laws ecclesiastical and the temporal laws of the land, and in conjunction with the chancellor of the diocese (Arthur Ducke) he therefore grants the prayer of the petition, and appoints the individuals therein named, as follows:—Roger Manwayring, D.D., Sir William Seager, Knight, Lawrence Whitaker, Zacherie Bethell, Thomas Shepherd, Hans Claxton, and Abraham Speckart, Esqrs.; Martin Basil, John Shelberry, Richard Bigg, James Pert, Humphrey Gardiner, William Mewe, Nicholas Bragge, Edward Robinson, Andrew Brown, John Brewer, Robert Johnson, Matthew Quiere, Robert Hope, Richard Sire, Edward Rice, Jeremie Cooke, Thomas Harvye, and William Chapman. These, including the rector and churchwardens, were to be the vestrymen, to manage the affairs of the parish peaceably and quietly; and as any of these should *decease*, or remove out of the parish, or become scandalous by drunkenness, whoredom, &c. others were to be chosen by the remaining vestrymen to succeed them. Thirteen at the least were to form a quorum, among whom the rector and churchwardens for the time being were to be always three. These were to act for the quiet and good of the church, parish, and poor; to incite to works of charity, and not to interfere in any ecclesiastical matters. Should they herein intermeddle, and should they do any act at their meetings in the absence of the rector, this instituted vestry was to be for ever void, as if it had never been granted.

The perusal of this precious *morceau* will convince the most superficial reader, that upon it is founded the vestry of St. Giles, which superseded the usual mode of election, and which, by the indolence of the successive parishioners in not asserting their rights, or not understanding them, has from that period become permanent. But although they became permanent as a body, they have not continued so in number;

the bishop *prescribed twenty-five in all, which was never to be exceeded, but they have since arisen to thirty-nine;* by which we may see how power innovates, when it becomes seated.

This instituting of vestries by mandate or faculty, was, it should seem, very prevalent about this period. We have already noticed one granted by the Bishop of London to St. Martin's in the Fields in 1662, in which forty-nine persons, together with the vicar and churchwardens, were named as a select vestry, and that number was to be kept up by elections, to be made by ten at least, of those forty-nine, together with the vicar and churchwardens. In the year 1673 this number of ten was reduced to seven by another faculty, and these faculties were acted upon ever afterwards. Ten out of the fourteen vestrymen, exclusive of the vicar and the churchwardens, who were present at the vestry holden next before the promulgation of the first faculty, were part of the forty-nine named in that faculty; and it was held, that as the vestry appointed by the faculty and since continued, was not inconsistent with the vestry previously existing by the custom, the custom was not destroyed by the parish having accepted the faculty, and acted upon it ever since, *the faculty not being binding in law, and the vestry having power at any time to depart from its direc-*

tions. (*Golding v. Fenn, 7th Barnwell and Cresswell's Reports,* 765.)

Formerly, under the common law, every parishioner who paid to the church-rate, or scot and lot, and no other person, had a right to come to these vestry meetings. But this must not be understood to exclude the minister, who hath a special duty incumbent upon him, and is responsible to the bishop, and therefore in every parish meeting he presides for the regulation and directing the same; and this equally prevails whether he be rector or vicar. (*See Chitty, &c.*)

Parton adds "the nature of the parish business they (the vestry) had to direct; their mode of managing it, and other particulars, are subsequently set forth in an answer to the bishop's mandate, dated 1635." Nothing is more extraordinary than Parton's conduct in withholding both the mandate and answer he alluded to, especially as he lays such stress upon them in reference to the authority of his vestry. The following is the answer in question, dated 6th of December, 1635:—

"The answer of the churchwardens of the parish of St. Giles in the Fields, to the Articles delivered unto them from the Right Reverend Father in God, the Lord Bishop of London.

To the first we answer—that our parish business of great moment, as the building and finishing the church, and fencing in the church-yard, and other things of the like nature, are propounded, debated, and ordered by a meeting of all the parishioners in general; *but the ordinary business of small moment, as assessments for the poor*, highways, choice of officers, and other such like occasions, are ordered by a select assembly of the parishioners, churchwardens, and other ancient inhabitants of the parish, which hath time out of mind been called a vestry.

To the second we answer—that we find in an ancient church book, mention of a vestry three score years past, which, when it had a beginning, we know not; but for the grant thereof from the Lord Bishop of London, or his chancellor, we do not certainly know, nor can find any, until the year of our Lord 1628, at which time it was granted by the then Lord Bishop of London, under the chancellor's seal.

To the third we answer—that we claim no power thereby more than it pleased the Lord Bishop of London by his said grant to permit unto us, and do make thereof no further use in chusing of the officers, and making of such rates and assessments as aforesaid, and in parochial matters of the like nature.

To the fourth we answer—that the fees and dues which we receive in our parish for ecclesiastical rites are contained in a schedule thereunto annexed, whereunto we refer ourselves; which fees and dues we receive not by any table of fees or dues, but by ancient custom and prescription, *time out of mind, as we are informed.*" (*Vide Vestry Minutes.*)

We have now gone through the two famous documents on which Parton has laid so much stress as applicable to his select vestry by prescription, and which was composed not of thirty-nine, including the rector and churchwardens, as he would have us believe, to give a colour to the number it now consists of, but of twenty-eight, as has been before adverted to. We discover that bishops' mandates have no validity, and they have been in several instances set aside, and the vestries founded on them, as at Twickenham and other places.

The answer above quoted was issued only eighty-eight years after the first presentation to the church and rectory, according to Newcourt and others; and it seems extraordinary, that the leading men in that day should possess no better information than what was contained in a book dated sixty years back, (1575,) wherein was mention of a vestry, but whether it was founded on prescription or election, or how it was constituted, or when it had a beginning, they knew not. They knew *clearly* that they were appointed by the mandate of a bishop seven years previously, and upon that they acted, but this was the limit of their knowledge on the subject.

The existence of the Vestry evidently cannot be traced to an early period; but it can be shewn from the bishop's books of this diocese, that rates and burials, &c. were settled in open vestry meetings, and especially the church-rate in 1623 was made at one of these meetings. The right of the parishioners to elect churchwardens and other officers has been long established by a British jury, as may be seen from numerous entries in the vestry minutes. The accounts, it will be there seen, were also audited by the parishioners, not vestrymen; and the vestry, it should seem, did not act as a body till the grant of the mandate, which was issued in the 3rd of Charles I. and prior to the rebellion.

In 1637, Messrs. Hope the churchwardens, and who seem to have been for years leading men, were requested to consult of, and propound to the vestry, certain orders for the better governing of the vestry business, and meetings. One of these was, " that they should severally subscribe ten shillings towards buying a velvet pall for the use of the poor, which themselves and families were to have the use of at their death, and such as refused to subscribe were to be deprived of the benefit of the same." There was another imposing penalties on vestrymen blaspheming the holy name of God, cursing, swearing, or otherwise indecently behaving himself.

One would have thought they would have exercised too much discrimination to have allowed members to be elected amongst them, capable of such debasement.

"In 1806, opinion of vestry: That in future no gentleman shall become a vestryman of this parish, during the time of his serving the office of churchwarden " Query—did this exclude his being so by virtue of his office?

"During the usurpation", Parton says, "no appointment of vestrymen appears to have taken place,* which, "he adds" was not extraordinary, considering that the then vestry were by the puritans honoured with the title of Dr. Haywood's *creatures*." They however managed, it appears, to protect their parochial rights, except as to the spoliation of their church ornaments, and electing a sexton that had been appointed by Mr. Case, the puritanical minister, and filling up the vacancies of their own body.

December 21st, 1681.—By the following entry in the minutes, it appears, that some of the inhabitants at this time were not quite

---

*Soon after the Restoration, an act passed requiring select vestrymen to take certain oaths, but it did not recognize any who assumed that right, there being an express clause to that effect in the act. See *Act 14th Charles II.*

On the 16th of October, 1663, the vestrymen appointed previous to the Interregnum, subscribed to all the conditions it exacted.

satisfied with the number and constitution of the vestry.

"Whereas Mr. John Morris, and Mr. Nathaniel Chandler, in behalf of themselves, and divers other inhabitants, have requested of the vestry, that some addition or alteration may be made to the present vestry; the vestry, upon debate thereof, do order—That the said John Morris, and Nathaniel Chandler, and the rest, do give in writing their desires touching the premises at the next vestry to be considered of. And it is further ordered, that there be a summons for timely notice to Mr. Dean Sharpe, and likewise to all the vestrymen, to desire them to meet at a time certain at the vestry-house; and that intimation be given in the summons of the occasion of that meeting."

"Whether these advocates for innovation," adds Mr. Parton, "afterwards discovered that the vestry, which had, as shewn, been time out of mind by custom and established usage invested with extensive authorities for the government of the parish, could neither increase their original number of THIRTY-SIX, nor with safety make any other alteration, does not appear. But some such reason did, in all probability occur, for they did not afterwards make any further application to the vestry on the subject."

These reflections of Parton comprize a most sophistical attempt to mystify a transaction which appears in itself both laudable and praiseworthy. These two patriotic men were no doubt aware of the usurpation of their rights as parishioners, and the baneful effects resulting therefrom, and were aroused to make an effort to rid the parish of the odious tyranny; but probably they were appalled by the expence, the unfavourableness of the slavish times they lived in, and perhaps the little support they met with from their fellow-parishioners.

Be this as it may, it is pleasing to know that a spirit of resistance existed at this remote period, which had for its object the lessening the parish despotism, which might have been productive of the happiest effects, had it been better advocated and persevered in. They are here called " innovators," who afterwards were supposed to have made the discovery, "that the vestry which had, as has been shewn, been time out of mind by custom and established usage invested with extensive authority for the government of the parish, could neither increase their original number of thirty-six, nor with safety make any other alteration."

The whole of this long sentence is made up of sophisms; and it is melancholy to contemplate such false reasoning, when emanating from an historian of intelligence and research. Neither has he "*shewn*," nor will it be ever "*discovered*," that the vestry has been *established by custom and usage, time out of mind.* It would seem that he purposely avoided the production of the mandate, and the answer to it, to conceal the cloven foot of his argument, knowing that the vestry had not been originally in number *thirty-six,* but, as has been shewn from the minutes, *twenty-two* only, exclusive of the rector and churchwardens, till it was afterwards varied.

The "*time out of mind,*" he knew had no proof beyond anno 1575, by the shewing of the vestry themselves in 1635; as stated in the answer alluded to, consequently at this period of "*innovation,*" as he terms it, the vestry could not have had an existence, judging by this hypothesis, more than 106 years. The vestry has clearly innovated from an elective body to a despotism, that infringed on those rights of which Britons make their boast; but we hope it is now for ever destroyed, for the future permanent advantage of the parishioners.

I contend then, that after the most careful and most unprejudiced inquiry, I see no claim the vestry ever had to its assumed power, other than usurpation; it clearly having no derivation from prescription, election, or act of parliament.

" We now enter on some particulars respecting the vestry of the younger part of the district, the parish of St. George Bloomsbury; its powers as defined by several acts of parliament, and its disputes with the mother parish of St. Giles.

u

The act of the 10th of Queen Anne, for Building Fifty New Churches, authorized the five commissioners therein appointed to nominate a certain number of inhabitant householders of each new parish to be enrolled in the Court of Chancery as vestrymen, to manage their several parish affairs and churches, in conjunction with the vestries of the old parishes from which they were abstracted; but should such parishes not have vestries, then they were to be modelled according to that of St. Martin's in the Fields.

Here then is the constitution of St. George's vestry, the powers of which we shall see described by Parton as so ill defined, as to leave it doubtful whether it was intended to conduct merely its ecclesiastical affairs, or those of the parish generally. Certain it is, that the vestries, of other new parishes put the former interpretation upon this comprehensive act, and continue to do so in their ministerial functions to this day.*

---

* Maitland took this view of the subject in his History of London, written a few years after the building St. George's Church, Bloomsbury, and unquestionably at a period when the acts of 10th and 11th of Anne were best understood. He states that "the vestry of St. George's Church, Queen Square, (one of the fifty by the way), like its neighbour St. George Bloomsbury, only regards church affairs, for all matters relating to the poor, (except about £100 per annum sacrament money, which is given to the poor at discretion), are still under the direction of the High Holborn liberty, from which it was taken." It is observable, in confirmation of Maitland's

Parton states, that " the commissioners for building fifty new churches caused one to be erected near Bloomsbury Market, and on the 8th March (no year), a Select Vestry was appointed for the new parish, consisting of an equal number of members with that of St. Giles. From this period the powers of the Vestry of the old parish were narrowed; but how far, was a subject of doubt for many years afterwards." It is admitted by this chain of argument, that the acts upon which the new parish stood, were at least very vague and difficult of comprehension; but we shall see more on these points as we proceed.

" 1733 (April 27th.) A committee was appointed to treat with a committee of the vestry of the new parish, on any matters that might occur relative to the two parishes. The matters then referred to were productive of repeated discussion, which in the year 1739 assumed a hostile shape; for, on the 23rd of April in that year, an application was made by the vestry of the new parish to the vestry of the old one, for a formal meeting of the two vestries, in order to ascertain the monies and rates to be assessed within the limits of the old parish,

---

position, that the poor (and other) rates are to this day managed in open vestry in that parish (Queen Square) conformable to the implied meaning of the Acts in question; no other construction having been given them during the lapse of now ninety years.

pursuant to a clause in the act of 10th of Anne. But the Vestry of the old parish declined such meeting; being of opinion that the officers and vestry of that parish were not obliged to so meet; the clause alluded to in such act seeming only to give them power, *if they should think fit to use it; and directions were given for appointing the officers, and making the rates (over both parishes) as usual.**

" The vestry of St. George Bloomsbury having resolved to resist the Scavenger's Rate, *made by the Vestry and Officers of St. Giles's,* and to try by a feigned issue the point in debate between the two parishes, the vestry of the latter parish, under the advice of Serjeant Wynne, declined such trial; and ordered, that all officers of that parish who should assist in collecting and levying the scavenger's rates in St. George Bloomsbury, should be indemnified at the charge of the parish of St. Giles: (and the vestry of the former parish passed a resolution to indemnify those who resisted payment.) *A rate for that purpose was accordingly made on the inhabitants of St. Giles, including that part of the*

---

* Nothing could be adduced more decidedly, to shew that the appointment of St. George's vestry was for no other definite purpose than the conducting its ecclesiastical affairs, as Maitland has argued; and, if this be admitted, it goes to prove that no legal vestry exists in that parish, in the extensive sense in which they have exercised their assumed powers.

parish then called Bloomsbury." Remark here, that this was imposed by the vestry of St. Giles alone!

" December 13th, 1739. A committee was appointed to treat with a committee of the vestry of St. George Bloomsbury, and to settle about the scavenger's rates, and also as to considerable demands made on behalf of the latter parish on the joint stock; when, after a long discussion, all matters in difference were (for that time) amicably adjusted to the satisfaction of both vestries; and the scavenger's and other rates were agreed to extend over both parishes as usual."

The following detail is very observable, especially as coming from Parton. "The construction of the several acts of parliament, by virtue whereof the parish of St. George Bloomsbury was created; the powers of each Vestry whilst acting in its separate capacity, and the separate interest of each parish (or rather portion of the old district) were for nearly forty years the subjects of frequent discussion, which was not always carried on in the most amicable manner; the object of the mother parish appearing to be, to keep the daughter in leading strings; whilst the latter, like other young ladies, sighed for emancipation."

" 3rd December, 1771. A proposal was received from the vestry of St. George Bloomsbury for a partial separation of the two parishes, relative to the nightly watch, which was referred to the joint vestry."

17th December, (same year.) Upon a proposition of St. George Bloomsbury vestry, in its separate capacity, it was resolved by St. Giles's vestry unanimously, " That any meeting of the vestries in separate capacities, for the purpose of considering of any application to parliament for powers to rate the inhabitants of their parishes to any parochial rate, is contrary to the customs and usages of these parishes, and to the intent and meaning of the statutes for establishing their united interests." Why, this point, which they here so furiously decry, had but a short time before been practised by themselves in their separate capacity against the meaning of the statutes! Where then was their consistency?

" 1772, January 3rd. The vestry of Bloomsbury having resolved to proceed in an application to parliament to obtain an act for establishing a nightly watch within that parish, it was by the vestry of St. Giles resolved ' that any attempt of a select vestry to separate two parishes united by law is dishonourable and unjustifiable.' Other resolutions of a like import, couched in strong terms, were passed, and a committee was appointed to oppose the intended application."

"17th July, (same year.) The committee reported, that upon an investigation into the customs and usages of the two parishes, by a committee of the House of Commons, it was resolved, that in levying the watch rate, the two parishes should be considered as one parish, in like manner as they are in collecting the poor and church rates; and that the bill had been altered accordingly."

"The several Acts for the support and management of the poor; and for paving, cleansing, watching, and lighting the two parishes, having removed all doubts as to the powers of the separate vestries, and the probability of their interests being separated; and it appearing to the vestry that the estate in Parker's Lane, with other estates and donations, were given to, or in trust for, this parish, long before the passing of certain acts of parliament, made in the 9th and 10th years of the reign of Queen Anne, by virtue whereof the parish of St. George Bloomsbury was, (so far as relates to *spiritual purposes only*) taken out and separated from the rest of this parish, it was resolved, 'that at the times of such devises and donations being made, and at this time the parish of St. Giles-in-the-Fields and that of St. George Bloomsbury, were and are one parish or district for all temporal purposes, and that the said devises and donations were intended to be for the benefit of the whole district, which before the passing of the said Acts did form the parish of St. Giles-in-the-Fields;' this vestry is therefore of opinion and do hereby resolve ' that the said several estates, funds, and donations, with the rents, interest, dividends, and produce thereof, be in future under the management of the said joint vestry, due caution being observed to prevent reversions and forfeitures."

Thirdly:—We are now to consider these conflicting vestries in their united or joint capacities, the latter appellation being now first introduced, and which is said to have originated with Mr. Serjeant Wynne.

From this period, 1772, a close union has been formed between the two vestries, and assumed the designation they now bear, "The Joint Vestry of St. Giles in the Fields and St. George Bloomsbury."

All the former bickerings between these anomalous bodies seem to have subsided very suddenly and unaccountably, both of them agreeing to take the affairs and burdens of office upon themselves quietly and peaceably, no doubt with the sincerest disinterestedness, thinking it would be too much to trouble their fellow-parishioners with the management of their own affairs.

Two years after this portentous event, it was found necessary to have a new act framed (the act of 14th George III.) to define their powers; and for other purposes; and this is the Act on which they have jointly founded their authority. (*See Abstracts of Acts.*)

This Act strikes me as miserably defective, inasmuch as it presupposes the existence of a Vestry legally sanctioned by prescription, or in some other constitutional way established; whereas, that portion of it applicable to the parish of St. Giles had no other claim to power than what it has acquired by assumption, and in its separate capacity it had always imposed rates on the whole district, as it appears to me, until 1772, when the coalition was formed.

In regard to the new parish, the vestry appointed by the commissioners for building fifty new churches, by virtue of 10th of Anne, were empowered to nominate, and did nominate a vestry selected from the inhabitant householders, who were, according to one of its clauses, enrolled in the Court of Chancery; but its powers, as Parton affirms, were very ill defined; nor does the Act of 3rd George II. appear quite calculated to remove the difficulty. We cannot therefore, on the whole, compliment the legislature of that period for enlightened views on the subject then before them. It has recognized these vestries in their united capacity, without considering that if the former one has no real foundation, the superstructure of the other, which has been erected upon it, will sink and fall with it.*

On reverting to the statute of the 14th George III. it is impossible to withhold astonishment on reflecting on the vestry's carelessness in not having it so framed as to meet future doubts on the subject: this they might probably have then effected without difficulty; but, secure in their fancied authority, they only sued for regulations, leaving themselves open to future animadversion as to the power they held, by an assumption too hateful to conciliate the respect of the parishioners.†

Secondly :—The making it imperative to fix the rates in conjunction with the churchwardens and overseers is truly ridiculous, as any opposition to the will of the vestry must always be

---

* It has been ruled that where acts of parliaments recognise vestries incidentally, they give no value to them, if they are constitutionally invalid. The act adverted to does not therefore invest the vestries in question with legal authority, if they cannot shew that they are so by prescription, by election of the parishioners, or that they derive their power from express parliamentary enactment.

† And it is equally remarkable, that during the disputes pending forty years between the parishes, no question was raised, as we are aware of, as to the validity of the old vestry. It was so natural to resort to this, as a counteraction to the tyranny it exercised over Bloomsbury.

unavailing, consisting, as they do, of sixteen only, whilst the Select in number amounts to seventy four. Hence the attendance of those officers degenerates into a mere nominal duty, and they are usually treated with as little ceremony as menials, when they have met on these occasions twice a year—the only opportunity the overseers have been allowed to enter that august assembly.

Thirdly:—The Act prescribes no rule for making rates and assessments, they are left to the caprice of the Select, and are exacted with the most disgraceful inequality, as I shall hereafter exemplify. The parties however who feel themselves aggrieved have the privilege afforded them of appealing to the Quarter Sessions at their own costs, whilst the respondents, who impose the rates complained of, pay theirs out of the parish funds.

With such disadvantages there is but little temptation to seek redress; and this and other reasons contribute effectually to induce the oppressed parishioner to sit down quietly under the injury, tamely suffering the money to be extracted from his pocket by this self-elected junto, having no voice in its distribution. Can despotism be carried farther than this in a state priding itself on its freedom?

Fourthly:—But nothing in the act exhibits such palpable inefficiency, as the clause which interdicts officers from furnishing contracts of

" goods, materials, or provisions for their own profit in the maintenance of the poor." It imposes no penalty on those who offend, and is therefore constantly violated with impunity. The offence being indictable, acts as a security to the offender; there being no instance, that I am aware of, of the vestry resorting to such a mode of punishment.

Having thus far adverted to the several acts of parliament applicable to these parishes, and which have invested the anomalous 'Select' with power, under the presumption of their being legally appointed by prescription or otherwise, we may now enter upon some historical and critical inquiries as to the exercise of that authority, added to some particulars of the opposition raised against them.

There can be but little doubt of these select vestries in their varied form, ruling the district of the united parishes during more than two hundred years; and, they have done so quite independant of the inhabitant householders. Whether this arbitrary power excited remonstrance and opposition on their part, we have no earlier instance than what is afforded us by the minute on record respecting Nathaniel Chandler and John Morris. It stands, however, as a solitary fact of a departure from that culpable tameness which in parochial matters have too much disgraced the spirit that characterizes Britons.

It is true, that a laudable resistance to the encroaching attempts of St. Giles's vestry, was exerted by that of St. George's Bloomsbury during many years, (forty); but it was, after all, power contending for supremacy, and, in point of fact, of no real utility to the mass of parishioners. That secrecy, which is always a sure indication of something wrong, has been the invariable conduct of these bodies, whatever changes have arisen in their constitution, and certainly at no trifling cost to the parishioners. If sickening disgust was produced in their minds at the conduct of these men " dressed" not " in a *little* brief authority," it resulted from surmises: nothing could be elicited from a conclave, which, shunning publicity, set investigation at defiance. A few patriotic individuals in these parishes were not unobservant of the unconstitutional nature of select vestries, and watched their proceedings with a jealous eye during many years.

At length, in April 1828, what was begun in infancy ripened to maturity, and an association was gradually formed, determined to investigate the receipts and expenditure in which they were so much interested, and examine the foundation of their acquired power. A placard, explanatory of these views, was issued April

4, 1828, bearing the signature of George Rogers, of 58, High Street, St. Giles, and pretty widely disseminated, which had the intended effect of rousing the inhabitant householders of both parishes, who added subscriptions to their names, on embarking in so good a cause. One of the first measures adopted was, that of waiting upon the vestry clerk, by deputation, to demand to see the accounts.

I was selected as one of the three on this occasion; and although we had heard reports on the subject, we were not the less surprised on being told, that there were no books of parochial accounts earlier than the date anno. 1822!

Some explanation may be necessary to elucidate this supposed *hiatus*, which I will endeavour to adduce here. Mr. Parton held the office of vestry clerk, virtually, during many years, inasmuch as he had been the principal manager for Mr. William Robertson, the former vestry clerk, who died in 1814. On his decease, he succeeded him entirely; and no man could possess more influence over the joint vestry than he did during the whole of his future life, which terminated in 1822. All the accounts of the parishes were in his grasp, whether it regarded the poor, lighting, watching, paving, the taxes, burials, or the department of the law. He was a leviathan in office, holding no less than fourteen at one time; and, as he was much troubled with gouty affections, he was incapable of active exertion, and his clerks were mostly in requisition to conduct his multiform duties.

Plausible, without much apparent capacity, the authority of the vestry might be said to be concentrated in himself; he dictated and arranged the assessments and rates, and audited the accounts; at least, his assurance to the vestrymen, that he had examined and corrected them, was never doubted, and their signatures were unhesitatingly given with implicit confidence. In this way, year after year, did this inefficient vestry pass the enormous accounts of two extensive parishes; and we have no proof of any other management, or rather mis-management, during nearly 200 preceding years, since this excrescence of a vestry has usurped the reins of our parish government.

When Parton died, his accounts were found involved in confusion, many of them having been written in pencil; added to which, they were soon afterwards said to have disappeared, and consequently the first books of receipts and expenditure bear no earlier date than 1822. What became of the antecedent ones was a mere matter of conjecture, and a variety of reports were put in circulation, concerning an event so disgraceful as to be without parallel in parochial annals.

Some contended, that the vestrymen, ashamed, for once, of their confiding negligence, and finding it impossible to reconcile the difficulties these books presented in regard to the application of the parish funds, consigned them to the flames. On the other hand, the vestrymen intimated that próbably Earle destroyed them whilst he had them in his custody, as successor to Parton, to avoid the exposition which implicated them both. Such was the conflict of opinion, about which it was difficult to decide; but the impression on the public mind was, that considerable sums were discovered in them, in the shape of defalcations; it cannot therefore be surprising, if the whole occurrence, mysterious as it was, excited a strong feeling of indignation. Nothing can better illustrate the evil of select vestries, it being more than probable that one formed upon an elective principle, would have proved an effectual check on the misapplication of the parish funds, and thereby rendered the destruction of the accounts, on the principle of "dead men telling no tales," unnecessary. And, as the election of the vestry would have been salutary to the parish interests, so would that of their clerk, who ought to be annually appointed, as a test of his integrity; for if his accounts, on auditing, should be found when the year expired, neither fair nor correct, he would be driven from his seat of office, as he ought to be.*

---

* In the pamphlet entitled "Refutation of Charges against the Vestry," referred to at page 268, some observations are made relative to the application of Messrs. Rogers, Laroche, and myself, May 16th, 1828, to inspect the parochial accounts at the vestry clerk's office, and credit is taken for the Vestry giving subsequent permission, under certain limitations. It then adds, " the same paragraph that imputes to the Vestry the refusal of inspecting accounts" (alluding to a placard of Mr. Rogers), states, that " no books of account of receipts and expenditure exist prior to 1822, except the banker's book." "That the accounts were not kept in the same systimatic order that has been observed for the last seven years is true, but some credit will be allowed to the *Vestry of the present day*, for regular accounts having been kept through that period; and the accounts of few parishes in London, of equal extent and population," (there are only two, Mary-la-bonne and Pancras), will be found in a better state. From the books, or means of making out such accounts prior to 1822, copious returns have been made to the committee of the House of Commons, recently sitting. In those accounts, the receipts and expenditure of the parishes are stated from 1774 to 1828, and the balances regularly brought forward; and this is a sufficient answer to the accusation of accounts having been destroyed." Being one of the parishioners who called on Mr. Robinson, to demand a view of the accounts, I aver, that he most unequivocally gave us, in substance, the information quoted by Mr. Rogers, and we each made memorandums of it at the time. I am unwilling to impute any improper motives for this evasion, but the fact is as Mr. Rogers has stated it; and as a lover of truth, I am bound to confirm it, although I have long ceased to have any direct communication with him. It is well known that the Vestry favoured the opinion of Earle's concealing the books, or destroying them; and had it not happened that one of his clerks (Mr. Ansell), gave a different version to this affair, it is doubtful whether the required returns would have been made

The direction of our parochial affairs, owing to the indolence of the Select, has usually devolved on the vestry clerks, who by an easy transition, became the masters instead of the servants of the parishes. Security never having been required of those officers until the appointment of Mr. Robinson, they have too often practiced abuses with impunity, aided by the incautious conduct of those from whence they

---

to the committee of the House of Commons in so copious a form. When Earle was dismissed, the Vestry resolved his clerks should participate in the exclusion, and Ansell was one of them; but, like a prudent man, having the custody of the books, he would not resign them until he had made a regular inventory of the whole. Ten days, he states, were thus employed, they were so numerous; after which he delivered them to Mr. Robinson, the new vestry clerk, and to Mr. Todd, the then churchwarden, taking their receipts and vouchers for the same.

He informed me that they consisted of an immense number, dated from 1617 to 1826, and that the vestry had refused to compensate him for this necessary and laudable trouble.

As to the regularity with which the accounts have been kept during the last seven years, the abstracts published by the Vestry, on which we shall have to remark, is the best comment on that assertion.

But "the Vestry considers it is concerned with the present, not the past state of the parishes." This seems to convey an imputation on a part of that body; who, having been more or less numbered with the select since 1794 (thirty-five years), have been mindful of their duties; for, had they not been so, the vaunting here implied, futile as it is, would have had no utterance. The conclusion of this defence, under the head of "Accounts," is lame enough, and the whole is a practical illustration of the absurdity of self-elected Select Vestries.

derived their appointment. It is well known that the vestry clerks were formerly entrusted with the payment of nearly all the claims of tradesmen and others, and we know the result has no ways proved beneficial to the interests of the parishes.

The vestrymen, in 1781 and 1810, published and revised some excellent regulations for the overseers and others, entitled "Hints and Cautions" but they omitted to prescribe plans for the safe distribution of the funds entrusted to their care, and especially in reference to the relief of the poor.

I was appointed, in 1814, an overseer of the parish of Bloomsbury; and, on attending the board at the Workhouse, I was struck with the manner of conducting the relief of the casual and other poor. On the table was spread out £40 or £50, in silver; near which sat the clerk with an elevated desk before him, ready to minute down the sums paid to the paupers. A churchwarden presided at the head of the table, and the then overseers sat with him, to direct the distribution of the money. Some of the poor had one shilling, others one shilling and sixpence, and some had more given them; and the clerk, who knew them, generally offered his opinion, which guided us in the amount. In this way we were engaged, usually, from two till seven o'clock, when we adjourned, after relieving from 400 to 500 of these paupers, who consisted chiefly of the lowest and most dissolute of the Irish people. But the worst part of the affair was, the not placing a check on the monies thus distributed; neither these, nor the balance left, ever went through the scrutiny of the officers, but every thing of this kind was left to the mercy of the clerk to settle as he pleased.

These boards for relieving the poor were regularly held, at least, five times a week, where the same confiding mode was always adopted; and certainly, if a man placed in that situation might be trusted with untold gold at first, such a careless system was well calculated to corrupt him. It was, in truth, a temptation almost irresistable, and I contemplated it as portentous of much evil, and in its tendency extremely mischievous to the vital interests of the parishioners.

Several of my colleagues viewed it with the same feelings, and we conferred together on a plan to remedy the evil, but so many obstacles presented themselves, and so many doubts prevailed as to our being supported in the attempt, that we passed through the year without effecting any thing, as I am ashamed now to acknowledge. An overseer generally goes into office, with no other qualification than inexperience, and he is glad to escape hastily from his duties to his business, and he travels through his term of probation, in subserviency to the church-wardens, knowing they have usually served the office of overseer and sidesman previously, which he presumes fits them essentially to direct his conduct. If submission to the judgment of others, without due consideration, is justifiable, it finds an apology here; albeit, I am far from vindicating such a prostration of the human understanding upon abstract principles.

Any clerk so situated, had an opportunity of appropriating large sums to himself, by setting down in his book one shilling and six-pence for one shilling, and so on, as the paupers were paid, and which book was placed, as the relief proceeded, out of the sight of the officers; besides which, he had the remnant of the silver, to enable him to set down the names of many who were not relieved.

Nothing was more easy than to abstract, for his own use, a considerable sum each board day, and there had long been strong suspicions of that practice at the period alluded to, and it reflects the highest disgrace on the Vestry, in allowing such irregularity to continue uncontrouled.

I mentioned this shameful abuse to Mr. Tuely, who, a few years afterwards, was appointed overseer; and going into office with the advantage of my information, he determined to try a different course, with the aid of his brother overseers. He succeeded in gaining their concurrence, and ever afterwards, on their entering the board-room, the money was counted, and attested by them all, and the same was done on the termination of each day's duties, and has been always continued.

This regulation was determined upon in the Vestry, and adopted in direct opposition to the Select, and no doubt it has been productive of much benefit to these parishes.

It was plainly the duty of these Select Vestrymen to have laid down such a plan as would obviate peculation; they alone possessed the power of effectual controul; and their not doing so, speaks volumes against the system of rule they assumed.

It appears to have been the practice for tradesmen and others to send the accounts, due to them from the parish, to the vestry clerk, and the natural way would have been for the "Select" to send them notice to attend in the vestry to be paid in person, on their tendering their receipts. Instead of this, they gave cheques upon the parish bankers to the vestry clerk for the time being, leaving the payments to his discretion. In this way sums to a large amount passed through his hands, thereby inciting temptation where security was never given. Such recklessness cannot be too highly censured, it was too much to expect human nature capable of resisting the lure afforded it, and the consequence has been most injurious to the parishes. Report says that these disinterested vestrymen formerly paid no rates, and who can deny that compensation was due to them for the eminent services they have so faithfully conferred upon the confiding parishioners!

CHAPTER IX.

Parochial Abuses continued—Poor's Rate and Misapplication critically examined—Partial and unequal Assessments—Audit Committee and Gallindo's Report—Whitton Estate, and Parish Jobs—Vestry Mismanagement—Progress of Reform, and a variety of miscellaneous information.

BEFORE we enter upon the extravagant waste of the public money of the parishioners, as evinced in the accounts extant, it is necessary the whole of them, as abstracted by order of the vestry, should be presented to the readers.

It is however necessary to premise, that the publication of these abstracts was never permitted till 1822; and as the books, prior to that date, have been withheld, we have no means of ascertaining what occurred at former periods. Even the abstracts in question were, not intended for the prying inquisition of the parishioners at large, they were distributed to the vestrymen, and to the officers only, prior to the determined opposition the vestry encountered in 1828. That select body, it should be remembered, resisted their being printed during many years, until the commendable perseverance of one individual amongst them finally triumphed. Mr. Parton used to present to the churchwardens a manuscript abstract annually, drawn up very loosely, and this comprised all the information he condescended to give, and they, and the Vestry, were the only persons favoured with it, meagre as it was.

Another extraordinary feature of this management, was the not appointing an audit committee until the year 1822, when they elected ten from each parish vestry, and the four churchwardens. The institution of such a committee, from their own body, was both suspicious and ill calculated to be useful to the parishes. Upon what principle but despotism, and a contempt for the inhabitant householders, could a body of men presume to sit in judgment on their own acts, by auditing their own accounts?

But without pursuing an inquiry into the injustice involved in such an appointment, about which every candid mind must come to the same conclusion, we proceed to give the analysis of the yearly accounts, reserving our farther observations on the glaring mistakes of this committee in their ministerial capacity.

The gross rental, as applicable to St. Giles's parish, is stated at much below the real amount, from a system of partiality which seems interminable in its operation, unless Bloomsbury insists upon a remedy in language not to be misunderstood. It is an incontrovertible fact, that whilst the new part of the parish is rated at nearly a rack rental, the old part is scarcely rated upon the average at three-fifths.*

It is competent for any parishioner to inspect the rate books whenever he pleases at the clerk's office, at the Workhouse, when he may make his own comparisons and comments as he notices the various assessments. From George Street to a few doors east of Kingsgate Street, comprising the north side of Broad Street, St. Giles, in a line east of Holborn, is in Bloomsbury parish, whilst the opposite or south side of those streets is in St. Giles's parish. He will find in almost all instances houses of the same description assessed on the former side at least two-fifths higher than the latter. Mr. Mills, the present churchwarden, lives at No. 110, High Holborn, and is assessed at £75, whilst an opposite neighbour, with premises equally extensive, is assessed at £36. Examine the rate book in reference

---

* The king's collectors are the assessors, and the poor's rate is regulated in these parishes by them, which is an inversion of the law; the king's assessment being usually founded on the rates made for the poor.

The irregularity of assessments tends to inflict great injustice upon the rate-payers who are fully assessed, in consequence of their having to pay the proportion unpaid by those who are under assessed.

to Lincoln's Inn Fields, Great Queen Street, Drury Lane, and all the intermediate neighbourhood from the vicinity of the Seven Dials south, to Great Russell Street north, and from the east side of Tottenham Court Road to near Chancery Lane, and there will be found abundant proofs of my position. The houses in the elder parish compared with Bloomsbury are as three to two, and yet the former is capriciously placed on a rental of only £126,196 : 10s. and the other at the excessive one of £137,949 : 10s.! A thoughtless parishioner of the favoured parish, uninformed by reflection, would say, yes, it is true that we are not placed on an equal footing with you, but consider what a number of small houses are found in our streets and courts. I admit the premises of this argument, but not the deductions drawn from them. Bloomsbury too has many small tenements, although it abounds with houses of consequence, but it has no legitimate claim to the honour of being taxed beyond the reasonable proportion of equity. Let the elder parish be viewed with just discrimination, and a greater number of consequential houses will be discovered, sufficient to counterbalance any weakness deducible from such reasoning. Take a survey of the streets already named, and then advance to the north side and part of the south side of Great Russell Street; from thence, after taking the adjacent street, proceed to Bedford Square, Gower Streets, Alfred Place, North and South Crescents, &c. &c. The result will convince a common observer, that under every circumstance, St. Giles's parish is assessed on the lowest computation at upwards of £40,000 a year too low.

This is a monstrous state of injustice, against which Bloomsbury has a just cause for complaint; and it is surprising to find such a disposition on the part of the favoured to blink this question. With patriotic exertions to lessen abuses, they have not shewn themselves hostile to this existing evil of the greatest magnitude. Nothing is more obvious on this subject than the constant selfish conflict of St. Giles's parish against Bloomsbury: it has been evinced during many years; nor can I hope that the interests of the latter will be fairly comprehended, now the triumph over the Select Vestry system seems completed. Accustomed to the privilege of being favoured in their assessments, these advocates for elective vestries, in the fruition of their hopes and expectations, will still deem it *ill timed* to place themselves on an equal footing with the younger parish. Let the inhabitant householders of Bloomsbury look to this, if they value their too long neglected rights, and let them no longer submit to a gross unreasonable partiality which oppresses them.*

---

* A placard was issued by Mr. Rogers, dated 1828, which contains this singular admission. "The consequence of this select and pernicious mode of parochial government, has been a system of jobbing, extravagance, and defalcation, and to such an extent, that, in order to support the expense, it has been necessary to assess the greater part of the houses, *particularly those in the squares and adjacent streets*, to such an exorbitant amount, that the sums paid for parochial taxation, absolutely exceed the demands of the government; consequently many reputable inhabitants have been driven from these to the neighbouring parishes, where the parochial funds are administered with economy."

In a letter from the same hand, addressed to the gentlemen of the Russell Institution, dated January 31, 1829; he says, "The contest hitherto has been almost wholly by the means and exertions of the tradesmen of the parishes, the gentlemen (with some few, but splendid exceptions,) having taken but little part in the matter; and this apathy appears the more extraordinary, as it is well known that the houses in the squares and the adjacent streets, *are rated most unjustifiably high, compared with the other parts of the parishes, and also with most disgraceful inequality, as compared with each other.* It cannot, for one moment, be supposed that the gentlemen of the parishes can be satisfied with a system, entailing upon them the enormous rates that they are now paying, or with that principle of self-election," &c.

Mr. Thiselton, in a pamphlet before referred to (see page 7), so long back as 1812, viewed this evil in the same light. He says, "a portion of the parish has been recently built upon, and some of the parishioners are rated even beyond their rack rent, while others are considerably below it."

Practical experience in my profession, has elicited numerous facts in corroboration of these sentiments; and, during nearly twenty years, have I complained of this shameful abuse. At the first general meeting of the inhabitant householders, held at the Freemason's Tavern, June 23, 1828, I moved a reso-

Almost invariably too highly rated,. there are discrepancies even in Bloomsbury which require correction, it being no uncommon case for houses, situate in Great Coram Street, and other streets adjacent, exactly of the same description and size, being placed unequally in the collector's books. In Bernard Street there are two gateway houses, exactly similar, the one is charged at £54, and the other at £36!! whilst there are two corner houses, num-

---

lution expressive of the evil, which passed without a dissentient voice. Strange to say, it was suppressed afterwards at a small meeting of the committee: the selfish members of St. Giles's parish were probably afraid of being placed on an equality with Bloomsbury, which, sooner or later, they must be, however repugnant to their views.

That Mr. Rogers, who had been my friend during many years, entertaining similar sentiments, should consent to such a procedure without giving me notice, is most unaccountable. In justice to myself, I feel it a duty to here enter my protest against conduct as inconsistent as it was offensive.

Having discharged my conscience so far, it is not my intention to add one more word on the subject; whilst, with a disposition averse to flattery, I hasten to bear testimony of my high sense of the integrity and active perseverance which that gentleman has displayed, in promoting the best interests of these parishes. To him we are indebted for the extinction of a vestry despotism, which, having no claims to the power assumed, had become odious by its conduct. Since he has taken the office of churchwarden, his vigilance, in connection with his worthy colleagues, in effecting reforms of abuses which had so long tainted the parochial government, are far above any praise of mine; and he, and they, have only to continue the good work, to live for ever in the estimation of their fellow parishioners.

bers 42 and 43, in the same street, of the same depth and frontage, except that the former has considerahle premises attached, extending into Everett Street; 42 is assessed at £72, the other at £90! Twenty years ago the inequality I complain of made a strong impression on my mind, and I made my way to the then vestry clerk, to remonstrate upon it. I was assured it was about to be regulated, and still the grievance exists in full force, as it ever will, if it is not resolutely resisted; and I presume to offer these few hints to the consideration of the occupants of the many respectable parts of Bloomsbury, because I am aware they have not, by their interference, made themselves acquainted with the extent of the evil they endure, under a system founded on shameful partiality. By this system, one householder is made the victim (if I may be allowed the term) of his neighbour, instead of applying that equal pressure by which the burthen should be borne by all.*

---

* If no other remedy can be applied, parliamentary interference ought to be sought for; indeed, it seems extraordinary that some general enactment has not been made to obviate an evil so extensively mischievous. It has recently been agitated at Manchester, Liverpool, Leeds, and other parts of the kingdom, and it was particularly recommended to the grave consideration of the legislature, by the committee who sat on the poor laws, in 1816.

According to Parton, who had the best means of obtaining information, "the number and expenses of the poor of this parish (St. Giles) at different periods, are only to be estimated by circumstances, except in occasional instances.

	£	s.	d.
In the year 1642, the amount received for church, parish, and poor, was	123	16	7
The whole disbursement for poor was £55 13 3			
Ditto for church and parish 41 6 3	96	19	6
So that there remains in the accountant's hands...	£26	17	1
1642. There was disbursed for the poor.....	173	3	4
1676. There was disbursed to them by the churchwardens ...£446 12 7			
Ditto ditto by the overseers...1320 0 0	1766	12	7
1677. The whole amount disbursed was	2163	3	10
1817. Its amount was no less than the enormous sum of............................	£39,116	9	0

If any one will be at the trouble to cast up the probable results of each year's receipt, founded on the assessments, he will find an average deficiency annually, amounting to upwards of £5,796 15s. 6d. arising from vacated houses and other causes, one of which is described thus emphatically by Mr. Rogers. "The assessing the houses so high, whereby many of the respectable inhabitants have been driven into the neighbouring parishes."

An audit committee has no claim to utility, if it sanctions accounts, and passes them without minute examination, aided by the production of vouchers. Without professing to know any thing of its former correctness, on reverting to the abstract ending Lady-day, 1827—the very first lines are as follows:—

	£	s.	d.
" To balance stated Lady-day, 1826............	6089	19	9
Deduct error, as adjusted in cash book, page 291	1774	5	4
Leaving real balance only	£4309	14	5

A more extraordinary statement was, perhaps, never put in circulation by men invested with ample power to scrutinize at leisure accounts under their charge as auditors. It is in truth a facetious specimen of the united abilities of no less than twenty-four vestrymen, if we include the four churchwardens, rendered so by virtue of their office. Did they think it part of their duty to exercise carelessness in their vocation? A schoolboy, with a competent knowledge of arithmetic, would have been inexcusable, had he made an error of less magnitude; and what excuse can they find for a mistake so flagrant? On every view of the subject, great inattention is apparant, whatever palliation is offered in its justification.

On turning to the cash book (page 291), I discovered that the auditors had admitted their incompetency, by calling in the aid of Mr.

Gallindo, the chancery accomptant, to correct their blunders, for which service he was paid from the parish funds, no less than £60! I copied his adjusted statement as follows, but I own I do not comprehend it, nor did Mr. Robinson's clerk, at the time I did so.

	£	s.	d.
September 30, 1826. By excess of balance at Midsummer, 1823	963	11	4
By difference paid Perry, £148 10s. 3d. By bankers	128	17	3
By ditto paid Warburton £290 13s. 6d. Ditto by ditto	153	10	0

1824. Deductions from alms-women, June	£174	12	0			
Ditto ditto, September	87	6	0			
Ditto, ditto, ditto	87	6	0			
1824. Ditto, March	44	13	0			
Ditto, ditto	174	12	0	568	9	0
In banker's hands				5542	12	9
In churchwarden's hands				300	0	0
In the governor of the Workhouse's hands				40	0	0
Apparent balance	£7656	18	1	£7697	0	4
Real balance	5882	12	9			
Error	£1774	5	4			

Such is the verbatim copy of their accountant's £60 report, which it should seem is entirely applicable to the late vestry clerk's deficiencies, part of which are best understood under the almshouse and audit committees report.*

---

* That report demonstrates that Earle had the collection of rents of that charity, and that from 1822 to 1826, he had not

The mal-appropriation of this servant of the "Select," is supposed to have amounted in the whole to full £2,000, and we see the admitted sum is not far short of that amount; and as he filled the office only four years, the loss to the parish was little short of £500 per annum!!

I found, on looking to another part of the cash book, the following entry, which ought to be recorded as another instance of misapplication. "May 18, 1827, Mr. B. Walker, repayment of money surreptitiously obtained from him by the late vestry clerk, by order of the vestry, 17th instant, £80."

This appropriation of the poor's funds, the property of the parish, is an utter dereliction of honest conduct, and cannot be too strongly reprobated; it is the act of adding one fraud to another, there being no semblance of justice in their paying private debts with funds not their own, but under their charge. In a moral point of view, I contend this is as unjustifiable as the frauds which they impute to Earle.*

---

accomp:ed for £700 2s. which is £131 13s. more than is set down in Mr. Gallindo's statement. I may add here, that Mr. Rogers and myself complained of this statement, as not evincing necessary clearness, when his report at large was refused us!

* I am most anxious not to misstate anything which comes under my notice, but, according to my view, the following result may be

We have now pointed out some of the mistakes of an audit committee, specially instituted to detect errors, instead of creating them.

It consisted of a number equal to any purpose for which it was formed, and it possessed the exclusive advantage of commanding all the necessary facilities, to enable them to fulfil their duties correctly. With all these opportunities, we find them blundering on from Midsummer, 1823, to Lady-day 1826, when they suddenly found it necessary to retrace their steps, with the assistance of an eminent accountant. It was to have been expected, that henceforward caution would have guided them, and that no future errors would have marked their conduct.—No such thing, for in the very next abstract issued to Lady-day, 1828, a more palpable one than the one complained of was inserted. On referring to the preceding abstract to Lady-day, 1827, it will be seen that the balance is stated as follows:—

drawn from the accountants statement, as applicable to the late vestry clerk.

	£	s.	d.
The defalcations admitted amount to	1774	6	4
Omission in almswomens' funds	131	13	0
Payment to Walker by vestry	80	0	0
	£1985	18	4

Query. Why have not Shelton's school rents, amounting to £162, and unaccounted for, been mentioned in the statement?

	£	s.	d.
Total expenditure	34395	13	2
Balance	6090	14	9
	£40486	7	11

	£	s.	d.
In the abstract of Lady-day, 1828, the above balance was brought forward in a reduced form, making it only	3878	2	1
Thereby sinking no less a sum than	2212	12	8

This extraordinary mistake might have passed unnoticed, but for the spirit of inquiry prevalent at this juncture, it never being intended to render these abstracts subject to general notice. The anti-vestry association deemed it their duty to circulate an exposition of it, and the public notice consequent thereon, is presumed to have induced the audit committee to recal the obnoxious document, and issue another, in which the original balance, viz. £6,090 14s. 9d. was restored!!!

"——————Power usurp'd
Is weakness when opposed; conscious of wrong,
'Tis pusillanimous and prone to flight."

After such specimens of incompetency, we may fairly pronounce the audit committee of the vestry essentially useless, and even worse than useless, because, in assuming to correct mistakes, it engenders them.

We will now notice somewhat in detail the abstract of the seven years receipts and expenditure: first premising, that the average number of paupers in the house during that period, will be found to amount to 888.

COMPARATIVE ACCOUNT

FOR

RELIEF OF

FOR THE

ENDING LADY-DAY 1823, 1824,

SUMMARY OF

	1822, Ending Lady-day 1823.	1823, Ending Lady-day 1824.
	£. s. d.	£. s. d.
In the House:		
Food	5,317 0 5½	5,904 2 6½
Fuel	125 1 0	1,639 0 2
House Expenses	596 17 2	605 6 3½
Clothing	3,074 1 3½	2,478 1 9
Infirmary	937 12 4½	996 3 9½
In the House	10,560 12 3½	11,622 9 3½
Out of the House:		
In Weekly, Monthly, Infant & Casual Poor, &c.	17,082 1 16½	17,503 16 9
Connected with the Maintenance:		
Salaries, Allowances, Law Expenses, &c.	4,399 4 6	5,713 9 4½
Not connected with the Maintenance:		
County Rate, Poundage, &c.	5,179 1 4	2,903 19 11½
	37,221 0 2	37,743 15 4
RENTAL OF THE PARISHES—	£.	£.
St. Giles in the Fields } St. George Bloomsbury }	263,616	263,234

N.B.—The Assessment is made on

OF THE EXPENDITURE

THE

THE POOR

YEARS

1825, 1826, 1827, 1828, AND 1829.

EXPENDITURE.

1824, Endg. Lady-day 1825.	1825, Ending Lady-day 1826.	1826, Ending Lady-day 1827.	1827, Ending Lady-day 1828.	1828, Endg. Lady-day 1829.
£. s. d.	£. s. d.	£. s. d.	£. s. d.	£. s. d.
7,072 6 5	6,428 0 2½	6,500 2 8¼	7,000 8 2	6,393 10 8
881 3 0	745 14 2	830 15 2	894 18 2	835 16 5
789 1 8	611 9 0	403 15 2½	650 16 11	639 4 8
3,149 19 8	2,301 13 6¼	1,554 11 3½	2,342 19 7	1,515 11 1
927 7 8	829 15 0	743 17 9¼	727 9 3½	649 2 8
12,739 18 5	10,919 11 11¾	10,033 2 1½	11,616 12 1½	10,682 5 6
18,211 19 11	15,465 4 4	17,452 6 10	19,354 11 2	21,085 2 4¾
6,048 6 3	5,150 13 5¼	3,358 4 10½	5,095 14 5¼	4,922 18 7½
4,551 6 2	3,950 4 3½	3,551 19 4	3,782 8 3	3,755 3 2½
41,551 10 9	35,390 19 8	34,395 12 2	39,849 6 0	39,848 9 5
£. 264,770	£. 264,770	£. 2, 7764	£. 240,822	£. 240,134

Nine-tenths of the Gross Rental.

* This is copied from the preceding Year, the Annual Return being lost.

Account of the Expenditure for the Years ending Lady-Day,

1822, 1823, 1824, and 1825.

In the House;	1822, Ending Lady-day 1823.			1823, Ending Lady-day 1824.			1824, Ending Lady-day 1825.			1825, Ending Lady 1826.	
	£.	s.	d.	£.	s.	d.	£.	s.	d.	£.	s.
Food:											
Flour for Bread, Puddings, &c....	2,027	19	0	1,397	0	0	2,275	10	0	2,096	10
Oatmeal, Barley, Peas, &c.	137	0	3	205	16	3	278	3	11	313	5
Meat	1,271	11	8	1,247	2	3½	1,530	4	7	1,430	15
Butter	41	19	7½	113	12	4½	66	11	6	83	18
Cheese	334	0	0	760	6	6	850	3	4	706	19
Milk	233	8	9	201	9	9	266	4	7	254	5
Grocery...............	218	4	0	273	11	3	288	6	5	248	12
Table Beer	1,247	4	0	1,149	12	0	1,132	4	0	847	4
Vegetables	53	13	5½	246	7	9	164	6	11	222	19
Salt & other Articles of the nature of Food..........	131	12	6	172	16	2½	87	4	0	65	9
Allowance to Officers in lieu of Tea, Sugar, &c and of Pence to Poor Persons in lieu of Meat ...	120	7	2½	146	14	2	149	7	2	158	0
Fuel:											
Coals	—			1,407	11	9	708	1	0	602	5
Candles...............	20	1	0	110	13	6	78	8	0	60	8
Oil	115	0	0	112	3	11	94	14	0	86	1
House Expences:											
Soap	117	0	0	114	0	0	181	0	0	188	10
Furniture...........	359	19	4½	367	18	2	422	10	8	320	13
Starch, Blue, Sand, Brooms, & other Incidents	119	17	9½	123	8	0½	105	11	0	102	5
Clothing:											
Clothes	356	11	1	227	16	10	353	6	9	223	11
Woollen Drapery	229	5	5½	85	12	9	35	5	3	—	
Linen Drapery ...	1,206	4	5½	1,107	18	5½	1,600	9	2	959	9
Hosiery & Haberdashery	342	0	10	393	13	3	539	0	7	432	6
Shoes, Leather &c	863	15	9½	623	10	0	552	4	2½	640	15
Incidents	74	4	3	109	10	5½	99	13	8½	55	10
Carried forward	9,622	19	11½	10,627	5	7½	11,812	10	9	10,080	16 1

	Ending Lady-day 1823.			Ending Lady-day 1824.			Ending Lady-day 1825.				
	£.	s.	d.	£.	s.	d.	£.	s.	d.	£.	s.
Brought forward	9,622	19	11¼	10,627	5	7¼	11,812	10	9	10,069	16
INFIRMARY EXPENCES:											
Wine and Spirits	213	16	10	238	19	6	154	8	0	102	9
Porter	272	1	5	289	16	10½	334	8	2	328	6
Drugs and Surgical Instruments	351	3	5½	271	13	6	251	18	8	234	11
Incidents	100	10	8	194	13	9	186	12	10	163	18
Out of the House:											
Weekly & Casual Poor	9,571	10	7½	8,382	6	9	8,980	17	0	7,585	19
Poor Housekeepers' Monthly Pensions	1,351	2	0	1,400	1	0	1,322	6	0	1,242	19
Poor Persons settled by Servitude &c.	2,306	14	0	2,287	2	6	2,196	12	6	1,725	15
Allowance to Mothers of Bastards	941	2	6	912	13	0	903	13	8	705	9
Infant Poor at Nurse in the Country	1,952	9	1	2,114	4	1	2,633	2	11	2,074	0
Lunatic Poor	59	3	7	1,052	14	9	799	12	4	728	12
Refractory Poor	318	16	2	551	5	11	702	13	3	614	6
Suspended Orders and Orders of Sessions	26	6	6	40	6	6	28	6	9	21	11
Pensioners residing in other Parishes	334	0	8	442	13	6	395	2	6	538	10
Occasional Allowances to Poor Persons	151	11	9	265	3	2½	207	16	8	135	10
Incidents	59	5	0	45	5	6	41	16	4	33	14
Connected with the Maintenance:											
Salaries	1,454	14	8	1,633	10	6	1,993	12	6	1,698	19
Wages to Servants, Gratuities, &c.	1,039	18	3¼	930	18	7	884	18	9	830	11
Law Expences	100	1	7	57	11	8	244	17	9	595	15
Removal of Paupers, Warrants, &c.	260	2	9	388	10	10	396	6	6	334	2
Funeral Expenses Coffins, &c.	176	15	0	240	3	4	295	1	10	220	5
Rent, Taxes, and Insurance	171	0	0	205	14	0	210	5	0	292	10
Building & Repairs	785	12	1½	1,498	16	1¼	1,163	17	10	476	11
Materials for Repairs done by Paupers	230	4	1½	425	6	2	98	16	7	13	8
Apprenticing Poor Children	99	0	4	177	5	0	392	15	7	328	12
Incidents	81	15	10	155	13	2	367	13	11	368	17
Carried forward	32,041	18	10	34,839	15	4½	37,000	4	7	31,465	14

	1822, Ending Lady-day 1823.			1823, Ending Lady-day 1824.			1824, Ending Lady-day 1825.				
	£.	s.	d.	£.	s.	d.	£.	s.	d.	£.	s.
Brought forward	32,041	16	10	34,820	15	4½	37,000	4	7	31,485	14
Not connected with the Maintenance:											
Collectors' Poundage	Deducted from the amount of Receipts.										
County Rate*	4,258	0	10	1,812	19	2	3,472	2	3	3,752	11
Expenses of, and Allowances to Churchwardens and Overseers	Included under Incidents.										
Fire Engines and Rewards, &c.	220	11	6	344	16	8	296	7	6	360	13
Bibles, Prayer Books, & School Books	31	13	9	—			—			—	
Printing, Stationery, Advertisements, &c.	152	4	4	247	2	0½	445	0	0	467	9
Incidents	409	11	8	499	2	1	344	16	5	274	10
Visitation Dinner	—			—			—			30	0
Total	37,221	0	2	37,743	15	4	41,551	10	9		
Rate per Pound.	s.	d.		s.	d.		s.	d.		s.	d.
First Half-year	1	9		1	9		2	0		2	3
Second Half-yr.	1	6		2	3		2	3		2	0
	3	3		4	0		4	3			

* It has been stated, on the authority of the Treasurer, that a County Rate of one halfpenny in the pound, produces the enormous sum of 19,000 £!

Account of the Expenditure for the Years ending Lady-day,

1826, 1827, and 1828.

In the House:	1826, Ending Lady-day 1827.			1827, Ending Lady-day 1828.			1828, Ending Lady-day 1829.		
	£.	s.	d.	£.	s.	d.	£.	s.	d.
FOOD:									
Flour for Bread, Puddings, &c.	1,777	3	6	2,302	9	2	2,286	16	6
Oatmeal, Barley, Peas, &c.	317	3	6	265	7	6	319	17	9
Meat	1,754	10	9	1,721	2	6	1,666	5	8
Butter	67	7	2	66	5	4	57	10	2
Cheese	671	16	8	702	10	6	671	19	0
Milk	264	7	1	342	16	0	268	10	6
Grocery	230	2	9	241	19	0	188	11	0
Table Beer	991	4	0	908	6	6	616	19	2
Vegetables	252	7	4	257	15	2	205	9	0
Salt and other Articles of the nature of Food	47	11	9	61	15	7	30	7	6
Allowance to Officers in lieu of Tea, Sugar, &c. and of Pence to Poor Persons in lieu of Meat	136	8	11½	130	0	11	241	5	5
FUEL:									
Coals	607	6	0	591	4	6	571	11	8
Candles	52	7	6	77	0	6	55	15	0
Oil	171	1	8	226	13	2	248	9	9
HOUSE EXPENCES:									
Soap	194	0	0	227	12	10	64	14	2
Furniture	245	7	3	360	8	9	453	4	6½
Starch, Blue, Sand, Brooms, and other Incidents	54	7	11½	62	15	4	19	5	6½
CLOTHING:									
Clothes	114	11	7	420	17	6	—		
Woollen Drapery	48	3	10	35	18	6	269	15	4
Linen Drapery	427	4	11	656	3	7½	628	0	2
Hosiery & Haberdashery	306	18	11	259	15	2	207	9	10
Shoes, Leather, &c.	506	17	7	717	0	2	364	11	4½
Incidents	70	14	5½	52	6	7	45	14	2½
Carried forward	9,265	4	4½	10,889	2	10	9,433	2	10

	1826, Ending Lady-day 1827.	1827, Ending Lady-day 1828.	1828, Ending Lady-day 1829.
	£. s. d.	£. s. d.	£. s. d.
Brought forward	9,289 4 4¼	10,689 2 10	9,433 2 10
INFIRMARY EXPENCES			
Wine and Spirits	98 8 0	111 14 8	100 10 6
Porter	263 1 7½	217 17 2¼	194 13 1½
Drugs and Surgical Instruments	281 12 1	271 12 6	149 8 10½
Incidents	100 16 1	126 4 11	204 10 2
Out of the House :			
Weekly and Casual Poor	9,417 2 9	9,710 15 7	10,267 8
Poor Housekeepers' Monthly Pensions	1,106 13 6	1,084 12 0	1,150 10
Poor Persons settled by Servitude, &c.	1,381 0 0	1,277 0 0	1,563 19
Allowance to Mothers of Bastards	490 15 4	1,225 15 9	1,932 15
Infant Poor at Nurse in the Country	2,311 18 0	3,315 17 3	3,056 8 2
Lunatic Poor	878 9 6	751 0 0	892 7 6
Refractory Poor	932 12 2	1,225 9 0	1,287 11 0
Suspended Orders and Orders of Session	55 5 9	31 16 0	125 12 9
Pensioners residing in other Parishes	681 7 6	519 10 6	482 16 5
Occasional Allowances to Poor Persons	162 2 3	194 2 1	214 3 2¼
Incidents	36 0 10	18 13 0	14 3 0
Connected with the Maintenance :			
Salaries	2,465 3 6	1,931 13 1	2,025 13 8
Wages to Servants, Gratuities, &c.	628 7 0	589 3 2	713 16 0
Law Expences	59 5 3	69 8 3	902 3 9
Removal of Paupers, Warrants, &c.	373 7 7	343 7 1	297 15 5
Funeral Expences, Coffins, &c.	154 4 5	248 15 5	79 3 1½
Rent, Taxes, and Insurance	180 8 3	198 17 3	231 6 0
Building and Repairs	267 7 0	850 10 5	118 19 10
Materials for Repairs done by Paupers	2 11 8	2 1 0	—
Apprenticing Poor Children	93 0 0	98 6 0	113 6 0
Incidents	114 10 2½	100 5 5½	80 11 3¼
Fees for Burials	—	559 10 4	360 3 4
Whitton Land	—	103 17 0	
Carried forward	30,843 13 10	36,066 17 9	36,693 6 5¼

	1826, Ending Lady-day 1827.			1827, Ending Lady-day 1828.			1828, Ending Lady-day 1829.		
	£.	s.	d.	£.	s.	d.	£.	s.	d.
Brought forward	30,843	13	10	36,066	17	9	36,093	6	5½
Not connected with the Maintenance:									
Collector's Poundage	—			311	13	11	460	11	0
County Rate	2,465	9	5	2,083	1	3	2,226	13	0
Expences of, and Allowances to Churchwardens and Overseers	—			162	5	5	182	13	11
Fire Engines & Rewards, &c.	288	5	0	130	5	0	260	0	6
Bibles, Prayer Books, and School Books	—			17	2	6	0	19	0
Printing, Stationery, Advertisements, &c.*	480	12	11	521	11	9	450	5	9
Incidents	298	6	9	281	16	8	123	4	2½
Alms Houses	9	5	3	298	14	8	31	14	10
Visitation Dinner	30	0	0	—			—		
Perambulation	50	0	0	—			—		
Interest to Bankers	—			75	17	1	—		
TOTAL	34,395	13	2	39,849	6	0	39,848	9	8
Rate per Pound.	s.	d.		s.	d.		s.	d.	
First Half-Year	1	10		1	8		1	6	
Second Half-Year	1	10		1	10		1	10	
	3	8		3	6		3	4	

* This item appears excessive, but some idea may be formed on the subject, when the following articles are said to have been consumed between the 1st of April and the 21st of October, 1828, viz. 177 quires of foolscap, &c. 10 ditto ruled ditto, 30 ditto blotting paper, 21 ditto blue ditto, and 10 ditto brown—Total 248. Ink 25 pints, and pens 1125, &c. &c. A pattern of writing paper, equally good, was produced at 6s. 6d. per ream, and pens at 2s. per hundred less than the prices charged, but the overseers refused to change on the ground of its being a mere matter of pence!!
Mr. Mills affirms, that on these items a considerable sum might be saved.

Under the head of "In the House," the total expense of supporting the inmate paupers amounts during seven years to £77,574 12s. 7½d. Average per year £11,082, being somewhat more than £12 9s. 6d. per head, which seems to be a large sum for so great a body, with all the advantages of their being congregated together.*

The expense of the monthly, casual, and infant poor, during the seven years, is £126,099 8s. 3d.

The average expense annually is £9,131 17s. for the support chiefly of Irish paupers.

The following statement is founded on a published account emanating from the late vestry, which does not quite agree with some calculations I had already made, but may be supposed more correct for the purpose intended.

---

* This will be found to amount to about 4s. 10d. per week for each pauper, without adverting to salaries, wages, and other particulars. Whilst at St. James's workhouse, the expense of each pauper is said to amount to no more than 3s. 9d. per week, which I own seems incredible.

Since writing the above, it has been ascertained that the Newington paupers are comfortably farmed at 4s. 6¼d. per head, for which every thing is found them; and Mr. Mott, the master, purposes to take ours at 3s. 9d. each, on account of their number amounting to upwards of 800. The present cost is calculated at more than 6s. each, including every expense! A saving might thus be effected of £100 per week.

335

	Rate in Pound		Money received within the year.			Money expended within the year.			Assessed Rental.	Observations.
	s.	d.	£	s.	d.	£	s.	d.	£	
Balance in hand, Lady-day, 1822.			1293	9	6					Total amount on assessments during the seven years 313163 19 11
From Lady-day										Amount collected 272686 9 6
1822 to ditto 1823	3	3	37320	4	10	37221	0	2	237255	
1823 1824	4	0	34464	12	4	37743	15	4	236911	Deficiency 40577 10 5
1824 1825	4	3	43546	13	7	41651	10	9	238293	
1825 1826	4	3	42769	18	11	35390	19	0	238632	
1826 1827	4	3	36176	13	6	34396	13	2	238990	Average of seven years, about* 5800 0 0
1827 1828	3	6	39687	11	4	39849	6	0	240822	
1828 1829	3	4	37338	6	6	39848	9	8	240143	
			272686	9	6	266000	14	1		
Leaving balance, at Lady-day, 1829, £6585 15s. 6d.										* As this includes sums received for bastardy, &c. the deficiency, probably, is at least £6000 a year.

FLOUR.—This item must necessarily amount to a large annual sum, being for the support of a numerous class of paupers. The total for seven years is £14,093 8s. 8d. and the annual average more than £2,000.

It appears that neither due care has been paid to the quality nor price of the corn, ground at the Workhouse, by the paupers. Mr. Mills says, " on the 1st of June I was sworn in churchwarden, and on the day preceding I went to the Workhouse and met the other three churchwardens, when we proceeded to examine the mills, which we found inferior to the old plan of the stones. We found much flour in the bran, and much grit in the flour. The baker confessed it was impossible for him or any other person to make a good loaf out of such flour. He also informed me that thirty sacks of bran had been sold, and afterwards returned, in consequence of Mr. Pinkerton, an overseer, having discovered, on calling on the purchaser, that the flour had not been properly extracted."

This imaginary bran has since, through proper attention, *produced no less than three full sacks of flour, of which bread was made, equal, at least, to that commonly used by farmers."* He farther remarked, that the food here purchased bore a good price, and ought to be of the best quality; among which, he particularly noticed the best Carolina rice, for which 35s. per cwt. was given, when good Patna rice could be obtained at half that sum.

TABLE BEER.—The Table Beer item is on the face of the abstracted accounts a most shameful affair. In 1822 the amount is stated at £1,247 4s. 0d. when the number of paupers was 917; and on the following year £1,149 12s. 0d., when the number was 993! In 1824 the sum was £1,132 4s. 0d. when the paupers were 1,023, being 106 more than in 1822, when the sum was £115 in addition; and farther palpable inconsistencies are shown on inspection. The amount is much reduced in the year 1828, being only £616 19s. 3d. paupers 804, certainly a less number than usual, but the expense is lessened, as may be seen on comparing the accounts, nearly one half. Is this one of the good results of the public opposition to the vestry?

By the " Rules and Regulations for the management of the Workhouse," I perceive that each adult pauper is allowed eleven pints of beer weekly; and on the calculation of one-third of the paupers being so allowanced, there does not seem much objection to this last amount, after the supply necessary for servants is taken into consideration. It is manifest, however, that most of the previous charges were extravagant and wasteful, or such a reduction could not have been effected.

The whole of the articles under the head of food, are well worthy the attention of the intelligent parishioner, and he will find, what appears to me enormous charges under other items.

COALS.—In noticing, in detail, some of the items of expenditure in the abstracts, the article of Coals deserves our attention. The charge for this useful necessary, during the utmost limit of our knowledge, (seven years from 1822 to 1828, inclusive), is £4,487 19s. 11d. £641 3s. in round numbers annually. This is equal, to the purchase of upwards of 300 chaldrons, they having been purchased some years at from 35s. to 38s. by contract. Be it observed, that they are stated under the head of "In the house;" and one of the regulations of the Workhouse, by order of the vestry, is, that "no fires, but those for culinary and medical purposes, be allowed before the 1st of October, nor after the 31st of March, except in very severe weather; and that not more than one peck of coals a day be allowed to each fire."—This would be about thirty-eight bushels annually to each fire; and probably there are fifty fires so apportioned: but suppose we double them, 106 chaldrons would amply suffice, there remains therefore about 200 chaldrons to account for; out of which we have to calculate the necessary consumption for cooking, baking, washing; fires for the governor, matron, apothecary, and the board. I am not aware of any other medium of fair consumption, nor have I any wish to misstate anything willingly.

Is it not true, that the vestry rooms, churches, school-houses, and alms-houses have been supplied from the same source, and under the designation of "*in the house?*" It would be well to inquire and learn if this be the fact; for, if it be so, it is nothing less than a surreptitious appropriation, and deserving of the severest censure. The present churchwardens will do well to look to this apparent abuse.*

FURNITURE.—There is a considerable annual charge for furniture for the Workhouse, which amounts in seven years to £2,630 2s. 10d. averaging yearly more than £375. In the absence of better information, it must seem to every one a most enormous sum for paupers, especially as it does not comprise blankets, or linen, for which there is also another extravagant item of account.

---

* An examination of the cash book, on this item, will convince the candid inquirer that the interests of the parishes have not been regarded, or the sum of £642 2s. 3d. would not have been abstracted from the poor's-rate, to pay three favoured parishioners for coals, at an expense of from 51s. to 60s. per chaldron, when contracts were made at from 35s. to 38s. Could we ascertain the whole particulars, the evil would probably exceed the calculation. This obloquy, be it remembered, attaches to the rulers of the parish, and not to the individuals alluded to.

LINEN DRAPERY is an enormous part of the Workhouse expenditure, the amount during seven years being no less than £6,767 10s. 8¼d. exclusive of Woollen Drapery and Hosiery. The consumption however is not commensurate, there being a heavy stock in hand, some of which has remained in the workhouse during the last six years. An inventory has been lately taken of it, and I was astonished on reading it to observe no less than seventy-two counterpanes, fit for the middle classes of society, but too expensive and ill adapted for paupers. The report is, that a tradesman in office a few years since, loaded the house with these goods, having little regard to the interest of the parishes.

It has been stated by an overseer in office at the time, that a much higher price was given for blankets, &c. than they could be obtained at, so that the parish suffers in a double sense, first in being unnecessarily glutted, and next by paying an extravagant price for the goods.

It will be seen that in 1823 and 1824 the items amount to £2,708 7s. 7½d. and on my mentioning this to one connected with the vestry, I was told, that it had been determined that the tradesman alluded to should never form one of that body. What a consolation for the parish! I contend, however, that the tradesman is less to blame than the vestry, who, assuming to themselves the guardianship of the parish purse, ought to have prevented such an abuse.

Nothing but determined vigilance on the part of those who have parochial duties to perform, can counteract the prevalence of fraud and peculation, and our present worthy churchwardens have evinced how much may be done by official attention to their duties. Mr. Churchwarden Mills keeps a journal, by which it will be seen that he often devotes to his official duties twelve and thirteen hours a day, and seldom less than nine. He has favoured me with a sight of this invaluable memento, and by his permission I quote the following entry :—" 16th October, 1829. The matron informs me the house is clothed four times a year, but many of the paupers state they have not had an article given them for nine or twelve months. Some had four or five pairs of stockings, three of which 1 ordered to be taken away where the latter number was found. Plunder seems to prevail every where. I have insisted on the clothing of the dead paupers to be returned, but have not as yet had a satisfactory account, either from nurses, matron, or governor, but I do purpose looking into that department."*

---

* The following order, issued by the churchwardens and overseers, 21st October, 1829, is well calculated to prevent

INFIRMARY EXPENSES. The amount for wine and spirits under this head, averages nearly £150 a year, and for porter more than £271, making a total of upwards of £421!! During the several last years, it is observable, how much these amounts collectively are reduced, and especially since 1825, proving demonstratively that the parishes have not been fairly dealt with.

	£. s.
From 1823 to 1825, three years inclusive, the wine and spirits are stated at	607 4 4
During the same periods the porter is stated at	896 6 5¼*
	£1503 10 9¼

During the four following years the wine and spirits amount to	413 2 2
Ditto ditto ditto the porter to	1004 8 6¼
	£1417 10 8¼

---

peculation:—"That in future no new article of clothing will be distributed to the inmates of this workhouse, until the old have been examined, and found to be fairly worn and delivered up, when a new article will be given out in its place.

* This sum is equal to 42,965 pots of porter, or 14,322 annually, or 275 pots weekly and 25 over, or about 40 pots per day. This is a tolerable allowance for sick people, and I should doubt whether half the quantity is afforded to the large number of patients in the Middlesex Hospital. I have examined the accounts of the Mary-la-bonne workhouse from 1817 to 1826, as ordered to be printed by the House of Commons, and find no mention of porter for the sick. There is however a charge for wine and spirits, and taking the last year, (1826.)

There is one circumstance very observable, namely, *that the two first years' charge for wine and spirits is more in proportion than double the amount of every subsequent year, with the exception of 1824, and that is not equal to three fourths of the least of the two!* If these articles were essential to the restoration and comfort of the sick, none of the friends of economy would suffer a murmur to escape them, but until this can be shown, every parishioner has a right to complain of the wasteful extravagance here exhibited.

The Infirmary is a small detached building, contiguous to the workhouse, instituted for the accommodation of sick paupers, and I understand the average is about fifty; and when it is considered how many of these, from the nature of their maladies, are debarred from the use of wine, spirits, and porter, suspicion cannot but attach to these enormous items.

The amount when recapitulated during seven years, is as follows:—

	£.	s.
The amount of the former is	293	6
For the latter	94	0
	£387	6

In our parish the porter, wine, and spirits will be seen to amount collectively in another instance to £485 18s. 3d. and to £528 16s. 4½d. annually.

	£.	s.	d.
Porter	1900	15	11
Wines and spirits	1020	0	6
Drugs and surgical instruments	1812	0	6
Incidents	1077	6	6
	£5810	9	4

So that, with the strongest indications of imposition somewhere, this Infirmary is stated to cost the parish, without salaries, food, &c. £830 a year.

SALARIES.—The items Salaries, Wages, and Gratuities, form another subject of inquiry, and until we are better informed, they savour rankly of jobbing with the parish funds.

	£.	s.	d.
Salaries for seven years	12,203	6	11
Wages and gratuities	5,617	12	9½
Total	£17,820	19	8½

Being an average of £2,545 17s. per annum!!

Now, we know that the vestry clerk had £1050 per year; and we are aware that the governor, matron, and apothecary to the workhouse, and several others, have salaries and wages: but when it is considered how many of the paupers are put in requisition for general purposes, it seems quite inexplicable how such large sums can have been fairly required.

The beadles and clerks of the paving, lighting, and burial boards, it is well known, are remunerated from other funds, as also were the watchmen and others. Even Parton, who has been deemed improvident, sets down for salaries and gratuities, for the year ending at Lady-day 1814, no more than £1087 7s. 0d.! as may be seen in a copy of his yearly manuscript abstract of that year, which I happen to possess. Does this heavy expense arise from the multiform duties, which formerly were concentrated in Parton, diverging to various newly created officers? If so, the experiment which was intended to produce greater economy has failed, and the sooner the old system under proper regulations is resorted to the better.

On looking at the annual item of Wages and Gratuities, it is worth while to notice the difference between the amount in 1822 and the subsequent years, and especially to compare that year with the year 1827. The former is £1,039 18s. 3½d.; the latter £589 3s. 2d. What can occasion such an amazing difference as this?

FEES FOR BURIALS.[*]—This is an item of expenditure which has been looked at in a very praise-

---

"[*] The burial ground of St. Giles's parish is situate near Pancras old church. It is under trustees appointed by the 43rd George III. which empowered them to borrow a sum not exceeding £10,000 for making, enclosing, &c. the said ground. About from two to three acres were purchased and appropriated here for the purpose about twenty-six years since, and it is conjectured (the trustees refused showing the books) that at least thrice that sum has been borrowed in defiance of the above act, and a fresh act was imposed in 1828."

worthy manner by the present churchwardens. Since they came into office not one farthing has been allowed for the burial of the paupers; nor ought there, if it be true that the clergyman has a salary for that purpose, and that ground has been allotted by donation during many years. The audit committee has afforded us a meagre account of these fees, and they can only be noticed from the statement of 1827 and following year. In the former the sum is £559 10s. 4d. and in the latter £360 3s. 6d. total in the two years £919 12s. 10d. Why this item has been withheld in the former abstracts we are at a loss to conjecture, whether it merged in the Incidents or in what way it was disposed of, we know not, but the amount given of two years is amply sufficient to point out the abuse. Taking the average of the two years, no less a sum than £2940 has been abstracted from the parish funds during the seven; an occurrence which we trust will never be repeated.

In the returns of St. Mary-la-bonne expenditure presented to the House of Commons, I find the item, " Burial of Paupers," the amount of which during seven years to 1826 inclusive is £1,156 3s. 11d. only. I have in vain sought for other accounts for coffins and fees, and therefore conclude that the whole is comprised under that head; certainly, by comparison, very moderate, considering the extent and population of this vast parish, and where we may infer there are more funerals of paupers than in any other in the metropolis.

BUILDING AND REPAIRS, which are said to be " connected with the maintenance," well deserves the notice of the inhabitant householders, involving as they do an expense of no trifling magnitude. The amount in seven years, including £772 7s. 8½d. under the head of " materials for repairs done by paupers," is £5954 2s. 0¼d. being about £860 per annum. Now, it is plain that the workhouse and its offices only can be said to be connected with the maintenance, and we are at a loss to conjecture how such a large sum could be expended upon them. In my researches, however, I found the following particulars of sums paid by order of vestry for repairs done to Bloomsbury Church, which throws some light on the subject, *but by what figure of speech they can be said to be so connected*, I am totally at a loss to learn.

REPAIRS TO BLOOMSBURY CHURCH.

1822.
December 4th. The joint vestry ordered payment of... 500
———— 12th. Ditto   ditto.................. 100
1824.
January 3rd. Ditto   ditto.................. 1050
May 18th. Ditto   ditto.................. 500

These payments therefore in seventeen months amount to £2150

Independent of other considerations, the money ought not to have been abstracted from any other fund than a church rate for the above purpose; but this did not seem to suit the views of the vestry; the parishioners would have been excited with alarm, especially as they knew the legitimate plan for making such a rate would require the assembling of them together. Mr. Rogers, who under a judge's order has had the exclusive privilege of inspecting the vestry minutes, gives the following statement:—

" Both our churches are stone buildings, with fittings-up of oak, and are comparatively new erections, yet the repairs and fanciful alterations are a source of never-ending expense to the parishes, and of profit to the Select and their connections; for example:—

One vestryman paints St. Giles's church and charges			£477	18	4	
A second charges for glazing			112	17	0	
A third ditto for iron work			174	4	6	
A fourth vestryman furnishes curtains			285	12	9	
			£1050	12	7	
A fifth vestryman paints Bloomsbury church	£595	0	3			
A sixth ditto puts in a new window to ditto	294	5	6			
A seventh ditto furnishes upholstery, &c.	174	6	3			
Others do smaller jobs amounting to	1497	9	9			
An eighth vestryman does glazing and charges	170	6	0	2731	7	9
				£3782	0	4

Then they assemble in their secret conclave, audit their own accounts, and pay themselves *by taking the above sum out of the money raised under pretext of supporting the poor.*"*

---

* The following is a statement of monies expended on Bloomsbury Church out of the poor's rate from 1781 to 1823.

		£.	s.	d.
1781.	Sum taken was....................	861	4	8
1791.	Ditto.............................	150	0	0
1793.	Ditto.............................	650	0	0
1794.	Ditto.............................	200	0	0
1796.	Ditto.............................	529	16	3
1803.	Ditto.............................	200	0	0
1806-7.	Ditto.............................	719	8	0
1809.	Ditto.............................	1812	5	1
1817.	Ditto.............................	500	0	0
1822.	Ditto.............................	1650	0	0
1823.	Ditto.............................	500	0	0
		£7772	14	0

Nearly equal to its cost, which was £9793.

Copy of some of the Items of 1822 and 1823.—

	£.	s.	d.
Winsland, Painter	595	0	3
Doyle and Son, Stained Glass	294	5	6
Ball and Son, Repairing Organ	145	2	0
Caldecot, Uphostery	174	6	3
Southgate, Bricklayer	128	0	7
Akers, Plumber	28	2	6
Yardley, Glazier	170	6	0
Morrell, Plasterer	67	17	2
Brown and Son, Masons.....................	151	4	4
Jeakes, Ironmonger	262	0	9
Banning, Surveyor	125	15	0
	£2142	0	4

" A churchwarden (in despite of the express provisions of an act of parliament) obtained the permission of the " Select" to do some repairs that he pretended were necessary at the workhouse to the amount of £200. Upon this permission, he jobbed on until his charge was swelled to upwards of £2000, which was paid him in sums of two and three hundred pounds at a time, *so as not to excite the attention of the more honourable part of the vestry who might happen to attend.*"

INCIDENTS.—These are items of no trifling magnitude in the abstracts when collectively considered, and exceedingly useful where concealment is desired. This single comprehensive word is regularly introduced six times under different heads, which seem sufficiently enormous, and strained to the utmost, without an appendage of so mysterious an import. During the seven years these abstracts have been published, their amount is £5809 16s. 7¾d. forming a yearly average of more than £829. But what a mass of these and other unintelligible matter will meet our inquiries, if the legacy of incomprehensible accounts left us by the former vestry clerks should be hereafter exposed to the public eye! Enough however has been exhibited to assure us of the utter incompetency and wanton extravagance of these guardians of the parish purse.

WHITTON.—This single unconnected word appears in the abstract of 1826, with the sum of £103 17s. subjoined to it, and from its novel character, excited much curiosity. I therefore took the earliest opportunity afforded me (5th June, 1828), of referring to it in the ledger, and there discovered that in the year 1824, the " Select" purchased a piece of land at the above place, with the intention of founding an establishment for the illegitimate parish children, which intention was afterwards abandoned, and a place was fitted-up in its stead, at Heston.

The following items of account will show that £103 17s. is but a small proportion of its expense.

	£.	s.	d.
"February 7th, 1824. Paid Mr. Winsland purchase money paid to Mr. Foster for land at Whitton	125	0	0
Interest from 26th June, 236 days..............	4	0	8
Paid Archer, Solicitor, for conveying land and concluding sale	43	16	0
Paid Mr. Turner, for conveying of ditto to trustees"	43	5	0
	£216	1	8

It appears, by this plain statement, that the land cost the parish £125, whilst the jumble of conveying and re-conveying, amounted to more than two thirds of its value. These sums have been altogether mystified in the abstract, being merged under the convenient head, "Incidents;" and the same remark equally applies to all the following items connected with it, except only the entry of £103 17s. which refers to plans and estimates for building the children's asylum.

"From July, 1823, to April, 1824.

"First charge, made by Mr. Abraham, Architect, of Keppel Street, for making out a plan and estimate, amounting to £4,950, for building a house at Whitton, capable of accommodating 300 infant poor 61 17 0
"Second—A like charge for another plan and estimate (4,800), for 275 only 24 0
"Third—A like ditto for another ditto ditto, for 290 children 19 10 0
"Fourth—A ditto for 250 ditto"................... 17 10 0
£122 17 0

Mr. Hardwick, an Architect, in Russell Square, was employed by the vestry to tax Mr. Abraham's bill, from which he deducted 19 0 0

Leaving the sum as in abstract £103 17 0

And any one would have thought the affair ended here, nor can it be divined why the remainder is withheld.—Mr. Abraham, subsequently produced another bill, under the head of omissions, the amount of which was 12 18 9
Mr. Hardwick's fee for taxing bill, as stated above... 5 5 0
By which the deduction became only 0 16 3

As per original charge.............................. £122 17 0

All the sums exclusive of £103 17s. connected with this improvident purchase, have been mixed up with the very dubious, but useful item, " Incidents;" whereas, if they had been set forth in an intelligible form, this Whitton job would have been seen to amount to no less than £338 1s. 5d.!! Who, on reading the solitary word " Whitton, £103 17s." could have fathomed such a wasteful transaction to the parish ?*

---

* In the Refutation, the following singular defence is offered in favour of this job. "There is nothing ambiguous or secreted concerning the land at Whitton; it was purchased with the intention of erecting thereon buildings for an infant establishment, but prudent reflection determined the Vestry to prefer hiring the premises at Heston, and to avoid the expense of building. It is not true, that the land was ever the property of a vestryman"—" and it is in the temporary conveyance only that he appears the possessor. The land is still the property of the parish, conveyed to trustees, and will return its cost." The reader will judge whether the transaction could have been conducted *more ambiguously*, and it is well known that some of the vestrymen expressed much disapprobation on the subject. But we are told, *the land " will return its cost!"* Nothing can be more improbable, as the following anecdote will show :—

May 1, 1829. Mr. Mills, the new churchwarden, accompanied by Mr. Newberry, went to view, at their own expense, the parish estate at Whitton. It was with some difficulty they found it; but at length, through the intervention of an old inhabitant, they arrived at the promised land. It is situate near the seat of Sir Benjamin Hobhouse, and was an allotment of waste land under an act of enclosure, and was purchased by Mr. Fisher by public auction, who soon found he had a very hard bargain, which he was anxious to get rid of. He was relieved from his perplexity by our vestry purchasing it;

There are many expenses stated in the abstract, worthy the special notice of the intelligent parishioners; such as printing, stationery, advertisements, law expenses, &c. that appear enormous in my view, and especially after examining the St. Mary-la-bonne expenditure, before quoted *(see page* 342), which gives a total on the three first items, during seven years (to 1826), of no more than £1,804 4s. 5¼d. whilst the amount of ours is £3,172 6s. 9d. within an equal period.

My object has been to "nothing extenuate, nor set down ought in malice," but to bring the merits of our vestry government fairly before the public, that the parishioners may, by past

---

pending which, a considerable portion of that body, accompanied by the officers, went in carriages to view it, and report says, their conveyance alone came to about £14. The natives were astonished, never having seen such a cavalcade before, and were at a loss to know what it was all about. Mr. Mills states, that, from his own knowledge of land, and from the information he obtained, the utmost value of it, when let, would be about sixteen shillings per acre. Archdeacon Cambridge had let land contiguous to it at a pepper corn for two years, and after that term, at that rental. He describes it as a square plot of barren heath land, "the worst I ever saw, and not above the value of £15 per acre. It never has been levelled, filled up, or cleared of its furze, nor enclosed, although the purchaser is bound to pay the expense of making and keeping the road in repair; and to make and maintain the north-east fences, none of which have been done. I paced it, and found it contained two acres, three roods, and twenty-seven perches of land." After this statement, is it credible that this "property of the parish *will'return its value?"*

occurrences, so appreciate them, as to decide what can be done for their future advantage. They are threatened with another appeal to a court of justice, to reverse the verdict of a jury which has decided against them, and it is essentially their duty to guard against the impending evil of a resumption, which experience has shown can only be fatal to their interests. Should a new trial be granted, and the vestry succeed in its object, a fresh enactment will be necessary for the future government of this extensive district, which must embrace a variety of measures calculated to obviate the abuses so much complained of. A vestry, chosen by the voice of the parishioners paying poor rates, is clearly the one best calculated for parochial usefulness, especially when selected from men of business and leisure. But, unless they are subject to re-election at stated periods, nothing effectually useful can be expected from them; they will degenerate like their predecessors, and become reckless of the duties they undertake to perform. A vestry of the description required, should assemble the inhabitant householders upon all important occasions, instead of agitating public measures without their concurrence.* If petitions to parliament,

---

* It has long been the practice of the select of these parishes, to fill up their vacancies by appointing resident Lord Chancellors, Lord Chief Justices, Recorders, and other high legal

addresses to the king, or any other circumstance which involved general interest became requisite, our former vestry, in its supreme wisdom, and in contempt of the ignorance of the parishioners, concocted all such matters in secrecy, after which their signatures might have the honour to be appended. Assuming to be every thing by a stretch of power, that body exercised it in wantonness, by placing legality at defiance in numerous instances. By the Act of 10th of Anne, and 14th of George III. it was specially provided, that the money raised for

---

characters, passing by men calculated to be efficiently useful. It is evident that these respectable individuals have other duties to perform, entirely precluding them from parochial affairs, however urgent. The present Judge Parke candidly acknowledged from the seat of justice, a short time since, that he was an unworthy member of St. Giles's vestry, not having attended during many years. Judge Bayley, thinking it incompatible with his function, resigned; and Mr. Justice Holroyd, for the same reason, refused to be placed on the list. It is well known that these, and other eminent persons, are considered honorary vestrymen, and are seldom summoned, nor have they been aware how many irregularities have been done under the sanction of their names. It has been said, the best security a parish has, is to be found in the wealth and respectability of its residents, who form its vestry. Nothing is more true if these were regular and vigilant in their duties, but the contrary is almost invariably the fact. In these parishes, where the joint vestries have consisted of seventy-two, exclusive of the rectors and churchwardens, it has often been with difficulty that thirteen have been collected together to conduct the business. A few individuals, and those none of the wisest, have therefore usually directed, at their pleasure, the affairs of the joint parishes.

the support of the poor, should be used for no other purpose, yet this body has constantly taken from that fund whatever they pleased for the repair of the churches, the support of the alms-houses, and for various other purposes, without any sentiments of remorse.

For all other parochial expenses than that of the poor, a distinct rate is necessary; but the "select" have never thought it worth while to attend to the letter and spirit of acts of parliament; it might have proved dangerous to their power to convene large assemblies, to make rates for specific purposes, and thus the illegal practice has continued, to the great detriment of the supine inhabitants.*

It is sickening to review the conduct of a vestry so constituted, as it is to reflect on the

---

* "Although it is truly said the churches are of stone, the effects of time will render repairs necessary; and the money for defraying such expenses has, for nearly a century, been taken out of the poor's-rate, *a practice not regular it is admitted, but, in effect, making no difference to the inhabitants,* who would have to pay the same amount, whether charged in a separate rate, or in a consolidated one under the denomination of that of the poor." *(See* " *Refutation,*" *page* 27.)

This defence of an illegal practice is replete with fallacies. The wisdom of our ancestors, so often urged, no doubt contemplated how many frauds would arise by a want of adherence to the distinctive rates. Will any one believe that nothing would have been saved to the parishes, had the law not been infringed? and does the practice of nearly a century render the evil less odious?

apathy so long prevalent in these parishes, where implicit submission has been carried to its extreme point; but for this we should not have to lament so many acts of delinquency. If the joint vestry had been composed of less discordant materials, their clerks for the time being would never have assumed such authority in the government of these parishes, nor would they have occupied their situations without giving securities commensurate to the trust reposed in them.

The choice of churchwardens, fearlessly determined to attend to their duties, will render the year 1829 memorable in our parish annals, and is highly honourable to the patriotism of the inhabitant householders. This was the only privilege remaining to them; the others were absorbed in the pride of vestry power, where regret has been audibly uttered, on the parishioners being legally invested with this solitary parochial right.

The inhabitants will hereafter know how many real reforms have been effected by these officers of their choice, who, surrounded by peculation, have laboured unintermittingly to promote economy, and the best interests of their constituents. Many of their praise-worthy acts have come under my notice, but to enter minutely into them, would, at present, be premature, and I refrain.

There are several points admitted by the late vestry, which have entered into this discussion, in which all must concur. They are to be found in their "Refutation." In page 10 it is remarked, that "it needs only be put to the understanding of rational men, whether, if the whole parish were competent, business could be transacted by several thousand persons assembled together?" Certainly not, and it will, therefore, be necessary to apply to parliament for the institution of an elective vestry, on a *broad comprehensive basis*; but I would not have the thousands shut out from its deliberations *on particular weighty occasions.** This is not, however, the affair of a moment, it cannot be effected until the meeting of that assembly; and as it is now announced that a bill is in progress, it is to be hoped that it will approximate, as nearly as possible, to the wishes of the mass of the inhabitants. They will, however, sedulously watch over their own interests, cautiously avoiding the recurrence of evils they have had to conflict with.

In page 25, under the head of assessments, we are told, "if the rating of the parishes is

---

* "If, in the application that may be made to parliament, a re-modelling of the constitution of the vestry is thought advisable, those who form that body, so far from opposing, will aid the advancement of such improvements, as deliberation, caution, and wisdom may sanction. Should such improvements be thought to consist in introducing the elective principle, the vestry will feel no repugnance to its adoption." (*See* "*Refutation,*" &c. *p.* 60.)

complained of, as being grievously unequal, what reason can there be for supposing the vestry would object to the remedy, by a general assessment? According to the showing of the complaints, the vestrymen would be benefitted by the equalization; the majority of whom, as asserted in the complaining passages, are resident in those *parts rated to such an exorbitant amount.** They know that the rates are unequal, but are convinced that all great changes must be gradual to be beneficial:" and again; "the vestry is desirous of gradually introducing a new assessment."

Here is an admission of the necessity of a new assessment, but it must be *gradual*. What is implied by this portentous word, I am at a loss to conjecture. Mr. Thiselton, it has been shown, complained of this monstrous evil in 1812; and I did so at an earlier period, when

---

* I am inclined to view this representation as being too hastily made. It can be easily demonstrated, that at least twenty out of the thirty-six of the late St. Giles's vestry, are considerably under-rated; and it is probable nearly as many, by fair calculation, may be selected from those of Bloomsbury, no less than twenty-two of them being residents in the old part of the parish. It is well known that many of these, and others, formerly vestrymen, were, and are greatly benefited by this. Mr. Peter Ludgate's house, No. 200, High Holborn, was never rated higher than £28 a year; whilst in Little Guildford Street, very inferior houses, to say nothing of situation, are rated at £33. Mr. Stable's immense premises were assessed at only £100; and, in respect to the living vestrymen, let the intelligent parishioners examine the rate-books and judge.

it was promised to be remedied. Twenty years have thus elapsed, without any alteration taking place, and still we are told it is to be *gradually introduced!* The truth is, it never will be *introduced* but by the efforts of the inhabitants, as was lately the case at Stratford-le-bow. On a moderate calculation, the elder parish has been paying somewhere about £8,000 a year less than her proportion, by which Bloomsbury suffers, not only in that instance, but also in respect to the king's-taxes; and ought such a state of things to continue?

Assuming that St. Giles's parish is assessed at two-fifths less than she ought to be, as compared with Bloomsbury (£45,360), the amount is annually, during the preceding seven years, at 3s. 9d. in the pound (that being the mean average), £8,437 10s. consequently the aggregate of that period amounts to £59,062 10s.!!!

This enormous disparity may be multiplied to a considerable extent (being applicable to former periods), before we can calculate with any precision the magnitude of the evil under which Bloomsbury has suffered, and yet its inhabitants have endured these exactions regardless of the injustice, or unaware of the consequences.

"He that is robb'd, not wanting what is stolen,
Let him not know it, and he's not robb'd at all."

There is a uniform utility in parochial government, when directed to small communities; therefore, whenever parishes have arisen to considerable extent and population, they ought to undergo a division; and this argument is especially applicable to our district. Bloomsbury ought to be entirely separated from the elder parish, as was evidently contemplated by the legislature in the Act of 3 George II. cap. 19 *(see Appendix)*, whatever objections may be offered against such a measure. The great obstacle to this, is the burthensome state of the poor, especially the Irish, who occupy a considerable portion of St. Giles's parish, from which it has acquired the cant appellation of the "Holy Land."* Excluded from the aid of the opulent parish of Blooms-

---

* 1816. Mr. Montague Burgoyne, in his evidence before a committee of the House of Commons, stated that he had taken much pains to ascertain the number of Irish residents in the two parishes; the result was, that in St. Giles's he found 2,348, men, women, and children, and in Bloomsbury only 35 ditto. Finegan gave evidence of there being 6,000 Irish in the neighbourhood of George Street, and 3,000 children. How are these accounts to be reconciled? The former gentleman stated, that after a most patient inquiry, he ascertained that there were, in 1815, 6,876 Irish adults in the metropolis, and 7,288 children, making a total of 14,164.

In one Court in Mary-la-bonne, containing only twenty-four very small houses, he states he found 700 of these poor people, in a situation likely to occasion contagion. There were but few of them who had not themselves begged, or employed some in their families to do so.

bury, the burthen would be extreme, and she has reason to deprecate such an event.

I would, nevertheless, have each parish, according to the implied intention of parliament, placed in an independent state, each conducting its separate affairs; and am persuaded, that an arrangement might be made combining mutual advantage.

If it be necessary to attach a portion of St. Giles's parish to Bloomsbury, to make the burthens equivalent; or if an annual sum, in aid of the elder parish be required, let such a measure be resorted to, conformable to the provision of the Act of 43 of Elizabeth; in my humble opinion, something of this nature would operate to the benefit of the whole district. No argument can be drawn against this from the two large parishes of Mary-la-bonne and St. Pancras; they are confessedly ill managed, as all overgrown bodies ever must be.

How weak and futile are the prejudices of man! the very naming of reforms, calculated to promote the best influence on society, have been always objected to, if they interfere ever so remotely on established institutions. The improvements in the arts, and the refinements of philosophy have been opposed, because mankind have wanted leisure or fortitude to scrutinize the object of their veneration, and the prejudices by which they have been blinded.

The proposition for the severing of these parishes, on the same principle, will, I am assured, be received with similar sentiments, and it is only by being accustomed to the sound, and giving scope to reflection, that the calmness of inquiry can be expected; and I am sanguine enough to believe, that at no distant period, the hints thus thrown out will be acted upon.

But whatever may be the event in this respect, the notice just issued of an intended application to parliament for a new parochial enactment, is a signal for due exertion to counteract any attempt to place us again on the old system. That the affairs of populous parishes must be administered by a few, in the nature of a committee, must be admitted, but whatever name is given it, it ought no longer to be a self-propagating body, irresponsibly constructed. On the contrary, it should be chosen at intervals, either wholly or partially, and its proceedings should be subject to the revision of the inhabitant householders.

As this new measure originates from a vestry odious to the parishioners, it becomes the more imperative to view it with jealousy; let them therefore, be on the alert, always recollecting, that if they act with the tameness of sheep, they may expect the wolves to devour them.

CHAPTER X.

Biographical Sketches of former Residents in these Parishes — Dr. Borde—George Chapman—Duchess Dudley—The Bedford, Montague, and Southampton Families—Mrs. Thomas—and the Revolution of 1688, &c. &c.

DOCTOR ANDREW BORDE—Grainger says, "was physician to Henry VIII. and an admired wit in his reign." He was the author of "The Breviary of Health," "Tales of the Madmen of Gotham," and of the work entitled "The Introduction of Knowledge, the whych doth teach a man to speak al maner of languages, and to know the usage and fashion of al maner of countries: Dedycated to the right honourable and gracious Lady Mary, daughter of King Henry VIII." Black letter, imprinted by William Copeland, without date.

The name of merry-andrew, since so familiar, is said to be first given to Doctor Borde, on account of his pleasantries. In the latter part of his life he grew serious, and took upon him the order of a Carthusian Monk, in the Charter House, at London.

He lived on the site of Dudley Court (see page 25), but it does not appear how long he was a parishioner of St. Giles.

GEORGE CHAPMAN, one of the earliest English dramatic poets, and the first translator of the whole of the works of Horace, was probably an inhabitant of this parish, he having a Grecian monument erected to his memory here, in St. Giles's church-yard, classically constructed by his friend Inigo Jones. The stone stands above ground, against the wall, much defaced. He died in 1634, aged 77.

DUCHESS DUDLEY, or DUDDELY—So celebrated for her charities, was a parishioner more than half a century. She was third daughter of Sir Thomas Leigh, of Stoneleigh, Warwickshire, Baronet. Her mother was Catherine, daughter of Sir John Spencer, of Wormleighton, Knight, and great grandfather to Earl Sunderland. The aforesaid Sir Thomas Leigh had by the said Catherine, John Leigh, Knight, who was the father of the Lord Leigh, Baron of Stonely. Alice married Sir Robert Dudley, Knight, in 1620, son to Robert Earl of Leicester, and for his excellent merits, created a Duke by Ferdinand II. late Emperor of Germany. She was, by letters patent, dated May 20, 1635, by Charles I. advanced to the title of a Duchess. She had five daughters, one only of which survived her, the widow of Sir Richard Levison, Knight, who was the picture of her mother in piety and goodness. The Duchess was born at Stonely, where there is a catalogue of her charities, to the reparation of the church, rebuilding it, and the ornaments of the altar. There her body lies entombed; and besides her charities to her native town, many others are recorded of her, and of her augmentation of poor vicarages. She purchased a fair house and garden for the incumbent of St. Giles, where her benefactions were neither few nor small.

Doctor Boreman, in his funeral Sermon, speaking of her, says, "She was a magazine of experience—her vast memory, which was strong and vigorous to admiration, was the storehouse and treasury of observation and knowledge of occurrences for many years; so that I have often said that she was a living chronicle, bound up with the thread of a long spun age. And in divers accidents, and things relating to our parish, I have often appealed to her stupendous memory, as to an ancient record. An enlargement of her estate she never desired by the addition of a jointure, but moving in the sphere of her own fortune, and contenting herself with the portion God had given her, she clave only to him. In short, I would say to any desirous to attain some degree of perfection, *vade ad sancti Egidij oppidum et disie Ducissam Dudleyam.*"—" Come to St. Giles, and inquire the character of Lady Dudley."

She is mentioned further in the Biographia Britannica, 1812, which in the preamble states, "That in the early part of James 1. a suit commenced against her husband, Sir Robert Dudley, Knight, and others, for pretending himself to be heir to the houses and lands of the Earldom of Warwick and Leicester, and that divers witnesses were examined in support of such claim. Whereupon by full testimony upon oath, partly made by the Lady Douglas, and partly by other persons of quality and credit, who were present at the marriage by a lawful minister; and that the said Sir Robert and his mother were owned by the Earl, as his lawful wife and son, as by many of such depositions appear. But a special order being made for sealing up the said depositions, did cause the said Sir Robert to leave the kingdom; whereof his adversaries taking advantage, procured a privy seal to be sent requiring his return, which he not obeying, because his honours and lands were denied, all his lands were seized to the king's use."

Sir Robert signalized himself in an expedition he fitted out to the River Oroonoco, in which he captured and destroyed several Spanish ships. In 1596 he was at the taking of Cadiz, and was rewarded with the honour of knighthood. In 1605 he had adopted legal proceedings to establish his legitimacy, but his father's widow defeated the attempt, on which he retired to Florence, thereby deserting his country and his amiable wife and five daughters. At Florence he seduced and carried off the daughter of Sir Robert Southwell, and was afterwards outlawed, and his estates were forfeited to the crown. Subsequently, he assumed the titles of Earl of Warwick and Duke of Northumberland. He devised plans for draining the neighbourhood of Pisa, and improving the port of Leghorn; and compiled a work entitled Arcano del Mare. He became chamberlain to the Grand Duchess, and was created a Duke of the Holy Roman Empire. He died at his seat, near Florence, in 1639, bearing the character of his family, for being clever and well informed, but unprincipled.

King Charles I. came into the possession of the estates, which had been purchased for a small sum by his brother, Prince Henry. They consisted of Kenilworth Castle, with its extensive chaces, &c.; but learning afterwards of the great injustice done her husband and herself and family by such alienation, and in consideration of the services of Sir R. Levison, and

Robert Holborn, Esq. (who married two of her daughters), the King granted to Lady Alice the title of Duchess of Dudley for her life, and to her daughters, the places, titles, and precedences of duke's daughters, for their lives, considering himself obliged to do much more for them, if it were in his power, in those unhappy times of distraction,

She died, possessed of the vast fortune of her husband's father, the Earl of Leicester, at her house, near the church, January 22, 1669, aged 90. Stow has given a minute account of her donations, under the article of St. Giles's parish.

Lord Herbert of Cherbury, in the county of Salop, eminent for his character and writings, resided in Great Queen Street, in a house still remaining on its south side, a few doors east of Great Wild Street. His chief work was "De Veritate prout distinguitur Revelatione," which has been treated with much respect, although it questions the utility of Revelation. It has been considered a book of much learning and argument, and has been answered by Gassendi. An incident which occurred, as he states, determined him to publish this work; and it may be mentioned as a remarkable instance of the power of imagination over an enthusiastic mind. He was in his chamber, doubtful as to the propriety of the publication, on a summer's day; and, as the sun shone clear, he took his book and knelt devoutly on his knees, and besought the Lord to satisfy him whether he should give it to the world or suppress it. "I had no sooner spoke," he says, "these words, but a loud, though yet gentle noise came from the Heavens (for it was like nothing on earth), which did so comfort and cheer me, that I took my petition as granted, and that I had the sign demanded." He makes the most solemn assertions in his life, written by himself, of the truth of this, and there is no reason to doubt his belief of it. He is said to have been the earliest English sceptical writer, and the work in question has been reported an extraordinary one, considering the time in which it was written; but one cannot but notice the inconsistency of the test which ushered it into the world. It was truly a surprising instance of vanity and self delusion, in one whose chief argument is against revelation, founded on the improbability that Heaven would communicate its will to a part of the world and not to the whole. He wrote also a "Life and Reign of Henry VIII." which has been considered an apology of that wicked Prince, rather than a fair representation. He joined the parliament in the turbulent times of Charles I. but afterwards quitted it, suffering greatly in his fortune in consequence. He was reckoned a man of great talent and bravery, and was open and generous in his disposition. He died at his house in Great Queen Street, in 1648, aged 77 years, and was interred in his parish church of St. Giles, where his epitaph particularised him as the author of " D'Veritate." His entertaining memoirs, written by himself, remained in manuscript until first printed by Lord Orford, at Strawberry Hill, in 1764.

We may here notice that Great Queen Street has been celebrated for men of high eminence and abilities. Here Sir Godfrey Kneller lived and practised his art, having among his numerous portraits painted those of no less than eight, monarchs, who sat to him. Many of the beautiful women of his day still survive in his colours. He died October 27, 1723; leaving considerable wealth, accumulated by his successful industry.

Doctors MEAD and RADCLIFFE were also parishioners, and resided in the same street, at the same period as Sir Godfrey Kneller. The medical works of the former are still in estimation; and the library of the latter, his munificent gift to the University of Oxford, is a noble monument to his fame. The former died in 1754—the latter in 1714.

LORD LISLE.—We have before mentioned the grant, &c. made to him; *(see page 21,)* and that he resided in part of the Hospital buildings. He was the eldest son of Edmund Dudley, who was executed with Empson in 1509: they were the rapacious agents of Henry VII. His mother was Elizabeth, daughter of Edward Grey, Viscount Lisle, who, five years after her mother's death, married Arthur Plantagenet, natural son of Edward IV. by Lady Elizabeth Lucy; and which Arthur Plantagenet was afterwards, in her right, created Viscount Lisle.

John Dudley was born 1502; and was on the reversal of his father's attainder, created Viscount Lisle, subsequently made Lord High Admiral, and was left one of the sixteen executors of Henry the VIII.'s will. Anno 1547, he was created Earl of Warwick, and had the office conferred on him of great Chamberlain of England, he was next made a Knight of the Garter; and in 1551, to complete his honours, was advanced to the dignity of Earl Marshal of England, and created Duke of Northumberland.

On the death of the Duke of Somerset, uncle of Edward VI. who fell through his intrigues, he became head of the council; and vested with this authority, had the address to prevail with the youthful Edward, to violate the order of succession, in order to set the crown on the head of his daughter-in-law, the Lady Jane Grey, who, after the king's death, was accordingly proclaimed queen. The accession of Mary, and the events which followed are well known. Arrested for the part he had taken in this transaction, he was, with his son the young Lord Dudley, convicted of high treason, and on the 22nd of August, 1554, fell like his father Edmund Dudley, on the scaffold, in the 52nd year of his age, unbeloved and unpitied.

Sir Roger L'Estrange, who was much celebrated as a political writer during the stormy reign of the Stuarts, as also for his gross inconsistency, is interred in St. Giles's church, and his monument was said to be the most remarkable one in it. He died at the advanced age of 88, in 1704.

Andrew Marvel.—The inflexible and disinterested Andrew Marvel, the early Latin secretary to the immortal Milton, lies also here. He was a fine example of incorruptible patriotism; of whom it is recorded, that in the hour of need he refused £1000 offered him by Charles II. although his necessities required immediately afterwards the loan of a guinea from a friend. Kingston-upon-Hull, his native place, was the borough he represented, and his constituents, highly sensible of his integrity, buried him at their expense. They also voted a sum of money to erect a monument to his memory, with a laudatory inscription, which, although devoid of party allusion, neither the one nor the other was admitted by a rector* belonging to a class of zealots, who occasionally impeach the intellectual character of the church of England.

As a curiosity, I here copy the intended epitaph, which was afterwards inserted on a monument at Kingston-upon-Hull by his constituents. They have, however, taken a liberty with the fact of his remains lying there.

EPITAPH ON ANDREW MARVEL, ESQ.

Near this place
Lyeth the Body of Andrew Marvel, Esq.
A Man so endowed by Nature,
So improved by Education, Study, and Travel,
So consummated by Experience,
That, joining the most peculiar graces of Wit
And Learning,
With a singular Penetration and strength of Judgment,
And exercising all these
In the whole course of his life
With unalterable steadiness to the ways of Virtue,
He became the ornament
And example of the age.
Beloved by good men, feared by bad,
Admired by all,
Though imitated, alas!
By few,
And scarce paralleled by any:
But a Tombstone can neither contain his character,
Nor is a Marble necessary to transmit it to posterity,
It is engraved on the minds of this generation,
And will be legible in his inimitable
Writings:
Nevertheless,
He having served near twenty years

---

* Scott seems to have been the rector alluded to.

aged 96 years. Her marriage is said to have given occasion to Cibber to introduce a scene in his play of "The Sick Lady Cured." Pennant says, she was kept on the ground-floor apartments of Montague House during his Grace's life, and was served on the knee to the day of her death. Of this first Duke of Montague we shall have more to add in the Life of Mrs. Thomas, *(see p.* 390.)

We shall here add, that the second Duke, John, son of Ralph, continued a parishioner during several years, and was, with his relative John Duke of Bedford, appointed a vestryman of St. George Bloomsbury in 1731. In 1733 he removed with his Duchess from Montague House, of which he only occupied one wing, to his residence at Whitehall.

RICHARD PENDRELL.—At the time of Charles II.'s escape and concealment in the oak, the Pendrells, who resided in Staffordshire, had the merit, by their fidelity and prudence, of being instrumental in effecting his deliverance. It is supposed that Richard, after the restoration, followed the king to town, and then settled in this parish, as being near the court. Certain it is, that Pendrell's name occurs in 1702 as overseer, which leads to the conclusion that Richard's descendants continued inhabitants here for many years. The grand-daughter of this Richard was lately living in the neighbourhood of Covent Garden, and is said to have enjoyed a small pension, part of the one granted to her ancestor. Richard Pendrell died in 1671, and had a monument erected to his memory on the south-east side of the former church. The raising of the churchyard, subsequently, had so far buried the monument as to render it necessary to form a new one to preserve the memory of this celebrated man. The black marble slab of the old tomb, at present, forms the base of the new one. Strype has recorded the inscription, which contains less poetry than sentiment:—

" Here lies
RICHARD PENDRELL,
Preserver and Conductor of his sacred Majesty, King Charles
the Second, of Great Britain,
After his Escape from Worcester fight, 1650,
Who died February 8th, 1671.

Hold passenger, here's shrouded in this hearse,
  Unparalled Pendrell thro' the universe!
Like when the eastern star from heaven gave light
  To three lost kings; so he in such dark night,
To Britain's monarch, lost by adverse war,
  On earth appeared a second eastern star;
A pole, a stem, in her rebellion's main,
  A pilot to her royal sovereign came:
Now to triumph in heaven's eternal sphere,
  He is advanced for his just steerage here,
Whilst Albion's chronicles with matchless fame,
  Embalm the story of great Pendrell's name."

The Annual Register of 1827 has the following announcement:—" Died, December 15th, 1827, at Eastborne, aged 70, Mr. John Pendrell, the representative of the preserver of Charles II. His son, who formerly kept the Royal Oak at Lewes, is now clerk at the Gloucester Hotel, Brighton."

ANECDOTES OF THE RUSSELL FAMILY—Intimately connected as this family is to Bloomsbury, and dear and illustrious as it is in the history of our country, it becomes imperative to enter into some particulars of it, and especially of its first introduction to this parish. The ancestors of the Russells are said to have had possession of a landed estate in Dorsetshire, at an early period, and in 1221, John Russell was constable of Corfe Castle. William Russell in 1284, obtained a charter for a market, at his manor, Kingston-Russell, and he was member for the county of Southampton, in 1307. Sir John Russell, his lineal descendant, was Speaker of the House of Commons in 1434, and in 1432. His son, John Russell, lived at Barwick, four miles from Bridport, when a further occurrence led him to wealth and honour. In 1506, Philip, Archduke of Austria and King of Castile, was compelled by a violent storm, to put into Weymouth, and was entertained by Sir Thomas Trenchard, who sent for Mr. Russell, knowing he understood foreign languages, having travelled abroad, to converse with him. The Archduke was so much pleased with him, that he took him to court, and recommended him warmly to the King, who made him immediately one of the Gentlemen of the Privy Chamber. He afterwards attended Henry VIII. in his expedition to France, and was present at the taking several towns, for which service he obtained some lands. In 1522, he was knighted by the Earl of Surry, for his services in Bretagne, and was created Lord Russell, in 1539, and afterwards Earl of Bedford. Francis, fourth Earl in lineal succession from the first, in the reign of James I. and Charles I. had four sons, and five daughters. His sons were, William, his successor, Francis, who died unmarried; John, a Colonel in the Civil Wars, for King Charles I. and Edward, whose son Edward went over to the Prince of Orange, in the time of James II. and was afterwards the famous Admiral Russell. The four daughters were, Lady Katherine, (the eldest,) who married Robert Lord Broke; the Lady Anne, afterwards wife to George Earl of Bristol; the Lady Margaret, married to James Hay, Earl of Carlisle; and the Lady Diana, married to Francis, Lord Newport.

William, Earl of Bedford, was at first Master of the Horse to the Parliament, and was mainly instrumental in gaining the Battle of Edgehill, where he commanded the reserve. Without entering minutely into the intermediate occurrences of his life, it is sufficient to observe that he assisted at the conferences, previous to the restoration, and bore St. Edward's Sceptre, at the coronation of Charles II.

He married Anne, daughter to Robert Carr, Earl of Somerset, and Francis Howard, he had seven sons, and three daughters; of the former, the eldest was the celebrated Lord William Russell, who married, as has been stated, at page 136, Rachel, daughter, and co-heiress of Thomas Wriothesley, Earl of Southampton, by whom he left issue one son, and two daughters* (*See page* 94.)

---

* Lady Rachel Russell, the eldest daughter of Lord William and Lady Russell, was married to William Lord Cavendish, afterwards Duke of Devonshire; and the second, Lady Catherine, married John Manners, Lord Ross, afterwards Duke of Rutland. Wriothesly the son, married Elizabeth, only daughter of John Howland, Esq. and succeeded his grandfather as Duke of Bedford, in 1700, and died of the small-pox, May 26th, 1711, aged 31. He was succeeded in the Dukedom, by Wriothesly, his son, who married Lady Anne Egerton, daughter of Scroop, Duke of Bridgewater, but dying without issue October 3rd, 1733, his only surviving brother, John, born September 30th, 1710, became the Duke. John, the Fourth Duke of Bedford, married to his second wife, Lady Gertrude, Daughter of John Earl Gower, and had issue one

Lady Rachel Russell was a most exemplary woman, and an ornament to her sex. She had the merit of reclaiming her Lord from the fashionable vices of the profligate court of Charles II. Her attendance upon him at his trial, and rendering him her best assistance, as his amanuensis, when counsel was refused, was highly creditable to her affection as a wife, and must ever render her an object of sympathy and veneration.

The following short note to him in prison, the day before his trial, is delightfully expressive of her zeal and anxiety on his account, combining, as it does, firmness with affection. *(Lady Russell to Lord Russell,)* endorsed, "To ask his leave to be at his trial."

"Your friends, believing I can do you some service at your trial, I am extreme willing to try, if my resolution will hold out—pray let your's. But it may be the court will not let me; however, do you let me try."

When judgment was given, the importunity of his friends, and the deep distress of a wife, whom he tenderly loved, prevailed upon Lord Russell to take another step to save his life. This was to write petitions to the King, and to the Duke of York, offering to live abroad, and never to meddle in the affairs of England. His Father, the Earl of Bedford, also sent a most affecting one full of submission, and offering pecuniary sacrifices, could his son's life be spared.

---

daughter named Caroline, afterwards Duchess of Marlborough, and one son, named Francis, who succeeded his father, as Duke of Bedford, and was grandfather of Francis, the late Duke. He died March 2nd, 1802, and was succeeded by the present John, Duke of Bedford.

All was ineffectual, and nothing remained, but to prepare for death. In his discourse in prison, he lamented the cloud which hung over his country; but he hoped his death would do more service than his life could have done.

The day before his execution, he received a few of his friends, and took his last leave of his children. On this occasion, the fondness of a father did not prevent him from maintaining the constancy of his temper. A little before he went to eat his supper, he said to Lady Russell, "Stay, and sup with me, let us eat our last earthly meal together." He talked very cheerfully, during supper, on various subjects, and particularly of his two daughters. He mentioned several passages of dying men with great freedom of spirit; and when a note was sent to his wife, containing a new project for his preservation, he turned it into ridicule in such a manner, that those who were with him, and not themselves able to contain their grief, were amazed. They could not conceive how his heart, naturally so tender, could resist the impression of their service. In the day time he bled at the nose, on which he said: "I shall not now let blood to divert this; that will be done to morrow." And when it rained hard that night, he said; "Such a rain to morrow will spoil a great show, which is a dull thing on a rainy day."

Before his wife left him, he took her by the hand, and said, "This flesh you now feel, in a few hour's must be cold," At ten o'clock she left him. He kissed her four or five times; and she so governed her sorrow, as not to add, by the sight of her distress, to the pain of separation. Thus they parted, not with sobs and tears, but with a composed silence: the wife wishing to spare the feelings of the husband, and the husband of the wife, they both restrained the expression of a grief, too great to be relieved by utterance. When she had left him for ever, he ran into a long discourse concerning this amiable woman: he said, " there was a signal providence from God, in giving him such a wife, where there was birth, fortune, great understanding, great religion, and great kindness to him, but her carriage to him in his last extremity, was beyond all—that he was glad that she and her children were to lose nothing by his death; and it was great comfort to him, that he left his children in such a mother's hands, and that she had promised him to take care of herself for their sake.

He refused to let his servant sit up in his chamber while he slept; and when his servant went to him at four, he was asleep as soundly as he had ever been in his life, and when his servant awoke him, and was preparing his things for him to dress, he fell asleep again. Dr. Burnett coming in, woke him, saying, " What, my Lord, asleep?" " Yes, Doctor," he said, I have slept heartily since one o'clock. He then desired him to go to his wife to say he was well, and slept well, and hoped she had done so. He remembered himself kindly to her, and prayed for her. He dressed himself with the same ease as usual, and said, he thanked God he felt no sort of fear or hurry in his thoughts. He told Burnet he was to give him his watch,*

---

* This watch, together with his sword, and other mementos, are still in the possession of the family. I was once shown them at the Bedford Office, Montague Street.

and as he wound it up, he said, "*I have done with time—now eternity comes.*"

As the carriage turned into Little Queen-street, that was conveying him to the place of his martyrdom, he said, "I have often turned to the other hand with great comfort, but now I turn to this with greater." As he said this, he looked towards his own residence,* Southampton-house, Bloomsbury, and Dr. Tillotson saw a tear drop from his eye. When at the place of execution, after the preparation of prayer, and conversing with the Sheriff, and those around him, he calmly took off his coat, waistcoat, and cravat, and drew a night-cap out of his pocket, which he had provided, fearing his servant might not be able to get up to him. The whole of these preliminaries he performed without the least change of countenance; and then being ready, he laid his head on the block. "When he had laid down," says Dr. Burnet, "I once looked at him, and saw no change in his looks; and though he was still lifting up his hands, there was no trembling, though at the moment in which I looked, the executioner happened to be laying his axe to his neck, to direct him to take aim: I thought it touched him, but am sure he seemed not to mind it." The executioner at two strokes cut off his head. This was in the middle of Lincoln's-Inn Fields.

Lady Russell, after the death of her Lord, removed to Woburn, where she mostly resided

---

* Lord William Russell resided here, and at Southampton House, Holborn, (on the site of Southampton Buildings,) alternately. This had belonged to the family of the Southampton's from the time of Wriothesley, Lord Chancellor, in Henry VIIIths. time.

for more than a twelvemonth after that event. In a letter she wrote to Dr. Fitzwilliam, dated 1st October, 1684, she thus pourtrays her melancholy feelings, when contemplating her return to Southampton House, Bloomsbury.*

"I have to acquaint you with my resolve to try that desolate habitation of mine, in London, this winter. The doctor agrees it is the best place for my boy, and I have no argument to balance that, nor could I take the resolution to see London till that was urged ; but, by God's permission, I will try how I can endure that place in thought—a place of terror to me!"

She spent her remaining long life in acts o charity and piety, and was held in great esteem by Archbishop Tillotson, and many other virtuous characters of her day. Among her other afflictions, she lost her only son, (May 26th, 1711, aged 31,) who inherited the title of Earl of Bedford, and whom she watched over with unceasing care. In the midst of health and vigour he fell a sacrifice to the small-pox, which at that period was regarded as the direst plague, neither inoculation or vacination, being known as mediums of arresting its ravages. She lived to see the sentence of her murdered Lord reversed, and so denominated by parliament, although her feelings were greatly shaken by the minuteness of the investigation it underwent in the Commons. It is well known, and generally admitted, that the greatest injustice was exercised to convict Lord Russell, by a

---

* Oldmixon says, "The Duke of York descended so low in his revenge against Lord Russell, as to desire this innocent Lord might be executed before *his own door, in Bloomsbury Square,* an insult the King himself would not consent to."

false construction of the law of treason, and the selection of the jury by a violation of the rules of decency, and the rights of the subject. Lord John Russell, (his elegant biographer,) admits that his ancestor was too violent against the Roman Catholics, which was the fault of the honest men of that day, whilst he treats the Rye-House plot as an infamous faction, and Lady Rachel was fully assured it had no other foundation than idle talk. She wrote a most touching letter to the King, after her Lord's death; and a collection of her letters, which do credit to her head and heart, was published in 1773. In these, she gives evident specimens of her calm magnanimity; there appears no triumph of expression, in the record she gives of the flight of King James II. and she passes over in silence the merited fate of Jeffries, whose rudeness and coarseness was so conspicuous on the trial.*

The mansion of the Earls of Bedford, before this union with the Southampton family, was at nearly the bottom of what is now Southampton Street, Strand, and was built principally of wood, as a town residence, and it remained so till 1704, under the name of Bedford House. It was inclosed by a brick wall, and had a large garden extending northward, nearly to the site of the present market place. The estate, com-

---

* Mr. Fox, speaking of the destruction of those eminent patriots, Russell and Sydney, says, they are " two names that will, it is hoped, be for ever dear to every English heart: when their memory shall cease to be an object of respect and veneration, it requires no spirit of prophecy to foretel that English liberty will be fast approaching to its final consummation." *See Fox's Life of James II.*

prising Convent, or Covent Garden, and the contiguous lands, belonged originally to the Abbots of Westminster, till the dissolution, after which it was granted by Edward VI. to the Duke of Somerset. It reverted, by patent, after the Duke's attainder, to John Russell, Earl of Bedford, and Lord Privy Seal, (March, 1552,) per Bill Dom. Regis. "of the gift of the Covent, or Convent Garden, lying in the parish of St. Martin's in the Fields, near Charing Cross, with seven acres, called Long Acre, of the yearly value of £6 6s. 8d. parcel of the possessions of the late Duke of Somerset, to have to him and his heirs, reserving a tenure to the King's Majesty in suage and not in capite." It was immediately after that the Earl built the mansion in question; and on Lady Russell's demise it was deserted, and Southampton House became the ducal residence, changing its name to Bedford House.* All the land where the

---

* "May 7th. The Duke of Bedford having disposed of the materials of Bedford-house for 5 or £6000, a sale of the furniture, pictures, &c. by Mr. Christie, commenced this day, when the most crowded assemblage were gratified with a last view of this design of Inigo Jones for the Earl of Southampton, father of the amiable relict of William, Lord Russell; from whence she dates many of her letters, published by Mr. Selwood, and resided in it till her death, 1723. The late Duke fitted up the gallery (which was the only room of consequence in the house) and placed in it Sir James Thornhill's copies of the Cartoons, which that artist was three years about, which he bought at the sale of that eminent artist's collection for £200. St. John preaching in the Wilderness, by Raphael, fetched 95 guineas. A beautiful painting, by Gainsborough, of an Italian Villa, 90 guineas. The archduke Leopold's gallery, by Teniers, 210 guineas. Four paintings of a battle, by Cassanovi, which cost his grace £1000, were sold

former Bedford House stood has been built on, the house being demolished, and the several streets have been named after the family, as Bedford, Russell, Tavistock, Southampton, Chandos Streets, &c. King and Henrietta Streets were named in honour of Charles I., and his Queen, being built on at an early period; and James and York Streets, in honour of the Duke of York, afterwards King James II.

SOUTHAMPTON FAMILY.—The Earls of Southampton became residents in Bloomsbury in consequence of their becoming proprietors of that manor, and, subsequently, of that of St. Giles. Wriothesley, Lord Chancellor in the reign of Henry VIII., is supposed to have been the first occupant of the manorial mansion, which had previously, with the manor, been in the possession of the family of the De Blemunds. Hence this residence took the name of Southampton House, until it became the property of the Russell family, when it assumed the name of Bedford House, to which we have before adverted. Wriothesley was created Earl

---

for 60 guineas. A most beautiful Landscape, by Cuype, for 200 guineas. Two beautiful bronze figures, Venus de Medicis and Antonius, 20 guineas; and Venus couchant, from the antique, 20 guineas. Another of the pictures was the duel between Lord Mahon and the Duke of Hamilton. The week after were sold, the double rows of lime-trees in the garden, valued one at £90, the other at £80; which are now all taken down, and the site of a new square, of nearly the dimensions of Lincoln's-Inn Fields, and to be called Russell Square, has been laid out. The famous statue of Apollo, which was in the hall at Bedford-house, has been removed to Woburn-abbey, and is to be placed on an eminence in the square between the abbey and the tennis-court and riding-house. It originally cost a thousand guineas."—*See Dodsley's Annual Register*, 1800.

of Southampton three days before the coronation of Edward VI. (1547) and having another mansion on the site of where Southampton Buildings stand, he resided at each house alternately. This latter house was called Southampton House, Holborn, to distinguish it from the former. He died 20th July, 1550, at his house in Holborn, and was buried at his parish church, St. Andrew's.*

His second son, Henry, succeeded him as Earl of Southampton, who being implicated in the intrigues of Mary Queen of Scots, and others, narrowly escaped the block. He left issue a daughter, married to Thomas Lord Arundel, of Wardour; and an only son, Henry, third Earl of Southampton, and the munificent patron of Shakspeare. He purchased the manor of St. Giles and united it to Bloomsbury, as before stated. (*See page* 135.) His son, the fourth Earl of Southampton, was Thomas, Lord Treasurer to Charles II. and father of Lady

---

* The following cruel account is given of this man, by Fox, in his Acts and Monuments. "Anne Ascue, a young woman of merit and beauty, was accused of dogmatizing on the real presence in the Eucharist. The Chancellor, Wriothesley, was sent to examine her with regard to her patrons at court, but she maintained a laudable fidelity to her friends, and would confess nothing. She was put to the torture in the most barbarous manner, and continued still resolute in preserving secrecy. The Chancellor, who stood by, ordered the Lieutenant of the Tower to stretch the rack farther, but that officer refused compliance. The chancellor menaced him, but met with a new refusal; upon which, that magistrate, intoxicated with religious zeal, put his own hand to the rack, and drew it so violently that he almost tore her body asunder. Her constancy still prevailed, and she was condemned to be burnt alive, and was carried to the stake with her limbs dislocated."

Rachel, the worthy and celebrated wife of Lord William, whom we have already spoken of. To this lady the manors above mentioned descended, being left to her, in her own right, by her father, who died in 1668.

ABRAHAM SPECKART, ESQ.—This gentleman ought to be mentioned for his useful services to the parish, especially in regard to the rebuilding the church in 1623, which has been already noticed. He resided near the church, in what was then termed Middle Row, (not the present building of that name), which appears to be at the time one of the most respectable parts of the parish; and was one of four parishioners living on that spot, to whom the favour was granted of a private entrance from their houses into the church-yard. Mrs. Dorothy Speckart, the widow, seems to have died some years after her husband, as a vestry minute of 1670 directs, " the late Mrs. Speckart's door into the church to be shut-up." Mr. Speckart's name, in the parish books, has always the addition of "Esquire" put to it, which was a title not then prostituted as now, and seems to infer that he was rather a private gentleman than a merchant or trader; his domestic establishment also, as enumerated in the assessment of 1623, was extensive. A greater proof, however, of this being the fact, and also of his opulence, was the circumstance of the consecration feast before mentioned being held at his house, which must have been no ordinary mansion to have contained so large and brilliant a company as assembled on that occasion.

HISTORICAL ACCOUNT OF THE REVOLUTION PLOT.—Bloomsbury has the honour to be the scene of a plot most momentous to the future welfare of Britain, yet it does not seem to be known to any considerable extent, nor properly appreciated. The subject to which I am referring is to be found in the biography of

MRS. THOMAS—the celebrated Corinna. She had undergone many vicissitudes, but above all, in her widowed state she had been the dupe of a visionary alchymist, whose scheming impoverished herself and daughter. Time and patience at last overcame the pangs this produced, and she began to stir among her late husband's great clients. She took a house in Bloomsbury, and by means of good economy and an elegant appearance, was supposed to be better in the world than she really was. Her husband's clients received her like one risen from the dead; they came to visit her, and promised to serve her. At last the Duke of Montague advised her to let lodgings, which way of life she declined, as her talents were not suited for dealing with ordinary lodgers; but, added she, "if I knew any family who desired such a conveniency, I would readily accommodate them." "I take you at your word," replied the Duke, "I will become your sole tenant; nay, don't smile, for I am in earnest: I like a little more freedom than I can enjoy at home, and I may come sometimes and eat a bit of mutton with four or five honest fellows, whose company I delight in." The bargain was bound, and proved matter of fact, though on a deeper scheme than drinking a bottle; and his Grace was to pass for Mr. Freeman of Hertfordshire. In a few days he ordered a dinner for his beloved friends, Jack, Tom, Will, and Ned, good honest country fellows, as his

Grace called them. They came at the time
appointed, but how surprised was the widow
when she saw the Duke of Devonshire, Lords
Buckingham and Dorset, and a certain Viscount, with Sir William Dutton Colt, under
these feigned names. After several times meeting at this lady's house, the noble persons, who
had a high opinion of her integrity, intrusted
her with the grand secret, which was nothing
less than the project for the revolution. Though
these meetings were held as private as possible,
yet suspicions arose, and Mrs. Thomas's house
was narrowly watched; but the messengers,
who were no enemies to the cause, betrayed
their trust, and suffered the noblemen to meet
unmolested, or at least without any dread of
apprehension.

The revolution being effected, and the state
become more settled, that place of rendezvous
was quitted; the noblemen took leave of the
lady, with promises of obtaining a pension or
some place in the household for her, as her
zeal in that cause highly merited; besides, she
had a very good claim to some appointment,
having been ruined by the shutting-up the Exchequer; but alas! court promises proved an
aerial foundation, and the noble peers never
thought of her more. The Duke of Montague
indeed made offers of service, and being Captain of the Band of Pensioners, she asked him
to admit Mr. Gwinnet, a gentleman who had
made love to her daughter, into such a post.
This he promised, but upon these terms, that
her daughter should ask him for it. The widow
thanked him, and not suspecting that any design
was covered under this offer, concluded herself sure of success; but how amazed was she

to find her daughter, whom she had bred in the most passive subjection, and who had never discovered the least instance of disobedience, absolutely refused to ask any such favour of his Grace. She could not be prevailed on either by flattery or threatening, and continuing still obstinate in her resolution, her mother obliged her to explain herself on the point of her refusal. She told her, that the Duke of Montague had already made an attack upon her, that his designs were dishonourable, and that if she submitted to ask his Grace one favour, he would reckon himself secure of another in return, which he would endeavour to accomplish by the basest means. This explanation was too satisfactory: Who does not see the meanness of of such ungenerous conduct? He had made use of the mother as a tool for carrying on political designs: he found her distressed; and as a recompence for her services, and under the pretence of mending her fortune, attempted the virtue of her daughter; and would provide for her on no other terms, but at the price of her child's innocence. In the meantime the young Corinna, a poetical name given her by Mr. Dryden, continued to improve her mind by reading the politest authors. (*See volume* XII. *of the General Biographical Dictionary.*)

Biographical Sketches of some of the Donors to the Charities in St. Giles and Bloomsbury.

HON. ROBERT BERTIE.—He was the son and fifth child of the great Robert Bertie, Earl of Lindsey, slain 1642, at the battle of Edgehill, and was born 1619. His elder brother, Montague, succeeded to the title, and was afterwards (as his ancestors had been) Lord great Chamberlain of England, and whose grandson, in 1706, (5th of Anne) was created Marquis of Lindsey. This family, afterwards the ducal family of Ancaster, resided for many years at the mansion called Lindsey, and subsequently Ancaster House, Lincoln's-Inn Fields. He, (Robert Bertie) was donor of £50 to the poor.

WILLIAM SHELTON, ESQ—Founder and endower of the Free School which bears his name, was a vestryman, and served the office of overseer in 1639. He was owner of a piece of ground on which the parish, during the plague of 1665, erected a pest-house. It is not known in what part it stood, but from the small sum it fetched, as stated in the parish accounts, it was probably a mere temporary building of timber. He seems to have been an illiterate man, from his prefixing his cross to his will instead of his name. He died 1673. (*See page* 251.)

WILLIAM BAINBRIDGE, ESQ.—(or BENBRIG, as he is called in the vestry minutes), gave the name to a street in St. Giles's parish. He was chosen a vestryman in 1669. He was the donor of £300 towards building a gallery in the church, the produce of which pew rents were to be given to the poor: this however has not been fulfilled, and an inquiry on the subject has been recently set on foot. (*vide p.* 266.)

WILLIAM WOODEN—the donor to the poor of the rent charge, issuing from the Hampshire Hog, was churchwarden during the plague 1665. He was elected a vestryman in 1672, but he vacated in 1675, probably from age, or an idea of his approaching death, as he obtained an order that year to erect a grave-stone for himself similar to Captain Hooper's, though his will is dated two years later. He had been a parishioner some years, having served the office of overseer in 1653.

ROBERT HULCUP, ESQ.—appears to have been a parishioner of much respectability, and besides his personal services as one of the directors of the parish concerns, was also a considerable benefactor to the poor at his decease. He was chosen vestryman in 1667, and continued so till 1682. He was churchwarden in 1671, having been overseer previously, and was on most committees for conducting the parochial affairs. His legacy of £80 was recovered, (after some trouble) for the use of the poor in 1686.

RICHARD HOLFORD, ESQ.—was the successor of the family of that name, who were in possession, by purchase, of some of the hospital estates after its dissolution, *(see page 75.)* The gentleman we are speaking of flourished during the interregnum, and great part of the reign of Charles II. The first mention of him in the books is anno 1653, as the donor to the poor of £4 per annum for ever; and in 1655-6 he is again mentioned as to the same gift, and the sum stated to be £5 yearly, instead of £4. In 1659 his principal donation (the Prince's Street estate), was secured by a deed of feoffment from him, therein described as Richard Holford, of the parish of St. Giles-in-the-Fields, to the then minister, Thomas Case, and other trustees. This estate still belongs to the parish. He seems to have had a monument in the old St. Giles's church.

BARTHOLOMEW OVERY, or IVERY—with his wife "JANE," were donors of the estate in the

Almonry, (which consisted of three tenements in *Great Ambrey, Westminster,* as his will expresses it) for the use of the poor. These were subsequently sold, and the receipts, Mr. Parton says, carried to the churchwarden's account for them. These donors lived in 1623 at Towns-end, St. Giles, but afterwards removed to Westminster, where Overy died in 1647. The churchwarden's accounts of that year thus notice the circumstance:—" 1647. Paid for the buriall of Bartholomew Overy, who died at Westminster, and desired to be buried at St. Giles's; who, by will dated 6th January, 1647, hath given to the poor of this parish, (after the decease of his wife Jane), three tenements, *(see above),* being college land."

AN APPENDIX.

The following Acts, being the most applicable to the United Parishes, are abstracted, with the idea of their proving useful, by conveying information to the inhabitants, many of them being unacquainted therewith. We begin with

The celebrated Act 43 of Queen Elizabeth, Anno 1600.

1. It provides, that the churchwardens of every parish, or parishes, to be called Overseers of the Poor, shall be nominated yearly, in Easter-week, or within a month after, under the hand and seal of two or more Justices of the Peace, in the same county where the parish lies.

2. That they, or the greater part of them, shall, with the consent of the Justices, set the children to work in their respective parishes, when their parents are known not to be able to keep and maintain them. Also, they were to set to work all such persons, married or unmarried, having no means to maintain them, and use no ordinary and daily trade of life to get their living by.

3. It then provides for the raising, by weekly taxation, or otherwise, such sums from the inhabitants, as shall be competent for the purchasing flax, hemp, wool, thread, iron, and other ware, and stuff to set the poor on work. Also competent

sums for the necessary relief of the lame and impotent, old, blind, and such other among them, not able to work: to put out children to be apprentices.

4. The overseers are then enjoined to meet monthly, together with the churchwardens, after the sunday afternoon service, to render an account of monies received and expended, &c. Penalty for not attending, 20s. unless lawful reasons for absence be given.

5. When any parish is unable to procure funds for the above purposes, *two Justices are empowered to tax, rate, and assess any other parish, or parishes, within the hundred; and if the said hundred shall not be thought able by the said Justices, then they shall be empowered, at their General Quarter Sessions, to assess other parishes within the county.*

6. The churchwardens and overseers are empowered to levy the rates by distraint, or to commit defaulters to prison, until payment is made; and, also, the Justices are to commit those who are able, refusing to work; and farther, also, commit to prison the churchwardens and overseers who refused to accompt.

7. Children to be bound apprentice; males not till they are twenty-four, and females not till they are twenty-one, unless they become married.

8. Cottages to be erected on any waste, or common, of any parish by leave of the Lord of the manor, for the convenient reception of the impotent poor.

9. Persons aggrieved by assessments, imposed by the churchwardens and overseers, may appeal to the Quarter Sessions—their decision to be final and binding.

10. The father, grandfather, mother and grandmother, and the children of every poor, old, blind, &c. person, not able to work, being of sufficient substance, shall, at their own charge, relieve and maintain such poor person, as shall be prescribed by the magistrates.

11. Officers of Corporate Towns, as Mayors, Bailiffs, &c. and Aldermen of the City of London, to have similar authority as Justices.

12. When parishes extend into two counties, or where they are partly in two liberties of any City, Town, or Place Corporate, the Magistrates, &c. shall only intermeddle with such portions respectively, with certain exceptions.

13. If Overseers are not nominated and appointed yearly, Justices, Mayors, &c. where such default occurs, are to be fined £5 towards the relief of the poor.

14. Directions are given how forfeitures should be employed and levied; Justices, at their General Sessions, holden next after Easter, are empowered to rate every parish to such a weekly sum as they think convenient, not exceeding sixpence, nor under the sum of a half-penny weekly; and so as the total sum of each amount not to above the rate of twopence for every parish within the said county; which sums, so taxed, shall be yearly assessed by the agreement of the parishioners within themselves, or in default thereof, by the churchwardens and petty constables of the same parish, or the more part of them; or, in default of their agreement, by the Justice, or Justices of the peace, in or near the said parish. Penalties are to be exacted.

15. Relief is next provided for prisoners in the King's Bench, Marshalsea, Hospitals, and Alms-houses. Twenty shillings at least to be sent out of every county, with other provisos, as to surplusages, &c. &c.

An Act for remydying some defects in the Act made in the 43rd year of the reign of Queen Elizabeth, intituled " An Act for the Relief of the Poor."

1. The preamble states that the former act contains some defects, whereby the money, raised for that purpose, was liable

to be misapplied; added to which, great difficulties and delays often occurred in raising the same. It then prescribes, that from and after the 24th of June, 1744, the churchwardens and overseers of the poor, shall yearly, and every year, within fourteen days after other overseers shall be nominated, and appointed to succeed them, deliver unto such succeeding overseers, a just, true, and perfect account, in writing, fairly entered in a book or books for that purpose, and signed by the said churchwardens and overseers, hereby directed to account, as aforesaid, under their hands, of all sums of money by them received or rated and assessed, and not received; and also, of all goods, chattles, stock, and materials that shall be on their hands, or in the hands of any of the poor, in order to be wrought, and of all monies paid by such churchwardens and overseers so accounting, and of all other things concerning their said office; and shall also pay and deliver all sums of money, goods, &c. and other things, as shall be in their hands, unto such succeeding overseers of the poor; which said account shall be verified by oath, or by the affirmation of persons called quakers, before one or more of his Majesty's Justices of the Peace, which said oath and affirmation, such said Justice and Justices is and are hereby authorised and required to administer, and to sign and attest the caption of the same at the foot of the said account, without fee or reward; and the said book or books shall be carefully preserved by the churchwardens and overseers, or one of them, in some public or other place in every parish, township, or place; and *they shall and are hereby required to permit any person, there assessed, or liable to be assessed, to inspect the same, at all reasonable times, paying six-pence for such inspection; and shall, upon demand, forthwith give copies of the same, or any part thereof, to such person, paying at the rate of six-pence for every three hundred words, and so on in proportion for any greater or less number.*

2. The next clause exacts the penalty of imprisonment, in the county goal, upon any churchwarden or overseer that shall

refuse to perform what is before required, therein to remain till they yield obedience fully to the conditions prescribed at large.

3. Overseers dying to be replaced by two justices, and executors to account in forty days to a remaining overseer or churchwarden.

4. Persons aggrieved by any rate or assessment made for the relief of the poor, or shall have any material objection to any person or persons being put on, or left out of such rate or assessment, or to the sum charged on any person or persons therein, or shall have any material objection to such accounts as aforesaid, or any part thereof, or shall find him, her, or themselves aggrieved by any neglect, act, or thing done, by the churchwardens and overseers of the poor, or by any of his Majesty's justices of the peace; it shall, and may be lawful for such person or persons, in any of the cases aforesaid, giving reasonable notice to the churchwardens and overseers of the poor of the parish, township, or place, to appeal to the next Quarter Sessions of the Peace for the county, riding, &c.

5. The justices there assembled are to receive such appeal, and to hear and determine the same, notice being given in due time. Reasonable costs to be allowed, as stated in an act made to remedy defects in the Poor Laws, in the 8th and 9th of William III.

6. Justices of the peace may quash the old rates, or make new rates and assessments, from which no appeal can be had, *as it had been formerly held*, from rates and assessments, the justices of the peace are required to amend the same, where they shall see just cause to give relief, *without altering such rates and assessments, with respect to other persons mentioned in the same; but if, from an appeal from the whole rate, it shall be found necessary to quash or set aside the same, then, and in every such case, the said justices shall, and are hereby required, to order and direct the churchwardens and overseers of the poor to make a new equal rate or assessment, and they are required to make the same accordingly,*

7. The next clause is for the more effectual levying money assessed for the relief of the poor, either in the parish where due, or any other part of that, or other county where the party is removed to, or has property, subject however to an appeal to the Quarter Sessions.

8. A clause is afterwards inserted to prevent vexatious actions against overseers, who made distresses in such cases.

9. Plaintiffs recovering in any action to have full costs, as in other cases; but they cannot recover for any irregularity, if tender of amends hath been made by the parties distraining, before such actions is brought.

10. Succeeding overseers may levy arrears to reimburse the former.

11. Persons removing out of parishes without paying rates are liable, as also are their successors, in proportion to the time they are occupants respectively, and they are liable to distraint severally.

12. *All rates and assessments hereafter made for the relief of the poor, are directed by this act to be entered in a book or books, to be provided for that purpose by the churchwardens and overseers of the poor of every parish or place, who shall take care that such copies be wrote and entered accordingly, within fourteen days after all appeals from such rates are determined, and shall attest the same by putting their names thereto. The books to be carefully preserved by the churchwardens and overseers for the time being, or one of them, in some public or other place in every such parish, &c. whereto all persons assessed may freely resort,* and shall be delivered over from time to time to the succeeding churchwardens and overseers of the poor, as soon as they enter into their said offices, to be preserved as aforesaid, and shall be produced by them at the General or Quarter Sessions when any appeal is heard or determined.

13. Penalties are prescribed against churchwardens and overseers, and others, who shall neglect or refuse to obey and

perform the several orders and directions of this Act, or any of them, where no penalty is before provided by this Act, or shall act contrary thereto. The penalty is stipulated not to exceed £5, nor less than 20s. for every such offence, to be levied by distress and sale of the offender's goods, &c.

14. The power of overseers to be the same as that of churchwardens, where there are none of the latter, and the penalties the same.

[The above is an abstract of an Act passed in 17th George II. cap. 3.]

Act 9th of Queen Anne, cap. 22. Anno 1710.

Entitled an act for granting to her majesty several duties upon Coals; for Building Fifty new Churches in and about the cities of London and Westminster, and suburbs thereof; and other purposes therein mentioned.

The preamble states, that the commons of Great Britain are desirous to aid her majesty's pious intentions to encrease the number of churches in and near the metropolis, for which purpose, they, with the consent of the lords spiritual and temporal, with the approbation of the queen's most excellent majesty, had enacted, that a duty of two shillings upon every chaldron and tun of coals or culm, should be paid from and after the 14th May, 1716, until the 29th September, 1716, and duties in other proportions at certain periods therein mentioned.

It is then stated, that the sums so arising shall be paid into the exchequer, to be appropriated to the building the said churches of stone and other proper materials, with towers or steeples for each, for purchasing sites for the same, and for burying places, and for houses of habitation for the ministers.

The sum of £4,000 to be applied out of the said duties for repairing Westminster Abbey, and £6,000 per annum towards the completion of Greenwich Hospital and its Chapel, and one Church, being one of the fifty to be built at East Greenwich in the county of Kent.

Her majesty was empowered to appoint commissioners for the purpose stated in the act. Money paid into the exchequer by way of loan to bear an interest of 6 per cent. within a certain period. One hundred chaldrons of coals for Greenwich Hospital annually to be exempt from duty. Other provisions are made as to surveyors' and other salaries, &c. under Act of King William III.

Act 10th of Queen Anne, cap. 11th.   Anno 1711.

Entitled an Act for enlarging the time given to the commissioners appointed by her majesty, pursuant to an Act for granting to her majesty several duties on Coals, for Building Fifty new Churches, &c. and also for giving the commissions farther powers for the better effecting the same, and for appointing monies for building the parish church of St. Mary Woolnoth in the city of London.

The preamble recites the purposes and particulars for which the former act was made, stating that the commissions appointed to carry the same into effect found the time mentioned too limited, and they are now empowered to continue their duties until the performance and finishing the building, &c. therein named. They were further empowered to make purchases of lands, and enter into contracts under the provisions of the act. Lands so purchased, with their tenements, &c. were to be conveyed to at least five commissioners.

They were empowered to provide cemeteries for the parishes, even out of their limits, if necessary. Provision is made for receiving loans and paying interest of 6 per cent. and for the treasury to issue money, &c.

The 8th clause is most important as it regards Bloomsbury parish. *It enacts, that it shall be lawful for the commissioners, or any five of them, by one or more instruments in writing on parchment under their hands and seals, to be enrolled in the high Court of Chancery, to describe and ascertain the true limits and bounds of the site of and belonging to each such new church, and house for the habitation of the minister of such new church, and church-yards and cemeteries for each respective parish, and also the district and division of each parish that shall be appointed for every church to be erected or constituted pursuant to this act or the said former act; and every such district or division so set out for a new parish shall, after such enrolment, and the consecration of such new church, be for ever deemed and taken to be of itself a distinct parish to all intents and purposes, excepting as touching the church rates, the relief of the poor, and rates for the highways, as is herein after provided; and the inhabitants within the distinct limits of every such new parish, shall from henecforth be the parishioners thereof, and subject to such taxes, rates, and assessments for the poor, cleansing the streets, and other duties within the said new parish, or the greater part thereof was divided and taken, are subject or chargeable with the same, and to be exempt within the space of one month after the consecration of such new church from the parish whence taken, and from all dependencies and contributions for or in respect thereof, except as is hereby otherwise enacted or provided.*

9. *The commissioners are in this clause empowered to take a district out of any large parish where any new church shall be made, and add it to a lesser parish adjoining, which shall be deemed part of the parish to which it is added, &c.*

10. Enacts that there shall be a rector in every new church, and a perpetual succession of such rectors. The morning preacher in any chapel converted into a new church shall be the first rector. *In every other new church the queen shall nominate the first rector, (except Stepney, see* 12th *of Anne, cap.* 17.) The land and hereditaments purchased for such church, &c. the freehold is appointed to be vested in the rectors of such new parish respectively, *and he is authorized to*

purchase lands to the value of £200 per annum for such church respectively.

11. *Empowers the commissioners to inquire of the right of patronage of the present churches, and agree with the patron who hath the right for the effectual dividing the parish and the tithes, oblations, dues, revenues, &c. All agreements on these points to be binding.*

12. Makes it lawful for persons to contract with the commissioners for any lands, &c. and for settling the right of patronage with corporations, &c. &c.

13. Provides that such bargains, &c. be sanctioned by the chancery, &c.

14. Provides that the crown shall present till such settlement of the right of patronage.

15. Enacts that the first and succeeding rectors shall be presented as other rectors are, and they and the churchwardens shall be subject to the ordinary.

16. Contains farther regulations as to the tithes, &c.

17 and 18. Regulates the distinct interest of proprietors of chapels as to their pews, &c.

19. The first churchwardens and overseers for the poor, scavengers, surveyors, and other officers for every new parish, to be chosen by the commissioners, and shall be fully invested with the powers and authorities as officers of the like description in any other parish in London and Westminster.

20. *It shall be lawful for the said commissioners, or any five of them, with the consent of the bishop or ordinary of the place, by instrument under their hands and seals, to be enrolled in the high Court of Chancery, to name a convenient number of sufficient inhabitants in each such new parish respectively, to be the vestrymen of each such new parish respectively, to be the vestrymen of such new parish, who shall have and exercise the like powers and authorities for ordering and regulating the affairs of such new parish, as the vestrymen of the present parish, out of which such new parish, or the greater part thereof, shall be taken, now have or exercise; and if there be no select vestry in such present*

parish, then as the vestrymen of the parish of St. Martin in the Fields within the liberty of the city of Westminster in the county of Middlesex, now have or exercise; and from time to time, upon the death, removal, or other voidance of any such vestryman, the rest or majority of them may elect a fit person, being an inhabitant and householder in the said parish to supply the same.

21. Provided always, and it is hereby enacted and declared, that all parochial customs, usages, by-laws, and privileges, as are now in force or use within any present parish which shall be divided by virtue or in pursuance of this act, shall and may, at all times after and notwithstanding such division, continue and be in force, as well in and for every new parish, of which the whole or the greater part shall be taken out of such present parish, as in and for such parish as shall remain to the present parochial church, and be used, enjoyed, and observed by the inhabitants thereof respectively, so far as the same shall not be repugnant to or inconsistent with the laws of this realm.

22. The commissioners in like manner are empowered, with the consent of the respective rectors, vicars, or ministers, churchwardens and overseers of the poor, and of the vestry, or twenty of the principal inhabitants of any present parish, in which there shall be no select vestry, from which any part or district shall, by virtue and in pursuance of this act be taken, and of such parish or parishes to which any such district or division so taken shall be appointed or belong, or else to or for such respective rectors, vicars, &c. and vestrymen or principal inhabitants, with consent of their respective ordinary or ordinaries, at any time or times hereafter, by instrument in writing under their hands and seals, to be enrolled in the high Court of Chancery, to make an effectual and perpetual division of such parishes or districts so divided as to the church rates, relief of the poor, and rates for the highways, and other parish rates within the same

respectively, and to limit and settle any certain annual sum or consideration for or in respect thereof, or for equality of such division, where there shall be occasion; and such division and settlement so made shall be for ever after binding, effectual, and conclusive, to all intents and purposes whatsoever.

23. Provides that until such agreement for such rates respectively shall take place, *they shall be levied as usual within the present parish.*

24. And for the better ordering, dividing, collecting, and distributing from time to time such rates within the present limits of every parish which shall be divided pursuant to this act, in the mean time, *and until such further division shall be made,* it shall and may be lawful to and for the churchwardens and overseers of the poor, with the vestry or principal inhabitants of each parish respectively, as aforesaid, to which any part or district of such present parish, after any division thereof to be made pursuant to this act, shall remain or belong, to assemble and meet together in the present parish church or vestry room annually, upon Tuesday in Easter week in the forenoon, or oftener from time to time as occasion may require; *and notice shall be given thereof on the Lord's day next before in the church of each such parish immediately after the morning service;* and to and for them, or the major part of them so assembled, to agree upon or ascertain the monies or rates to be assessed within the limits of such present parish for the relief of the poor, and other parish rates within such limits, or the repair of any church to which any part or district of such present parish shall, when divided, belong; and to divide, ascertain, and apportion such monies and rates to and upon every part or district of such present parish so divided respectively, with regard to the value of the lands and estates therein assessable to the same, which monies or rates so to be divided or apportioned, shall be assessed, levied, and collected in each such district accordingly, by the proper officers of the respective parish to which such district

shall remain or belong, and by such ways and means as the officers of the present parish might have assessed, collected, or levied, the same if such division or this act had not been made; and also to divide, ascertain, and distribute such monies and rates so assessed and collected through the present limits of such parish, in just and reasonable proportions to and for every such part and district respectively, as the same shall be divided separately and apart for the relief of the poor, and repair of the highways, and other parish rates within such part or district, and for the repair of the respective church to which such part or district shall remain or belong, with regard to the wants and occasions of each such part or district, for the uses and purposes aforesaid respectively; *and all such proportions so to be distributed, shall be employed and applied to the proper uses and purposes for which the same was assessed and shall be distinctly accounted for by the officers of the respective parish to which such district shall remain or belong.*

25. Enacts that in default of such yearly agreements, &c. the parish officers for such districts shall assess all rates.

26. Provides that this act shall not invalidate any ecclesiastical law, or destroy the rights of the Bishop of London.

The remaining clauses are not very important, being chiefly applicable to the issue of monies, repairs of Westminster Abbey, &c. referred to in former act.

Act of 3rd George II. cap. 19, entituled " An Act for providing a maintainance for the Minister of the new church near Bloomsbury Market, in the county of Middlesex; and for making more effectually an Act, passed in the 4th year of his late Majesty's reign, for empowering the Com-

missioners for building the fifty new churches, to direct the parish church of St. Giles in the Fields, in the said county, to be rebuilt, instead of one of the said churches.

The preamble recites the particular nature and purpose of the Acts of 9th and 10th of Anne, in respect to the building the fifty new churches.

It then refers to the successive Acts of the 1st of George I. and the 1st of George II. cap. 8, applicable to the Acts of Anne, and authorising a fund of £360,000 for the said building, in lieu of certain former provisions.

It then proceeds to state, that "a site for a church had been purchased, and a new church built thereupon, near Bloomsbury Market, in the parish of St. Giles in the Fields, in the county of Middlesex; and a site for a house for a minister hath also been purchased, and a house built accordingly thereupon, near the said new church; and a district, or division for a new parish to the said new church hath been laid out, and the bounds and limits thereof ascertained and described by a writing.

The inhabitants of the old parish are next stated to be willing and desirous to give the rector of the new parish £1,250 which the treasurer to the commissioners is requested to receive and apply under the same controul as the £3,000 before mentioned.

These sums are specified to form a fund for the rector of Bloomsbury's maintenance, by the purchase of lands, tenements, &c. in fee simple; the rents and produce to be so applied annually to him and his successors, and also the surplus fees, perquisites, Easter offerings, and other dues, and the house for his and their habitation.

A churchyard was also to be purchased by the said commissioners, and they and the vestry were to affix the burial fees for the rector, which were to be binding.

The vaults under the church and vestry room, seats and pews, were vested in the churchwardens and their successors, for the public uses of the said new parish, under the directions of the vestry.

The parish clerk for the time being is declared a member of the corporation of the parish, with all its privileges.

The rights of the rectors of St. Giles not to be intrenched upon, and the lecturer to be chosen by the rector and vestry.

The Act then adverts to the 4th of George I. empowering the commissioners to rebuild the church of St. Giles, and to afford assistance for the same, amounting to £8,000, on or before the 24th of June, 1730, the same to be vested in thirteen trustees therein named, who were to manage and lay out the same, the particulars of which were to be given hereafter to the said commissioners, &c.

And in the mean time, and until an effectual division and separation of the said parishes can be had and obtained, according to the powers and directions given for that purpose, by the said act of the tenth year of her late Majesty Queen Anne: Be it enacted by the authority aforesaid, that from and after the 25th day of March, 1731, the churchwardens and overseers of the poor, and other parish officers, for the said new parish, shall be annually chosen and appointed, at such time and times, as such respective churchwardens and overseers of the poor, and other officers, are annually chosen and appointed for the said parish of St. Giles in the Fields: and all rates for the relief of the poor of both the said parishes shall be made by the overseers of the poor of both parishes jointly, and when confirmed as the law directs, shall be levied and collected by the overseers of the poor of the said parishes respectively upon the inhabitants of each parish, and the money so collected shall be accounted for by the said respective overseers, and shall be applied and disposed of in such manner as if this act had not been made: and the workhouse, or house of maintainance for the poor of both parishes, now standing in the district of the said old parish, is hereby deemed, declared, and shall be taken to be for the joint use and benefit of both parishes, and shall be repaired, supported, maintained, and managed from time to time, as shall be thought necessary by the vestries, and at the joint expense of both parishes, anything herein contained, or any law, usage, or custom to the contrary notwithstanding.

14. provides that the rights, titles, and claims of his grace Wriothesley, Duke of Bedford, are to be respected as if this act had never been made.

Actions in reference to this act must be commenced within three months after the fact committed.

The expenses and charges of obtaining this act, were to be paid by the treasurer of the commissioners for building fifty new churches.

All judges, justices, and others, are enjoined to consider this a public act.

The following Act (the 14th George III. cap. 62) being that under which the United Parishes have been chiefly governed, is inserted at considerable length.

An Act for the better governing and employing the poor, and making and collecting the poor's-rates, within the parishes of St. Giles in the Fields, and St. George Bloomsbury, in the county of Middlesex.

1. Whereas the poor within the parishes, &c. are very numerous, and are supported at a great expense, and the powers for making and collecting the rates for the relief of such poor are not sufficient for those purposes:

And, whereas the poor belonging to the said parishes might be better maintained and regulated, and the rates for their relief more properly made and collected, if some farther and other powers were given for those purposes; may it therefore please your Majesty that it may be enacted, and be it enacted by the King's most excellent Majesty, by and with the advice and consent of the lords spiritual and temporal, and commons in this present parliament assembled, and by the authority of the same, that such number of substantial householders in the said parishes of St. Giles in the Fields and St. George Bloomsbury, not exceeding eight for the said parish of St. Giles in the Fields, and not exceeding four for the said parish of St. George Bloomsbury (who, by any law now in being, are liable to serve the office of overseer of the poor,) shall be nominated yearly, on some day in Easter week, or within one month after Easter, under the hands and seals of two or more of his Majesty's Justices of the peace for the county of Middlesex, dwelling in or near the said parishes, and the persons to be nominated as aforesaid, together with the churchwardens of the said parishes, shall be overseers for the year then next ensuing, and until others shall be nominated to, and shall have accepted the said office; and shall, within three days after such nomination, and notice thereof, given or left at his or their place of abode, take that office and duty upon them, upon pain that every such person refusing or neglecting so to do, shall forfeit the sum of ten pounds; and any two justices of the peace for the said county, are hereby authorised to nominate some other fit person or persons to the said office, in place of him or them refusing or neglecting as aforesaid; and the person or persons so nominated, in the room of such person or persons, shall take such office and duty upon him and them, under the like forfeiture of ten pounds for every such refusal or neglect, to be recovered in manner herein after mentioned; all which said forfeitures shall be paid to the treasurer, who shall be appointed to receive the monies for the relief of the poor of the said parishes, and be applied for and towards the relief of such poor.

2. And be it further enacted by the authority aforesaid, that the vestrymen of the said parishes, together with the

said churchwardens and overseers of the poor, are hereby authorised and required to assemble and meet together in the vestry-room belonging to the said parishes, upon the first Tuesday in the month of June in every year, or within twenty-one days afterwards, and at any other time or times, as occasion shall require. And they, or the major part of them so assembled, shall make a rate or rates, assessment or assessments, for the relief of the poor of the said parishes, upon all and every the lands, houses, tenements, buildings, and hereditaments, within the said parishes; which said rate or rates, &c. shall be paid by the persons inhabiting or occupying the said lands, &c. respectively, at such times, and in such manner and proportions, as the persons making any such rates or assessments shall thereby direct and appoint.

3. And whereas there are divers houses, tenements, and hereditaments within the said parishes which are let in separate apartments, or ready furnished, by which means the payment of the parochial rates for such houses may be evaded. It then goes on to state, that in such cases the landlords or proprietors of such occupations shall be liable. Tenants are compellable to pay who occupy furnished houses, or under any similar tenure, where the landlord is subject to rates and taxes, the same to be deducted afterwards by the tenant from the landlord's rent.

4. Ambassadors, or other public ministers of foreign courts are not liable, but the lessor, landlord, or owners of houses so occupied, are compellable to the payment of the rates, to be recovered in the usual way.

5. Forfeitures incurred by refusing to serve the offices of churchwardens and overseers, and rates not paid, may be recovered by distress and sale, with costs.

6. Vestrymen, in number seven or more, may cause actions to be commenced and prosecuted in the name of the collector of the rates, or other proper officer, in any of his Majesty's courts of law at Westminster, against all persons from whom

arrears of rates are due by virtue of this act, or they may recover the same in the court held for the recovery of small debts, within the county of Middlesex.

7. Seven or more vestrymen shall and may at their meetings, held from time to time, elect and appoint collectors from the resident householders from each and for each parish respectively: also one or more persons to be treasurer or treasurers, and also such other officers and servants as they shall find necessary for the due execution of this act; and shall take such security as the said vestrymen shall think proper for the due execution of their respective offices; and shall and may remove such collectors, treasurers, and officers, or servants, at their will and pleasure.

8. The collectors to be allowed, from the monies they receive, not more than three-pence in the pound. The treasurer or treasurers, officers, or servants to be allowed for their services such sums as the said vestrymen in their discretion shall think proper.

9. Collectors and treasurers to account at all times when required by the vestrymen, or any seven of them, to render full, true, and perfect accounts, verified upon their oaths respectively, of all monies by them received and paid by virtue of their said office, and shall pay over any money remaining in their hands to such person or persons as the said vestrymen, or the major part of them present at any meeting shall, by writing under their hands, authorize and appoint to receive the same. In case of non-compliance on the part of any of the said collectors or officers, they shall be committed lawfully to the common goal, without bail or mainprize, until he or they shall have made a true account on oath, and shall have paid such sums as appeared to be remaining in their hands, &c.

10. Vestrymen may lawfully make rules and regulations for disposing of the money that shall be raised and received for the relief of the poor of the said parishes, and for the better maintenance of them, governing and employing them, as to them, or any seven of them, shall appear necessary and expe-

dient, and may from time repeal or alter any of them in such manner as they, or any thirteen or more of them shall think proper, all which rules, &c. shall be of the same force and effect for the purposes thereby intended, as if the same were enacted in the body of this act; provided that such rules, orders, and regulations ARE NOT REPUGNANT TO THE LAWS OF THIS REALM.

11. And be it further enacted by the authority aforesaid, that no vestryman, churchwarden, or overseer of the poor for the time being, or any other person appointed by the said vestrymen to any office under or by virtue of this act, shall, during the time of such office, provide, furnish, or supply for his or their own profit, any goods, materials, or provisions, for or towards the employment, use, support, or maintenance of the poor in the workhouse of the said parishes.

12. Penalties are set forth on persons who shall buy or receive in pawn any clothes or apparel from persons in the workhouse.

13. And be it further enacted and declared by the authority aforesaid, that the several laws relating to the office of overseer of the poor, and for the relief and maintenance of the poor, shall still continue in force within the said parishes, except where the same are declared to be altered by this present act.

14. The expenses of this act to be defrayed out of the first monies to be raised by the rates herein before directed to be made.

15. Persons aggrieved may appeal to the Quarter Sessions, and it is lawful for the justices there assembled to hear all such appeals, and award reasonable costs to the party in whose favour the same shall be determined. Their order to be final and conclusive.

16. Persons making distress for poor's rate not be deemed trespassers from any defect or want of form in the warrant, or from other irregularity, but the person aggrieved by such ir-

regularity, shall or may recover full satisfaction for the special damage sustained, and no more, in an action on the case.

17. Proceedings not to be quashed for want of form only, or be removed by certiorari to any of his majesty's Courts of Record at Westminster, or by any other process.

18. Actions against persons for any thing done in pursuance of this act must be commenced within six calender months next after the fact committed, and not afterwards, the same to be laid and brought in the county of Middlesex. The defendants may plead the general issue, and give this Act and the special matter in evidence, at any trial to be had thereupon. Defendants, should the jury find for them, are to be entitled to treble costs, and the same should the plaintiff discontinue the action, or become non-suited.

19. This Act to be considered and taken to be a Public Act by all judges, justices, &c.

A List of the Joint Vestry of the Parishes of St. Giles in the Fields and St. George Bloomsbury, 1829.

ST. GILES.

Rev. James Endell Tyler, B.D. Rector, 24, Bedford Square.
Rt. Hon. Lord Chief Justice Best, 29, Bedford Square
[13 Feb. 1823.
Hon. Mr. Justice Park, 32, Bedford Square   [8 Feb. 1823.
John Soane, Esq. 13, Lincoln's Inn Fields [11 Feb. 1802.
William Beckett, Esq. 75, Gower Street [14 Feb. 1805.
Henry Meux, Esq. 19, Great Russell Street [11 Feb. 1813.
Lewis G. Dive, Esq. 3, Tavistock Street [10 Feb. 1814.
William Harrison, Esq. 45, Lincoln's Inn Fields [9 Feb. 1815.
Henry Burrows, Esq. 20, Gower Street [11 Feb. 1819.
Thomas Sumpter, Esq. 10, Thornhaugh Street [10 Feb. 1820.
Richard Latham, Esq. 18, Great Russell St. [10 Feb. 1824.
Nathaniel Saxon, Esq. 39, Gower Street [16 Feb. 1824.
James Carden, Esq. 24, Bedford Square [10 Feb. 1825.
Richard Woodhouse, Esq. 17, Bedford Square [8 Feb. 1827.

John Shaw, Esq. 28, Gower Street [8 Feb. 1827.
William Oldnall Russel, Esq. 14, Gower Street [8 Feb. 1827.
Henry Combe, Esq. 2, Caroline Street [14 Feb. 1828.
C. B. Williams, Esq. 59, Lincoln's Inn Fields [14 Feb. 1828.
J. F. Pike, Esq. 30, Bedford Square [14 Feb. 1828.
James Parkinson, Esq. 46, Bedford Square [14 Feb. 1828.
William Keene, Esq. 29, Alfred Place [14 Feb. 1828.
Joseph Moore, M.D. 9, Lincoln's Inn Fields [12 Feb. 1829.
Mr. Samuel Remnant, 15, High Street [18 Dec. 1794.
Mr. John Waddell, 25, High Street [13 Feb. 1812.
Mr. Richard Hilhouse, 116, Great Russell St. [10 Feb. 1814.
Mr. Joseph Holdsworth, 266, Tottenham Court Road
[8 Feb. 1816.
Mr. William Hughes, 247, Holborn [13 Feb. 1817.
Mr. George Robinson, 2, Great Queen Street [11 Feb. 1819.
Mr. William Henry Savage, 30, Gt. Queen St. [16 Feb. 1824.
Mr. Charles Ward, 164, Drury Lane [10 Feb. 1824.
Mr. Yeeling Underwood, 8, Great Turnstile [10 Feb. 1825.
Mr. Andrew George Bachhoffner, 69, Monmouth Street
[9 Feb. 1826.
Mr. Samuel Page, 232, Holborn [8 Feb. 1827.
Mr. John Doyle, 229, Holborn [8 Feb. 1827.
Mr. William Parker, 233, Holborn [12 Feb. 1829.
Mr. Egerton Cutler, 16, Great Queen Street [12 Feb. 1829.
Mr. T. G. Hough, 7, Tavistock Street [12 Feb. 1829.

CHURCHWARDENS.

Mr. George Rogers, 58, High Street.
Thomas Wakley, Esq. 35, Bedford Square.

BLOOMSBURY.

The Rev. John Lonsdale, B.D. Rectory House
Right Hon. Lord Tenterden, 28, Russell Sq. [11 Feb. 1819.
Francis P. Stratford, Esq. Charlotte Street, Bedford Square
[14 Feb. 1811.
Bernard Bosanquet, Esq. 12, Montague Place [10 Feb. 1814.

Augustus Warren, Esq. 24, Charlotte Street, Bedford Square
[9 Feb. 1815.
John Jortin, Esq. 7, Charlotte Street, Bedford Square
[12 Feb. 1818.
James Loch, Esq, Bloomsbury Square [12 Feb. 1818.
William Rothery, Esq. 1, Vernon Place [12 Feb. 1818.
Robert Ray, Esq. 10, Montague Place [11 Feb. 1819.
William Pratt, Esq. 59, Russell Square [10 Feb. 1820.
John Hall, Esq. 5, Russell Square [14 Feb. 1822.
John Griffin, Esq. 21, Bedford Place [13 Feb. 1823.
John Rawlinson, Esq. 38, Russell Square [12 Feb. 1824.
Samuel Mills, Esq. 20, Russell Square [10 Feb. 1825.
Thomas Day, Esq. 28, Montague Street [10 Feb. 1825.
John Baker, Esq. 66, Torrington Square [10 Feb. 1825.
George Man Burrows, M.D. 9, Montague Street
[9 Feb. 1826.
William Groom, Esq. 24, Russell Square [9 Feb. 1826.
Thomas Gotobed, Esq. 82, Great Russell Street [9 Feb. 1826.
John Miles, Esq. 25, Southampton Row [9 Feb. 1826.
William Flower, Esq. 7, Upper Bedford Place [8 Feb. 1827.
Henry Ellis, Esq. British Museum [14 Feb. 1828.
Samuel Brown, Esq. 24, Bloomsbury Square [14 Feb. 1828.
Bary Hutchinson, Esq. 52, Russell Square [12 Feb. 1829.
Mr. James Hall, 38, Southampton Row [30 Dec. 1795.
Mr. John Meabry, 1, Broad Street [9 Feb. 1815.
Mr. Thomas Harris, 52, Great Russell Street [12 Feb. 1818.
Mr. Henry Langley, 3, Charlotte Street, Bedford Square
[11 Feb. 1819.
Mr. Luke G. Hansard, 10, Bedford Square [8 Feb. 1821.
Mr. Francis Keysell, 7, Broad Street [13 Feb. 1823.
Mr. Nicholas Winsland, 44, Great Russell St. [12 Feb. 1824.
Mr. John William Willis, 138, High Holborn [12 Feb. 1824.
Mr. James Hansard, 7, Southampton Street [10 Feb. 1825.
Mr. James Donaldson, 8, Bloomsbury Square [10 Feb. 1825.
Mr. James Holmes, 12, Montague Street [9 Feb. 1826.
Mr. James Davies, 8, Plumtree Street [8 Feb. 1827.
Mr. W. Edwards Caldecot, 53, Great Russell St. [19. Feb. 1829.

CHURCHWARDENS.

Mr. Thomas Brown, 167, High Holborn.
Mr. William Mills, 120, Holborn.

Select Vestries.

The general odium into which these irresponsible juntos, have fallen since the aggrieved parishioners have viewed them with inquisitive jealousy cannot be better illustrated than by noticing some of the abuses connected with them in several districts of the metropolis, as announced in the public papers.

" ST. ANDREW'S, HOLBORN, May, 1828.—A meeting of the parishioners took place yesterday, when the report of the committee appointed to inquire into the expenditure of the parish was received. It stated that Dr. Lushington had given it as his opinion that all charges for dinners and refreshments as connected with parochial affairs are illegal. It then alluded to the charges made by Mr. Hicks, who, in his double capacity of sexton and grave-digger, received legal dues amounting to £250, together with various sums for dressing the pulpit, digging graves for the poor, employing men to attend on a Sunday, &c. &c. making an additional rent of nearly £100, out of which he had to pay £30 to Mrs. Perrey, the late sexton's wife. Among the items embodied in the latter sum was £26 for washing surplices, being £19 10s. more than was paid at the present moment by the parish of St. Sepulchre. There was also a charge of £9 for dog's meat, while the committee had only been able to ascertain that not one shilling had been paid on account of such provender. The committee recommended the discontinuance of all parish dinners, the separation of the offices of sexton and grave-digger, and the curtailment of all extra fees to Mr. Hicks; and observed, that the various circumstances which they had to complain of were caused by the officers of the parish being appointed by the *Select Vestry*."

" CHRISTCHURCH, SPITALFIELDS.—An item was charged in the parish account of £80 (1826) for carving and gilding the legs of the communion table, and a certain other sum was charged for a cloth to cover them, so that the parishioners were prevented from viewing the elegant work which was paid for out of their own pockets. There was another item for repairing hinges amounting to £50."

St. George, Hanover Square.—The following case of oppression is taken from the Examiner, September 14th, 1828.—" For nearly half a century I have lived and paid parochial rates in the above parish; but being a widow, the expense of bringing up a large family necessitates me to let a part of the house I occupy, which is situated in the out-ward; the frontage, however, being without any pavement, and the traffic past it daily increasing, I found it next to impossible to procure lodgers who would brave the mud and mire accumulated during the winter months. I, in consequence, applied to those in authority in the parish to pave the front, but without effect; and, in order to remedy the increasing nuisance, I had it paved *at my own expense*. But judge my surprise, when the very next time the collector came round, I was for the first time charged with a *paving rate!* Well knowing that the parish had not laid down any pavement, even within *half a mile* of my residence—*at least*, half a mile by measurement—I thought it a mistake, and caused inquiry to be made at the vestry on the subject; but the answer was, that it was quite contrary to vestry etiquette to listen to any complaints, until all demands (just or unjust) are complied with by the unfortunate applicant. The long period I had been a parishioner, and my never having applied to the vestry before, was pleaded as a reason why they should hear my appeal: but the *gentlemen (?)* present ridiculed this; and although all other rates were tendered, nothing but the whole would be received.

Considering that a voluntary compliance with this gross fraud (for I think it nothing better) would be establishing their right to further extortion, I refused payment, and the consequence was an *execution* on my goods! I now considered that I had, at least, established my right to be *heard* at the vestry; but no such thing—they had got the money—and the vestry-clerk, with an air of triumph and self-importance, refused to set the appeal down for hearing, alleging that it had already been heard. So that I am now left at the full liberty to go to law with the parish for redress. This, I apprehend, never could have happened but in a vestry self elected, and irresponsible for their actions, however nefarious; but as I understand there are several respectable and even *titled* names to be found in the list, I do trust they will disavow all participation in a transaction so disgraceful, and afford me justice (*not law*) at as cheap a rate as it is to be had."

ST. GILES, CRIPPLEGATE.—" The resistance to the Select Vestry System, now so generally prevalent, has been already productive of the most beneficial results. A striking example to other parishes and ministers has just been afforded in that of St. Giles, Cripplegate. The office of evening lecturer having become vacant, there were no less than ten candidates for the situation. A very sensible address from a parishioner was suddenly sent round, recommending that an eleventh should be put in nomination, and that this should be their vicar himself! There were two special grounds set forth—1st. " That if the duties of the lectureship be necessary at all, it is incumbent on the vicar to fulfil them. At the time of his ordination he declared that he ' thought in his heart he was fully called to the priesthood;' he professed to ' receive the Holy Ghost;' and solemnly engaged to be ' diligent in prayers and in reading of the Holy Scriptures, laying aside the study of the world and the flesh.' Now the duties of the lectureship either are necessary or they are not. If they are not, we cannot do without an evening lecturer, the appointment of whom is an indirect reproach on our vicar." Secondly, That of economy; and a computation was made that the total annual amount of the vicar's emoluments from the parish was £2,300. " For this sum" (continued the address) " he, either by himself or deputy, reads prayers and preaches (that is, reads) a sermon of the length of half an hour every

Sunday, and once on certain holydays, as they are called—
say that he reads sixty such services and sermons in the year,
and that he is employed each time an hour and a half, he is
then, for the sum of £2,300. employed throughout the year,
ninety hours, or three whole days and three quarters of another day; and he receives for each service and sermon of one
hour and a half long, the sum of £38. 6s. 8d. sterling, being
about the value of eight quartern loaves for every minute of
time he is engaged. Those who regularly hear the said sermons will be best enabled to judge whether or not they are
worth the money." The address was also accompanied by an
intimation that by law, according to the article " Offerings"
in *Burn's Ecclesiastical Law*, no greater sum could be exacted
than 2d. per head as Easter offerings, though a much larger
sum was generally paid, and that further payments were per-
fectly voluntary. Other addresses were, it is said, in readi-
ness, and a canvass in preparation to support this nomination,
when intelligence was received that the vicar had very wisely
agreed to allow a sum for a lecturer, and moreover that he
should be chosen by the parishioners. This of course has
given the greatest satisfaction." (*November* 16*th*, 1826.)

ST. GILES IN THE FIELDS AND ST. GEORGE
BLOOMSBURY.—It is well known that the action, Rogers
versus Tyler, had for its object the establishing the right of
the parishioners to sit in vestry; and when the order was obtained to enable the plaintiff to examine the vestry minutes,
many discoveries were made and published, not much to the
credit of the " Select." The following is copied from the
address of the committee to the parishioners, June, 1828—
" The last vestry clerk was a defaulter to a very large amount,
without one shilling security having been taken for the money
with which he was improperly entrusted, *and the whole transaction concealed by the Select*, whose pretended abstract of
accounts does not make the least allusion to the great losses
thereby entailed upon the parishes."

"The cash accounts during the time of the previous vestry clerk are in such a state, that they cannot be audited, or even understood. The numerous additions of receipts and disbursements of the poor rates for upwards of two years, amounting to ninety thousand pounds, are still in pencil marks.!!

"Of three-quarters of a year's receipts and disbursements, there is not a vestige of an account produced!!

"To carry on the defence to the action above alluded to, £200 were abstracted from the funds raised for the support of the poor, and thus stimulated, the vestry attorney put in by singular industry no less than fifteen special pleas, covering the surface of one hundred and seventy-five folios! These the Court of King's Bench on the 25th November, 1828, reduced to less than half, whereby the "Select" incurred personally the needless and vexatious expense to which they resorted for obvious purposes."

ST. JAMES, WESTMINSTER.—Mr. Hobhouse in his motion, 28th April, 1829, for the appointment of a committee to inquire into the abuses of Select Vestries, which was agreed to after some opposition by Mr. Peel, made the following remarks:—

"That during ten years the guardians of the poor drew up their accounts in one room, and audited them themselves in another! Also, that accounts were furnished sufficient not only to cover the table, but to fill up the hollow under it, from whence, however, very little satisfaction could be derived, and it was of little use to appeal to the magistrates, who were either vestrymen themselves, or intimate with that body."

At a meeting of the parishioners at Cauty's rooms, 24th Dec. 1828, Mr. Fores, the chairman, stated that £12 10s. had been charged the parish for an accountant's-teaching the clerk of the workhouse how to keep his books! The visiting the infant poor at Wimbledon was charged in 1817 about £30, but in 1827 the amount was £85! He and two of his friends had paid the very same visit, and the cost had been no more than 7s. 6d. £100 per annum was paid to the assistant preacher twice over, owing to an error in the acts of parliament. Among other abuses, there was a sum of £24,000 which had not been credited in the accounts, and of this the vestry had been brought to admit £15,000, so that sum had been already saved to the parish by the exertions of the committee appointed by the parishioners, &c.

ST. MARTIN'S IN THE FIELDS.—We have already alluded to some extraordinary decisions in reference to this parish, (*vide page* 281, *&c.*) the vestry of which attracted the notice of the parishioners and legislature as early as 1741. Daniel De Foe wrote a pamphlet about 1720, entitled "Parochial Tyranny, or the Housekeeper's Complaint against the Exactions, &c. of Select Vestries," in which he published a bill of expenses of the vestry of this parish in 1713, which contains the following items:—

	£.	s.	d.
"1713. Spent at many meetings on visitations	65	0	4
Ditto at taverns with ministers, justices, overseers, &c.	72	19	7
To clerks paid	10	0	0
Ditto for examining poor	170	16	10
Boards for grave-digger	4	2	0
Sacrament bread and wine (no bill)	88	10	0
Paid towards a robbery !!	21	14	0
Spent for dinner at Mulberry Gardens	49	13	4
Ditto going to Hicks's Hall about bastard children	2	7	0
	£486	3	1

	£.	s.	
1818. The balance charged this parish for churchwardens' dinner was	56	15	0
1819. It was	44	10	0
1823. Ditto	30	15	6
1826. Ditto reduced to	14	0	0

which was handed over to Mr. Cuff out of the parish funds

1827. The amount paid was.................. 27 2 6

The sum of £48. 12s. 9d. was paid to Messrs. Wood and Co. for Archdeacon Pott's Sermon on the death of Queen Charlotte. It appears it did not sell, and the parish was robbed to pay the loss.

6th January, 1813. The sum of £5. was charged and paid for a petition of the vestry against the Catholics,—a most impudent act; for, although they had a just right to petition if they pleased, they had none to defraud the parish to defray the expense.

ST. MARY-LA-BONNE.—" The committee on the bill to reform the *close* Select Vestry of this parish met again yesterday. Sir Thomas Baring was chairman of the committee, among whom we observed Mr. Hobhouse, Colonel Freemantle, Messrs. Wood and Waithman, Mr. Bernal, and several other members, together with Mr. Ross, Mr. G. Smith, now vestryman, and also Colonel Graham, formerly a vestryman, and then of the house of Fauntleroy and Co. of Berners Street.

Among other things, the building of a chapel, and afterwards taking a great part of it down to convert it into a church, at a great and wasteful expense, was clearly proved. So was the paying of the late venerable President of the Royal Academy £800 for a design for a window, which he executed as a transparency, the first perhaps he ever thought of painting in his life, and the placing of it as a *centre-piece* for the organ! Also the payment of £300 for a fine group of figures by Rossi, for the pediment of the chapel, which were never used, and are now lying somewhere about the stone yard of the parish.

The best joke was, they had taken a fine gold figure of an angel playing on a lyre which had been placed at the top of the organ (and as nobody could tell what had become of it, the counsel for the vestry said it had gone to the devil), and had placed in lieu of it, under the auspices of the present Reverend incumbent, a crown on a cushion, supported by a *mitre* on either side.

Great interest was excited by the following detail of a grand perambulatory dinner which was laid before the committee:—

	£	s.	d.
Temporary cellars and coach hire	14	0	6
Ale and Porter	72	12	6
Hams	20	7	6
Wine, 39 dozen (468 bottles)	121	1	0
Meat, 164½ stone, at 1s. per lb.	65	16	0
Grocery, cheese, eggs, &c.	16	12	5
Vegetables and lemons	22	14	0
Ribband for cockades	23	16	3
Table linen	4	8	11
Brass cocks and cork screws, with brushes, &c.	7	17	6
Earthenware	59	11	5
Man cook and assistants	5	5	0
Female assistants and cabbage nets	6	10	10
Wands and gilding	1	5	0
Penny pieces	2	2	0
Waiters	8	0	0
	£452	0	10

Only a few of these items, amounting to £86 odd, appeared in the book under the name of perambulation. All the rest were disguised, and entered as provisions for the poor, clothing for the poor, furniture, &c. one article charged to the account of repairing and cleansing the streets, a very small part being for making good damage done to fences, &c. during the day.

The upholsterer's bill for dressing the church amounted to the enormous sum of £2150.

It seems they had two suits, one for ordinary and another for extraordinary occasions, one of cloth and silk lace, the other of crimson silk Genoa velvet and gold lace.

The dresses for the pulpit cost	£320
Ditto for reading desk	139
And for the clerks	99
	£558

Dressing the communion table	260
Chairs and kneeling stools	260
Seven hassocks	108
Curtains for the organ gallery	93
Churchwardens pews	166
	£887

Among other statements made to the House of Commons, the following may be mentioned:—

'The accounts are rendered so intricate, which the vestry audit, that for the year 1825 a surplus appeared in the account in favour of the parish of £26,000, when in fact there was a deficiency of £21,000, leaving a sum of nearly £47,000 unaccounted for! and next year they borrowed of their treasurer, without law, as temporary loans £64,000.

A few years ago, when money was to be had at 3½ and 4 per cent. the vestry refused to obtain it at that rate, and thereby pay off a large debt created at a higher interest, because the money had been borrowed mostly of vestrymen.

They were in debt nearly £500,000 when the bill to regulate them went to parliament, and they refused to render any account of the receipts and expenditure, till Alderman Wood obtained an order of the house as follows:—

	£.		
Amount of rates collected during 9 past years	1,442,619	19	6¼
Expense of collecting 6d. in the pound, (the king pays 3d.)	20,257	8	4
Gratuities to officers and clerks, exclusive of salaries	138,477	18	11½
Provisions for workhouse	75,593	19	3½
Wine for ditto	2,854	3	8
Spirits for ditto	612	15	6
Medicine for ditto	6,667	9	3
Medical herbs for ditto	889	8	9
Clothes for one year for poor	3,268	6	8

Great interest
perambulatory

Temporary cell
Ale and Porte
Hams..........
Wine, 39 doz
Meat, 164½
Grocery, che
Vegetables
Ribband for
Table linen
Brass cock
Earthenwa
Man cook
Female as
Wands an
Penny pi
Waiters

Only
in the b
were di
for the
of rep
for ma
    Th
the e
    It
for e
othe
The
Dit
An

Dressing the communion table.................... 3
Chairs and kneeling stools _____ 5
Seven hassocks.................................. -
Curtains for the organ gallery _____ -
Churchwardens pew.............................. 7

Among other statements made in the report,
the following may be mentioned:—

' The accounts are ....
............, that for the year 18.., ...
count in favour of the ....
was a deficiency of £......., ...
£47,... .... for the next year; but ....
their treasurer, ...

A few years ago, ... purpose
per cent the vestry refused to .... : a .... en-draper
thereby .... at too sensiti
come the .... robably broken
They were a .... own ' Success to
regulate .... elect parishioners n
any account of his .... hve-mile visit to a
Wood .... n; but surely no man
.... his own stomach, can bl
.... apting to smuggle a bill thro
.... ive secured them the full enjoy
.... with creature comforts."—Mo
3.
.—The following is stated to be the cos
w Church:—

	£.	s.
or ground on which it stands	6,695	0
ontractor, on account of contract.......	45,647	0
.o for extras	13,909	3
itto for Terra Cotta work...............	6,248	19

Raw material for ditto, each succeeding year (average)	2,800	0	0
Money for lunatics	14,831	7	6
Casual Poor	137,784	19	7
Money paid for bastard children	32,891	17	5¼

Besides the current expenses, it appears that the parish is saddled with a large annuity interest upon bonds for paving, church, and other rates amounting to £136,212."
(See Examiner, May 4th, 1828, and February 1st, 1829.)

ST. PAUL's, COVENT GARDEN.—" 1817. The parish paid Bourdillion, son of a vestryman, £115 8s. for burying the rector.

1828. The sum of £80 was taken off the account charged by Roach, the former vestry clerk, although he was warmly supported by Sir R. Birnie and Mr. Halls.

The feast of eighteen of the parishioners, with the rector at their head, which took place at Norwood in 1826 is well known:—" The auditors appointed by the non-select parishioners of St. Paul's Covent Garden, to audit the accounts of their defunct Select Vestry, had scarcely commenced their labours yesterday, when they stumbled on the following entry:—

	£.	s.	d.
' 1826, August 1st. Paid chaise-hire, turnpikes, refreshments, and other expenses on visiting the children at nurse'	34	12	6

Now the auditors, not being sufficiently select to comprehend how such a sum could be necessary for visiting a few pauper children at Norwood, called upon the vestry clerk, (Roach) for an explanation thereof, and he forthwith furnished them with a *voucher*, as follows:—

	£.	s.	d.
' Dinner and dessert for eighteen *gentlemen*	9	9	0
Lemon	0	1	0
Ten bottles of Bucellas	3	0	0
Two bottles of Sherry	0	12	0

	£.	s.	d.
Punch	0	12	0
Soda	0	16	0
Four bottles of Champagne	2	8	0
Twelve bottles of Port	3	12	0
Five bottles of Santerne	2	0	0
Ice for wine	0	2	0
Rose water!	0	2	0
Glass	0	5	6
Noyeau	0	18	0
Tea and coffee	1	7	0
Three servant's dinners	0	7	6
Waiters	0	9	0
Coach-hire and turnpikes	8	11	6
Grand total	£34	12	6

The *rose water* seems to have been had for the purpose of bathing the nasal appendage of a worthy woollen-draper of the party, whose olfactory nerves are somewhat too sensitive for pauper visitations, and the *glass* was probably broken by some gentlemen too zealously knocking down ' Success to the Select Vestry System !' What the non-select parishioners may say to this expenditure of £35 in a five-mile visit to a few pauper bantlings, remains to be seen; but surely no man who entertains a sufficient respect for his own stomach, can blame the ex-Select Vestry for attempting to smuggle a bill through parliament, which would have secured them the full enjoyment of a system so replete with creature comforts."—*Morning Herald, March,* 1828.

St. Pancras.—The following is stated to be the cost of St. Pancras New Church:—

	£.	s.	d.
" Paid for ground on which it stands	6,695	0	0
Ditto contractor, on account of contract	45,647	0	1
Ditto for extras	13,909	3	6
Ditto for Terra Cotta work	6,248	19	10

Architect's commission, clerk of works, and incidents	4,307	0	7
Warming and ventilating church	391	11	0
Organ	1,087	0	0
Scagliola work and gilding	897	8	2
Clock, three bells, and furniture	2,742	5	0
Communion plate, bibles, prayer-books, and consecration	1,004	10	7
Laying-out and planting ground	251	0	0
Extra works, security given	3,000	0	0
	£86,280	18	9
Deduct remission of duties	3,579	11	1
Grand total of this job...	£82,701	7	8

" These are some of the consequences of worshipping and adoring God at the public charge."

(*See Morning Herald, September*, 1828.)

Rogers v. Tyler, Clerk.

An intimation has already been given in the Preface why I abandoned the intention of publishing the details of this important Trial, and other matter has been substituted. A short notice of it seems, however, indispensable in a work intended to form a record of events for the future guidance and use of the parishioners, which I here insert:—

21st July 1829. (Adjourned Sittings at Nisi Prius in Middlesex after Trinity Term, before Mr. Justice James Parke, and Special Juries.)

Counsel for the Plaintiff—
Mr. Campbell, Mr. Evans, and Mr. Richards.

Counsel for the Defendant—
The Attorney General Sir James Scarlett, Mr. Patteson, and Mr. Thesiger.

The List of the Jury:
David Henderson, St. John's Wood;
John Strutt, Manor Place, Chelsea;
Thomas Boutiffee Shelton, Lisson Grove South;
Joseph Jellicoe, Upper Wimpole Street;
Joseph Shappe, Dean Street, Soho;
Alexander Still, Leicester Place;
William Stretton, Lisle Street;
George Stephenson, Oxford Street;
Charles Tett, Dean Street, Soho;
Thomas Thornton, Ditto;
George Taylor, Litchfield Street;
Evan Thomas, Macclesfield Street.

This was an action formally brought to recover damages of the defendant, The Rev. James Endell Tyler, B.D. for an alleged assault committed by him upon the plaintiff, Mr. George Rogers, in the Vestry-room of the parish of St. Giles in the Fields, on the 4th of June 1828, but substantially to try the question of the legality of a Select Vestry in that parish.

Lord Tenterden, being himself one of the select vestry of St. George Bloomsbury, which by act of parliament is incorporated with St. Giles, declined trying the cause; his place was therefore occupied by Mr. Justice James Parke.

Mr. Campbell, Mr. Evans, and Mr. Richards appeared for the plaintiff; the Attorney General (Sir James Scarlett) Mr. Patteson, and Mr. Thesiger were engaged for the defendant.

Mr. Richards opened the pleadings. George Rogers was the plaintiff, and James Endell Tyler, clerk, the defendant.

The declaration alleged, that the defendant had assaulted the plaintiff in the vestry-room of the parish of St. Giles in the Fields, and had turned him out of that room. The defendant pleaded not guilty, and also a justification, on the ground that the plaintiff had no right to be present; and that when desired to retire he refused, and that then the defendant turned him out. Also, that there existed a select vestry, of which the plaintiff was not a member. There were also pleas founded on the separation of the parish of St. George Bloomsbury from that of St. Giles in the Fields, in the reign of Queen Anne; and their union, as far as concerned the maintenance of the poor, in the reign of his late Majesty: but they were not considered by the plaintiff's leading counsel as material. The plaintiff replied, that the defendant had committed the assault of his own wrong.

The trial was continued, by adjournment, till ten minutes past six on the following day (July 22nd,) when the Jury retired, and, after an absence of an hour and a quarter, returned a verdict for the plaintiff. Damages 40s.

The case towards the conclusion excited considerable interest, and on the announcement of a general verdict for the plaintiff, the majority of the auditors expressed their feelings of satisfaction in a manner which is usually considered indecorous in a Court of Justice.

Attorney for the Plaintiff—
Mr. Eldred, Southampton Street, Bloomsbury Square.

Attorney for the Defendant—
Mr. Turner, Bloomsbury Square.

On the 9th November, Sir James Scarlett moved the Court of King's Bench for a new trial, when a rule *nisi* was granted.

INDEX.

	Page
Alms-Houses, history of, since 1656, and misapplication of their funds, &c.	241—258
Aggas, his plan of London, 1560, noticed	40—41
Adulation and superstition of the clergy	103,4,5—8
Ansell, his account of parish books	305—306
Audit Committee, blunders of censured	321—325
Assessments, inequality of investigated, and erroneous admission of "Refutation," &c.	359—361
Acts of Parliament applicable to Joint Parishes, abstracts of, &c.	396
Apostles washed off the organ-loft	108
Burton St. Lazar Hospital, its dissolution & final sale in 1828	15—21
Bricks, introduced by the Earl of Arundel	47
Buildings, proclamations to restrain	42,46—48
———— progress of, till Interregnum	48
———— new ones, ordered to be pulled down	54
———— extension of, in St. Giles's, to VI. of Anne	58—62
———— accumulation of, in Bloomsbury	142—146
Burton, James, his vast enterprise & extraordinary abstract	143—148
Babington, his plot, and execution in Lincoln's-Inn-Fields	55
Burial Ground, for the sole use of the poor, purchased	122
———— purchase of, at St. Pancras	123
———— of St. Giles's, Pennant's disgusting account of	123
———— of Bloomsbury, and remarkable trial	155—160
Britton, his dimensions of Metropolitan Squares	171
Baltimore House, and serious charge against Lord Baltimore	173—174
Benefactors to St. Giles's second church, 1635	99—101
Bloomsbury, its derivation, manor, and boundaries	134—138
———— formed into a separate parish, 1724	150
———— its church, built by Hawksmore	1730—ibid.
———— church criticised by Ralph and Walpole	152—153

INDEX.

	Page
Bloomsbury, rector's list of, shortly noticed	154
———— church, expensive repairs to ditto	347—349
———— vestry, appointed under 10th. of Anne	154
———— new streets, &c. enumerated	180—181
———— Dispensary, notice of	265
———— Square, and criticisms by Ralph	138—139
———— Market, Maitland and Strype's account of	139
Baynbrigge's, bequests to St. Giles's poor	266
Biographical sketches of residents, &c.	365—395
———— ditto of charitable donors	392
Bedford House, in 1801	176
———————— demolition of, in 1802	386
———————— Dukes of, enumerated	379
———————— John, Fourth Duke, his splendid gift	161
British Museum, instituted 1759	162
Its collections, & a cursory notice of its future improvements, &c.	16²
Burgoyne Montague, his census of Irish Poor, &c.	362
Brunswick Square, short notice of	179
Cobham Lord, persecution of, and cruel death	26—30
Cottages in Birchin Lane, 1372	36
College of Surgeons in Lincoln's-Inn Fields	170
Churchwardens, their origin and duties	222—224
———————— election vested in parishioners of St. Giles by legal decision, 1670	225
———————— memorable election of, in 1829	356
Charity Schools in Museum Street, accounts of, Bedford Chapel, Ditto George Street, &c. &c.	264—265
Cromwell, Oliver, his donation to St. Giles's poor	197
Drury Lane, its country blacksmith's shop	38
———— derivation of, and ancient state	46
———— its present state contrasted	56
Doomsday Book of William I. scarcely notices London, and remarks upon	2
Doomesday Book, a parish record	95—96
———————— lost, and advertized for in 1828, and found	98
Duchess of Duddelye, her munificence to St. Giles's Church	100
Earle, his defalcations, &c.	303,4—332—334
Freeman, his prophetical epigrams	183
Foreigners, influx of, in 1580, and 1697	43—60
Fielding and Hogarth, on the depravity of St. Giles's, 1749,	201—202
Faithorn's Plan of London in 1658	61

INDEX.

	Page
Graunt, Captain, his remarks on London, 1661	59
Gwynne, Nell, born in St. Giles's Parish	59
Griggs, Mrs. her affection for cats	186
Gallows of St. Giles, and remarkable custom	9—10

Harley, Sir Robert, his extreme zeal against images and crosses...109
Hospital of St. Giles, for lepers, founded in 1117 6
——— site of, dedication, &c. ....7—9
——— donations to, charters, &c. ....13—15
——— dissensions of its inmates, and decline ....15—17
——— dissolution of, and grant to Lord Lisle, 1545 ....21—23
——— devolves afterwards to Sir Wymond Carew ....22—25
——— its capital mansion, site of, &c. ....ibid.
——— its estates, lay in 63 parishes and places 88
——— church, the resort of the inhabitants 89
——— its high altar, and other particulars 91
——— repairs to ditto, 1617, when parochial ....ibid.
——— ordered to be pulled down in 1623 ....ibid.
Heywood, particulars of his ceremonies, and complaints against...105
Housling people, signification of 43

Infant Poor, neglect of, in 1810, as stated by Mr. Thiselton 239
——— Heston, establishment for, in 1827 837
Irish Poor in St. Giles's first mentioned, 1640 194
——— expense of annually ....
Items of parochial expenditure, during seven years ....354—366

Kingsgate Street, noticed in Pepy's Diary 146

Leprosy defined, and some account of ....4—6
London, its unseemly aspect anciently 40
Lighting and cleansing streets first adopted 57
Lying-in Hospital in Brownlow Street 365
Lincoln's-Inn-Fields, its Square, &c. ....50—5
——— Walpole's sarcasm upon 54
Laud, Bishop, his superstitious ceremonies, 1630 ....103—104

Montague House, Evelyn's account of, 1676, burnt down in 1696 ...161
Montague House, Lady Russell's account of ditto 284
Mandate and parochial answer to ditto ....278—284
Mary-la-bonne, black forest 39
Manwayring's obnoxious sermons in St. Giles's Church 102
Morris and Chandler oppose Vestry, 1681 ....287—288
Monuments, two remarkable ....123—124

INDEX.

	Page
Overseers first appointed by act 43rd. of Elizabeth	226
———— their duties, how performed in joint parishes	307

Pestilence, destroys 50,000 in London	17—18
Parish, defined by Jacob, &c.	8
Paving of Holborn, &c. 1417 and 1542	38
Population of St. Giles's in 1550, &c.	100
———— of united parishes	186—189
Parish assessment, 1623, &c.	97
Paul, Peter, and Barnabas, turned out of church	108
Parish entries, curious extracts	196—280
Pennington unsaints the churches	109
Parsonage-house of St. Giles's given by Duchess of Dudley, 1646	124
Pound and Cage, where formerly situate	125
Plague of 1665, originated in St. Giles's, particulars of	126—132
Petty, Sir Wm. on the extension of London	182
Pauperism and mendicity, early notice of	191—194
Pavement Chalkers, and other mendicants	209—210
Poor Laws, observations upon	213—220
—— number, and expenses of, from 1642 to 1677	220
Poor's receipts and expenditure, from 1776 to 1815	220
Poor, expense of, in 1725, £4,200	226
—— shameful mode of relief of, exemplified	307—308
Parochial and charitable estates, stated	260—261
———— abuses, and disparity of assessments	313—320
Prescription, and legal decisions thereon	272—276
Parton, his defence of the vestry discussed	282—289
Prince's Square, smallest in the world	55
Parishes of St. Giles and Bloomsbury, reasons for separating	362—364
Places of worship in united parishes	183—186

Queen Street Great, mansions of nobility there	57—58

Restoration, and replacing the King's Arms	110
Russell Square, its extent, &c.	171
———— retrospections thereon	176—177
Riots of 1780 noticed, in connection with Bloomsbury Square	178
"Refutation of charges against the vestry," commented upon 268, 305, 350,	353—359
Rogers and Thiselton, their remarks on assessments	317—318
Russell Institution, described	168—170
Resurrection Gate erected, particulars of, 1687	123
Revolution of 1688, concocted in Bloomsbury	389

INDEX.

	Page
Seven Dials, formerly Cock and Pye Fields	61
St. Giles, a Grecian saint, Butler's account of	36
St. Giles's manor described	1
———— village, first mention of	56
———— suburb village, &c.	32—35
———— antique cross in Henry III's. reign	38
———— civic hunt, in 1562	40
———— encrease of, and progress	42—44
———— contains the largest and smallest squares in the world	55
———— early inns, account of	63—65
———— ancient six divisions	65—81
———— first institution as a parish, 1547	82
———— village so called in ancient deeds	83
———— parish not mentioned in Doomesday Book, 1066	82
———————————— in the valor of Pope Nicholas, 1291	84
———————————— in the nona rolls, 1341	84
———————————— in any of the hospital charters down to Edward III	84
———————————— in the confirmatory Bull of Pope Alexander, in reign of Henry III.	88
———— so termed, but seven times out of 102 grants and obits	88
———— new church, consecrated by Bishop Laud	103—104
———— early repairs and decay	111—115
———— church, application to parliament to re-build, and	
———— protest against	115
———— present church erected, 1733, and criticisms upon, by Ralph	117
———— rectors' list of, during 282 years	119
———— church-yard, land given to poor	120—122
———— manor purchased by trustees of Lord Southampton, 1617	135
———— church, reparations done to	348
Suburbs, early state of, according to Pennant and others	3—32
St. Mary-la-bonne, origin of	38
Sexton, his singular tenure in 1670	122
Statue of Francis Duke of Bedford, Russell Square	175—176
———— of the Right Hon. James Fox	177
Sidesmen, their office and duties	226
Shelton's School, founded in 1668, history of, and mal-appropriation of its funds, &c.	251—259
Stevenson's extraordinary evidence on mendicity in St. Giles's	202—212
Statue of George I. epigram upon	153
Traditional story of "the forty footsteps"	175
Turnstiles, books anciently printed there, &c. 1637	56

INDEX.

	Page
Tolls, the first grant of, in St. Giles's	30
Tottenhall, an ancient mansion in St. Giles's	37—66
Tyburn, village of, a place of execution, &c.	10—11
Tresilian, Judge, barbarous treatment of at Tyburn	ibid.
Torrington Square described	179
Thanet House, where formerly situated	137
Trial, Rogers ver. Tyler, concisely adverted to	430

Vestry, definition of, by Shaw, Burn, &c. .... 267—271
——— legal decisions upon .... 274—276
——— origin of St. Giles's, 1617 276
——— open, one for building second church, 1623 .... 96—277
——— select, list of, in 1620, and at other periods .... 277—281
——— Parton's fallacious account of, discussed 272
——— regulations against blasphemy, &c. .... 284—285
——— clerks, a list of, and short account of .... 228—230
——— of Bloomsbury, its first institution, &c. 290
——— disputes of with that of St. Giles .... 290—295
——— unites with ditto after 40 years variance 295
——— joint, obtain the act 14th George III. and other matters relative thereto, to discussed .... 296—401
——— formidable opposition to in 1827, decision against, 1829 267—301
——— impolicy of electing judges and others 355
——— illegal appropriation of the poor's funds 357
——— arguments for an elective one 359
——— doings in several metropolitan parishes .... ib.

Wickliffe's remarkable tenets 26
Workhouse, a general one, for various parishes, 1649 .... 230—232
——————— one for labour, first instituted in St. Giles's 232
——————— present one, account of, founded 1724 234

𝔉𝔦𝔫𝔦𝔰.

Marshall, Printer, Kenton Street, Brunswick Square.